PSYCHOTHERAPY and the Highly Sensitive Person

Improving Outcomes for That Minority of People Who Are the Majority of Clients

Elaine N. Aron

Routledge
Taylor & Francis Group
New York London

Routledge
Taylor & Francis Group
711 Third Avenue
8th Floor
New York, NY 10017

Routledge
Taylor & Francis Group
27 Church Road
Hove, East Sussex BN3 2FA

Printed in the United States of America on acid-free paper

International Standard Book Number: 978-0-415-80073-0 (Hardback) 978-0-415-80074-7 (Paperback)

Library of Congress Cataloging-in-Publication Data

Aron, Elaine.
Psychotherapy and the highly sensitive person : improving outcomes for that minority of people who are the majority of clients / by Elaine N. Aron.
p. ; cm.
Includes bibliographical references and index.
ISBN 978-0-415-80073-0 (hardback : alk. paper) -- ISBN 978-0-415-80074-7 (pbk. : alk. paper)
1. Psychotherapy. 2. Sensitivity (Personality trait) I. Title.
[DNLM: 1. Psychotherapy--methods. 2. Personality. 3. Self Concept. WM 420 A769p 2010]

RC475.A76 2010
616.89'14--dc22 2009053531

Visit the Taylor & Francis Web site at
http://www.taylorandfrancis.com

and the Routledge Web site at
http://www.routledgementalhealth.com

Contents

Preface

Infants each have a unique temperament. We know parents are not imagining things when they say "He's such an easy baby," or "She's more active than her brother was." Obviously infants grow into adults, keeping their temperament, but when we see an adult patient it is far more difficult to sort out what is nature and what is nurture. We know the basic traits are still there and deserve to be considered as an unchanging substrate of patients, but how can we help them have a good relationship with their genetic makeup, especially when it means being highly sensitive?

High sensitivity as defined in my research (Aron & Aron, 1997) is found in about 20% of the population (Kagan, 1994; Suomi, 1991, studying primates), so no doubt some of your friends and family members are highly sensitive as well as a large percentage of your patients. They are observant of subtleties and bothered more than others by high levels of stimulation, such as loud noise, places like malls, extreme temperatures, or a long day of sightseeing. They have strong emotional responses and need more downtime. They are usually thoughtful and observant. About 70% are introverts, and in certain ways may seem more vulnerable, yet thrive in their own way. (For a more expanded sense of the trait, turn to Appendix A, the Highly Sensitive Person [HSP] Scale.)

WHY A NEW TRAIT, NOW?

This trait is not new, of course. It is found in both humans and animals (Sih & Bell, 2008; Suomi, 1991; Wilson, Coleman, Clark, & Biederman, 1993; Wolf, van Doorn, & Weissing, 2008), so it has been around a long time. It has been given a variety of names, depending on the focus of the research in which it has been studied—for example, in infants, "low sensory threshold" (Chess & Thomas, 1987); "slow to warm up" (Thomas, Chess, & Birch, 1968); "affective negativity" (Marshall & Fox, 2005); "inhibitedness" (Kagan, 1994); "differential susceptibility" to both positive and negative environments (Belsky, Bakermans-

Kranenburg, & Van Ijzendoorn, 2007); "psychobiological reactivity" (Boyce et al., 1995; Gannon, Banks, & Shelton, 1989); "biological sensitivity to context" (Boyce & Ellis, 2005). "Sensitivity" seems to provide an umbrella that captures well the underlying innate survival strategy behind the trait, a tendency found in the immune system as well as the central nervous system, not only in humans but also in over 100 animal species (Wolf et al., 2008), from fruit flies and fish to canines and rhesus monkeys. This strategy allows one to process information thoroughly before responding.

HOW DOES THIS TRAIT RELATE TO PSYCHOTHERAPY?

Although this trait is found in 20% of the population, the actual occurrence is probably closer to 50% of patients in most practices. Individuals display this trait mainly if they had a troubled childhood, which makes them more prone than nonsensitive persons to depression, anxiety, and shyness; although those who had good childhoods do not display these problems any more than nonsensitive persons (Aron, Aron, & Davies, 2005; Liss, Timmel, Baxley, & Killingsworth, 2005). Indeed, there is considerable evidence that sensitive children benefit more than other children from good childhoods (for reviews of this growing literature see Belsky et al., 2009; Boyce & Ellis, 2005). This is one of many reasons not to think of this trait as a disorder, and why the title of this book is *Psychotherapy* and *the Highly Sensitive Person*—not *for*.

An equally important reason so many highly sensitive people seek therapy is because they may believe they have a disorder even if they do not. They are a poorly understood minority and they do not even understand themselves, so they come seeking an explanation for why they seem to be so different.

They are also more likely to come to treatment and want more sessions than other patients because they are more open and interested in things psychological, more aware of symptoms and their long-term consequences, and better able to see and overcome their initial resistance. They also need to stay longer because it takes more time to establish trust with them, and they need to understand and adapt to their trait as well as work on their presenting problem. They also gain more if they process their therapy experience longer, and probably they enjoy it more. Overall, needing and appreciating more and longer treatment, they will be a higher percentage of a general patient population at a given time.

With so many sensitive patients coming to counselors for so many reasons, it is crucial that we know how to distinguish sensitivity from the many disorders that it could be mistaken for. At the same time, we need to appreciate that sensitivity is often present along with other problems and disorders, so we need to know how those problems look different in sensitive patients and how understanding their sensitivity can improve our work with them. The purpose of this book is to clarify these issues while suggesting ways you can adapt to these patients' needs.

WHAT WILL I GAIN FROM THIS BOOK?

First, you will receive a speedy yet thorough education about high sensitivity. Although this book is intended to be a solid academic and professional book, it is written to save you time, with summaries at the beginning and end of each chapter and "bottom line" summaries of each section. There are also case illustrations and sample dialogues throughout. The first chapter gives you a feel for the main characteristics and the scientific research behind the trait (there is a fuller description of the research in Appendix C), and the second chapter helps you with the central task of recognizing when someone who comes for counseling is highly sensitive. The third, fourth, and fifth chapters provide ways to help these patients with their most typical problems and to adapt your work together so that you have the best outcome possible. The sixth, seventh, and eighth chapters focus on relationships and work, with the final chapter's focus on helping you identify sensitivity amid the vast array of other possible personality variations, including variations among the highly sensitive.

More generally, from this book you will gain the ability to improve greatly the quality of life of all the sensitive patients in your present and future practice. You will be able to inform them about their trait, validate it, and thereby permanently improve their self-esteem while helping them separate their innate temperament from the rest of what is going on for them. They will learn from you the advantages of this trait and how to handle what could become disadvantages. With many, your understanding of this core trait, so often overlooked or misunderstood by other professionals, will be the basis of their trust in you and the success of your other treatment goals.

Perhaps your most satisfying gain will be in seeing many of these patients benefit more than others from your psychotherapeutic efforts. As I stated previously, there is a growing body of research showing that sensitive children have a "biological sensitivity to context" (Boyce & Ellis, 2005) that allows them to derive more than other children from a supportive, enriching environment. Although they are sensitive to negative environments, children with a heightened sensitivity to psychosocial processes "might also be better able to notice when social cues denote encouragement and acceptance" (p. 420). It seems very likely that excellent psychotherapy would have the same differentially positive effects on sensitive adults, helping them turn vulnerability into a susceptibility to the good all around them.

STILL, ISN'T THIS "HYPERSENSITIVITY" AN IMPAIRMENT?

The question naturally persists, largely because the above-mentioned research on the normalness and benefits of the trait is not yet well known. Plus, therapists do not see a cross section of all sensitive persons because those raised in good environments are often adapting well, blending in, and unobtrusively selecting to place themselves in the situations in which they perform best and avoiding the others. You hardly notice them, even if you know them well. They are not the ones you think of when you think of high sensitivity.

On the other hand, due to their heightened vulnerability, there are more sensitive persons than others experiencing psychological distress and these sensitive individuals stand out. Suffering and sensitivity are paired in our minds. Even among nonpatients, we tend to notice sensitive people only when their feelings are being "too" easily hurt or "too bothered by a little bit of noise." Further, being a minority, they are not normal in the sense of being like most people (and like most therapists). The highly sensitive truly are different. On the HSP Scale there are people who answer yes to every question and those who answer no to all of them. That is a considerable range in behavior, but it is all normal.

Further confusion arises because high trait sensitivity can resemble certain disorders. For example, the highly sensitive have stronger emotional reactions, which could be mistaken for cyclothymia—and it does become that in some sensitive people. Their desire to pause to check before entering a novel situation can appear to be, or become, shyness. Their preference to revise cognitive maps after a failure rather than plunging immediately ahead again (Patterson & Newman, 1993) could be mistaken for compulsiveness, or their desire to consider all the consequences of a course of action could appear to be chronic anxiety—and again, some sensitive people do develop these disorders.

Above all, the potential for becoming overstimulated that accompanies the trait can lead to overarousal in the very situations most important to anyone, and overarousal (or underarousal) in anyone leads to discomfort and poor performance in the short run and reduced self-esteem and risk taking in the long run. Hence, if one confuses some natural consequences of the trait with the trait itself, it can seem to be nothing but a disorder or syndrome. Yet the trait itself is not an impairment. Indeed, it can yield rich benefits.

IS THIS LIKE BEING BORN SHY?

Sensitivity gives a more accurate sense of what underlies behaviors we label as shy, anxious, inhibited, reactive, neurotic, or withdrawn. These terms are applied after observing individuals, especially children and animals, who are not doing anything unusual that can be seen, so we try to hypothesize the cause of this inaction. But terms like "shy" do not cover all the possibilities. Strictly speaking, shy means fearing social judgment. How can we be certain that a child who hesitates before entering a classroom is afraid? The term *high sensitivity* comes closer to explaining a strategy of learning about one's environment through observing rather than exploring, while allowing for the fact that if a sensitive child's learning has been that rejection is likely to occur after entering a classroom, that child is more likely to become shy.

The term *sensitive* is also hopefully less negative, or rather has at least as many positive as negative implications. After all, the term for a trait does determine how we view it, and there are no truly neutral terms. For example, spontaneity as a trait is positively viewed, whereas impulsivity is negatively viewed, likewise with persistence versus stubbornness or extroversion versus lacking boundaries. In the case of this trait, most terms for it focus on what it sometimes but not always leads to, social withdrawal, fear, rumination, low self-esteem, shyness, and pessimism. In fact, none of these are inherent results of sensitivity, but they can arise through an interaction of the innate trait with various life experiences and difficulties. Since there are many sensitive persons without these negative characteristics, using these negative terms mislabels them in a way that harms these individuals, misdirects researchers, and confuses clinicians.

ISN'T THIS ACTUALLY INTROVERSION?

Sensitivity and introversion are the same in the way that Carl Jung (1921/1961) first used the terms: a preference to understand an experience subjectively, through comparison with other experiences, rather than explore its objective qualities. Also, research on introversion (Koelega, 1992) repeatedly finds that introverts are more sensitive in many senses than extraverts. But all of us, even Jung, then proceed to talk as if all introversion were social introversion. Although roughly 70% of sensitive persons are social introverts, 30% are actually social extraverts who do reflect considerably on their experiences and need more downtime than other extroverts in order to do this. They would be left out by equating sensitivity with introversion, and this is a group that especially needs to be understood.

Sensitivity appears to be more fundamental and innate, while introversion results from various causes, sensitivity being only one. Introversion and extroversion are still useful terms, but when sensitive patients are called sensitive, their therapists grasp a little better their underlying makeup. Equally important, patients feel more understood and helped because they recognize more of their experiences in this term, beyond their social behaviors.

WHY WOULD THERAPY NEED TO BE ANY DIFFERENT FOR SENSITIVE PERSONS?

It begins in a therapist's waiting room and office—sensitive persons react strongly to their environment and you can easily make a room comfortable for them if you realize this. Their initial session will be different—they will be more nervous than others would be, which can be wrongly interpreted or heightened in ways that make them suffer unnecessarily.

As therapy progresses, these patients will benefit most from being treated gently and not being overstimulated. No one learns well when overaroused. With these patients that happens more easily, so you need to adjust your style to them. They are also more sensitive to criticism and prone to shame. These reactions can be avoided by stating whatever you need to say in a softer way than you might with others. These are only a few ways.

ISN'T THIS MORE OF A POPULAR SELF-HELP IDEA?

This subject first appeared in my book for the layperson, *The Highly Sensitive Person,* which was published in 1996, before the first empirical research appeared in 1997. That book received considerable public attention, but for me it has been first and foremost a research topic. I never intended to write a popular book on sensitivity or anything else. But at the time that I began the research I was affiliated with the University of California at Santa Cruz, and they wrote a press release about it that was featured in the Sunday section of the local newspaper. Although only my name appeared in print, in the next 2 weeks hundreds of people had located me, calling or writing and wanting to know more. I agreed to give a talk at the public library and the crowd was standing-room only. Afterward, there were many requests for some sort of course on the subject. I had no idea what to teach beyond what I had already reported at the library. But I agreed to provide a small course and found myself listening more than teaching as a few dozen sensitive persons compared notes about how they managed their lives.

Soon I had pages of "coping strategies" that I shared during three more courses. However, I was definitely not interested in a career of giving self-help seminars, so it seemed best to meet the obvious need for this information by writing a book. Indeed it seemed like almost an ethical obligation, given the strength of interest and of the as-yet-unpublished research. When the book became a bestseller, there were many more opportunities to reach sensitive people and help them through *The Highly Sensitive Person's Workbook* (1999), *The Highly Sensitive Person in Love* (2001), a natural topic given that my husband and I have collaborated for years on research on attraction and closeness, and *The Highly Sensitive Child* (2002). The last seemed necessary as I further explored the statistical interaction of a poor home environment and sensitivity leading to adult anxiety, depression, and shyness.

Providing the general public with the information they need has left me little time to add to the research or attend conferences to discuss it, which would have led to more studies by others and the critical mass being achieved that makes an idea well known in academic circles. Hence, some may still see it as not a serious topic within academic psychology.

WHAT ABOUT THE AUTHOR?

I am highly sensitive myself, and while my own sensitivity could seem to threaten my objectivity, it does mean that I know the trait from the inside, which has been useful given that sensitivity involves so much nonobservable behavior. Further, being a psychotherapist who gradually became a specialist in treating sensitive patients, I have thousands of hours of clinical experience working with this group. I also have as many hours teaching, interviewing, and consulting with the larger, nonclinical population of highly sensitive persons, allowing me to compare the two. I have tried to use all of this material as objectively as possible, and being a skeptical type myself, there is an equal chance that I have been overly conservative.

USING THIS BOOK

The ideas presented in this book should be equally useful, whatever your theoretical orientation. I have tried to avoid advocating a particular overall approach, even if my own approach may show through at times. Its suggestions could become homework in brief cognitive behavioral therapy or insights gradually gained for use in longer-term psychodynamic work. Illustrations are more often of complicated long-term patients, assuming you do not need as many examples of working with those only needing counseling about the trait.

The cases are composites (and thus names are pseudonyms). I have wondered if this solution is quite right, given that a composite creates a person who might never exist. But perhaps all clinical descriptions have that problem.

Please notice the appendices. While at first it seemed sensible to begin with the research, it also felt wrong to force readers at the outset to digest several chapters of what might not interest them. Therefore, the details of the research are presented in Appendix C.

Chapter 2, on assessment, seemed to require some mention of the American Psychiatric Association's *Diagnostic and Statistical Manual of Mental Disorders* (*DSM*) categories—how sensitivity might be mistaken for various disorders and how a patient's sensitivity might change the "look" of some disorders. But it, too, seemed likely to be a burdensome beginning, so that material became Appendix B.

TERMINOLOGY

"High sensitivity," "sensitivity," and "sensory processing sensitivity" are used interchangeably. However, "sensitive person" refers to someone who is part of the group of all highly sensitive persons in the general population, and "sensitive patient" refers to someone in the subset of those who seek psychotherapy. That distinction is important.

My choice of "patient" more often than "client" is best explained by the reflections of Patt Denning, in her Preface to *Practicing Harm Reduction Psychotherapy* (2000/2004).

> When I call someone my patient, I feel a different, more profound responsibility in my role as therapist. I am aware that this person has come to me in pain and often with a large amount of fear. … I promise to offer myself as an anchor and an active helper, realizing her vulnerability and taking care not to use it to demean her or gain control over her life. Somehow, for me, the word "client" does not convey this sense of awesome responsibility, respect, and intimacy. (pp. xx–xxi)

ACKNOWLEDGMENTS

I wish to acknowledge my own patients and the many other sensitive persons I have met. They have taught me so much of what is in this book. The entire concept would never have reached so many, with such clarity and empirical validity, without the help of my husband, Art Aron. Jim Nageotte, an earlier editor, was also very helpful. George Zimmer at Routledge is the final reason you are reading this book. He was always enthusiastic about the project.

There were others who collaborated with us on the research, most notably Kristen Davies, Hal Ersner-Hershfield, and Jadzia Jagiellowicz. I received valuable clinical suggestions from Chauncy Irvine, Carole Kennedy, Gary Linker, Ellen Nakhnikian, Ellen Siegelman, and many others.

I owe so much to my dear friend and colleague Jan Kristal, who died too soon to share all that she knew about temperament. I dedicate this book to her.

CHAPTER

1

Highly Sensitive Patients

Who They Are, Who They Aren't, and Why It Matters

> I believe in aristocracy, though—if that is the right word, and if a democrat may use it. Not an aristocracy of power … but … of the sensitive, the considerate. … Its members are to be found in all nations and classes, and all through the ages … there is a secret understanding between them when they meet. They represent the true human tradition, the one permanent victory of our queer race over cruelty and chaos. Thousand of them perish in obscurity, a few are great names. They are sensitive for others as well as themselves … considerate without being fussy, their pluck is not swankiness but the power to endure.
>
> **—E. M. Forster, "What I Believe," in** *Two Cheers for Democracy*

This chapter provides an understanding of the highly sensitive person who is not necessarily a patient, before turning to those who are. It provides a definition of high sensitivity, differentiates it from disorders requiring treatment, and compares it to other well-known personality traits. There is a list of characteristics of sensitive persons and, finally, a discussion of the research indicating that sensitive persons with difficult childhoods do indeed evidence more vulnerability than others to depression, anxiety, and shyness.

"I've always been shy." "Everybody says I'm way too sensitive." "I don't get it. There're people with far worse childhoods and they don't need therapy. They aren't depressed and anxious." Therapists often hear these statements in their first session with a patient, and they consider various hypotheses about the underlying cause. Is the shyness enough to be social phobia? Is "too sensitive" a sign of a personality disorder? Why *is* this person suffering so much, given his or her history?

Many clinicians have applied the term "sensitive" to a patient or seen the word casually used in the literature. For example, "Individuals who are over stimulated by parental needs, or who are especially sensitive by nature, may perceive both pain and pleasure intensely" (Perera, 1986, p. 34). And on the first page of the first chapter of *The Inner World of Trauma*, Donald Kalsched wrote: "In most cases these patients were extremely bright, sensitive individuals who had suffered on account of this very sensitivity some acute or cumulative emotional trauma in early life" (1996, pp. 11–12). Yet these authors, like most clinicians, do not venture to define the term.

DEFINITION AND PREVALENCE

Sensitivity, high sensitivity, and sensory processing sensitivity are terms used in this book to identify a single innate temperament trait expressed as an awareness of subtleties in stimuli as well as a potential to be overwhelmed by too much stimuli (Aron & Aron, 1997; there is a full discussion of the research on this trait in Appendix C). This enhanced perception is not a quality of the sense organs, but rather of a brain exhibiting a strategy of processing information especially deeply. Hence, the observable behaviors that result from this strategy are quite varied, as you can see from the range of items on the HSP Scale, which is presented in Appendix A.

Sensitivity is found in about 15 to 20% of the population (Kagan, 1994; Kristal, 2005). Interestingly, it has been found in about the same percentage in most animals as well, from fruit flies (Renger, Yao, Sokolowski, & Wu, 1999) to primates (Suomi, 1987, 1991), although its genetic form and expression of course vary with the species. Its distribution is bimodal rather than normal (Kagan, 1994; Korte, Koolhaas, Wingfield, & McEwen, 2005); that is, individuals tend to have the trait or do not have it. There are not many in the middle.

Biologists now refer to two general strategies in animals, giving rise to two innate personality types with various names, such as bold versus shy (Wilson et al., 1993), hawk versus dove (Korte et al., 2005), or unresponsive versus responsive (Wolf et al., 2008). The former are usually the majority. Their strategy is to move quickly and forcefully if necessary toward feeding and mating opportunities without much prior observation of the situation. Compared to the more impulsive or bold 80%, the sensitive minority evolved a survival approach of avoiding risks by carefully observing the subtleties in a situation before acting. Both strategies—"think first" and "act now"—can be successful, depending on conditions in the environment.

In humans, the more sensitive strategy of scanning the environment and attending to details of stimulation has been observed in functional magnetic resonance imaging (fMRI; Jagiellowicz, Xu, et al., in press) and more generally in thinking and feeling before and during a behavior. This strategy allows for a greater awareness of subtleties and consequences. This in turn leads, for example, to high levels of conscientiousness and creativity. On the negative side, this elaborate processing creates a greater potential for being overstimulated and troubled by stressful life events.

As for gender, there are as many sensitive men as women born (Buss, 1989; Rothbart, 1989), and while perhaps the presence of testosterone has some later effect, for the most part they experience sensitivity differently according to the culture in which they live. If the culture disapproves of a man being sensitive, these men generally learn to cover up their sensitivity in order to appear more like a typical male. On the HSP Scale (Appendix A) they tend to score a bit lower, even though gender-biased items have been removed from the scale. For example, originally there was a question on the scale about crying easily, which many respondents assented to, but men did so much less. In fact, sensitive men were actually a little less likely than other men to say they cry easily. Yet eliminating items like this did not change the overall effect of gender, which was that men scored lower. This is probably due to their overall impression of the scale. Sensitive men definitely have different issues than sensitive women and overall probably face larger problems. The issues for both genders are discussed more in Chapter 5.

Bottom Line: Sensitivity is an innate trait found in 20% of humans, and in most animals as well. It seems to result from a strategy of processing information carefully before acting, and results in an awareness of subtleties but also in being easily overstimulated. There are as many sensitive men as women, but the men hide this trait more and usually have more difficulties with it.

SENSITIVITY IN CLINICAL PRACTICE

High sensitivity is a normal variation in innate temperament. It has a high prevalence and bestows many benefits. It is not a diagnostic category. Rather, it is orthogonal to mental disorder. Some sensitive persons have diagnosable disorders, as do some nonsensitive persons. Most do not, just as most nonsensitive persons do not.

The highly sensitive have been found, however, to be more vulnerable to depression, anxiety, and shyness if they have had difficult childhoods, but with a good enough childhood evidence is no more indicative of this trait than in nonsensitive persons (Aron et al., 2005; Liss et al., 2005). Indeed, as mentioned in the Preface, sensitive children appear to benefit more than others from good childhoods (for reviews of this growing literature see Belsky et al., 2009; Boyce & Ellis, 2005). Still, many do have impairments to varying degrees, especially mood and anxiety disorders.

On the other hand, you will see highly sensitive persons who have no disorder but have been diagnosed with one, and some will have a disorder but will have been misdiagnosed. (You may also see a few patients who think they are highly sensitive, having read about it, and probably are not but rather do have a disorder.) Specific *DSM* diagnoses that might be confused with sensitivity are discussed in Appendix B. An example is autistic spectrum disorder. Sometimes it is said that the trait described here is at the high end of this spectrum. The criteria for an autism disorder or Asperger's syndrome, however, have no overlap with high sensitivity as defined here and found in 20% of the population. Many autistic persons are distressed by high levels of specific kinds of stimulation, but they can be unfazed by other types, especially social cues. In contrast, sensitive persons can tolerate high levels of stimulation without becoming utterly confused or violent, and they use increasingly appropriate ways of reducing stimulation as they mature. Further, the sensitivity in autism is due to faulty use of sensory information, not processing it to deeper levels. Sensitive persons do not perseverate in the way that the autistic do, and they evidence high levels of empathy as well as adequate to excellent social skills, especially in familiar environments.

Sensory integration problems are also confused with sensory processing sensitivity. But sensory integration dysfunction or disorder refers to specific soft neurological problems that usually respond well to treatment. Some sensitive persons (and indeed most sedentary people whatever their temperament) might improve through these treatments. However, they will not eliminate the characteristics listed below.

An illness is something you hope to change or lessen. Although the lives of sensitive persons can improve with knowledge about their trait and they can learn ways to adapt, no treatment will eliminate innate high sensitivity, nor is there any reason to want to do that given its advantages in some contexts.

Bottom Line: High sensitivity as described in this book is not a disorder.

A DIFFERENCE LIKE GENDER AND ETHNICITY

A better way to think of this trait is that it is a widespread individual difference, much like gender, but found in a minority of people, much like a particular ethnicity. Given that many people answer yes to every item on the HSP Scale (see Appendix A), while many others answer no to every item, a case could be made that this difference is a factor at least as potent in its effect as gender and ethnicity. Further, it is a largely invisible difference, and these create unique social difficulties for those who have them (Frable, 1993).

As with gender and ethnicity, there are specific problems associated with being highly sensitive, some of them due to the trait itself, such as being easily overaroused, and some due to the culture in which it is found. For example, in China, elementary school children with the trait are popular with peers; in Canada they are not (Chen, Rubin, & Sun, 1992). Thus, depending on the culture, sensitive persons may have high or low self-esteem.

There are also disorders that have nothing to do with sensitivity itself, yet the trait gives the disorder a certain flavor. For example, a certain number of sensitive persons with panic disorder improve with relative ease once they understand the role of overstimulation in their symptoms, whereas panic attacks in nonsensitive persons are less likely to be resolved in this way.

Bottom Line: This trait has an individual-difference effect similar to gender or ethnicity.

COMPARISON TO OTHER PERSONALITY TRAITS

The HSP Scale overlaps with but is not identical to measures of introversion (see Aron & Aron, 1997, and Appendix B), in that roughly 30% of sensitive persons are found to be extroverts. This figure depends on the measure of introversion used (correlations range from .12 to .52, Aron & Aron, 1997), as these measures in themselves do not correlate well.

As for neuroticism, the correlation is generally higher. One reason is that, again, highly sensitive persons with a troubled childhood are more likely to be depressed, anxious, and shy—that is, have more negative affect (the general definition of neuroticism as a personality trait)—compared to nonsensitive persons with the same level of childhood difficulties and traumas. In any random sample, some sensitive persons will have had difficult childhoods, and they raise the mean of neuroticism scores for the entire sensitive subset unless childhood environment is statistically controlled for.

Shyness shows the same pattern but is present only if there is also negative affect (Aron et al., 2005). That is, sensitive persons are more likely to be shy if they had difficult childhoods *and if* that resulted in high levels of negative affect. Not every sensitive person's poor childhood leads to negative affect. Shyness and negative affect are the results of unfortunate experiences, not the trait itself.

Bottom Line: High sensitivity is not the same as introversion, neuroticism, or shyness.

A LIST OF DISTINGUISHING CHARACTERISTICS

The deeper processing common to all highly sensitive persons leads to the characteristics listed below. Except where indicated, this list is based on my own published data or that of others, or in some cases my extensive experience, clinically and in research interviews. No sensitive person will have all of these, but should have a broad variety of them, as opposed to having a few (only staying on the sidelines or only being conscientious), which could be due to something other than a fundamental genetic difference.

- Preferring to be on the sidelines in a situation for a while before entering it, and generally exploring a situation more by observing and reflecting rather than by moving about within it. "Sometimes I wish people would leave me alone to sit in a corner and watch before I get involved." "I like to check things out first—see what I'm getting into."
- Being very aware of subtleties or small changes. "I noticed that on your answering message you now refer to yourself as 'Doctor'—would you prefer that I call you that?" "That picture (carpet, hair style, etc.) is new, isn't it?"
- Wanting to consider every detail and possible outcome before acting—"do it once and do it right"—as opposed to the majority's tendency to decide more quickly. This results, for example, in being slower than nonsensitive persons at making decisions, more aware of risks and benefits, and being seen as slow but accurate. "I'm terrible at making decisions." (In fact, they are slow but their decisions are usually good.) "I'm a real perfectionist."
- Being more aware of the thoughts and emotions of others, due to gaining more information from nonverbal cues and guessing correctly because of intuiting the likely effects of a situation on others. "Sometimes I feel like I can read other people's minds." "I'm really affected by other people's moods."
- Having been harmed more by bad environments in childhood or adulthood, but possibly gaining more than others from unusually supportive environments (skilled parenting or teaching in childhood or thoughtful management in adulthood).
- Acting more conscientiously due to being heavily attuned to causes and consequences—how things came to be as they are and how they will turn out, depending on what is done. They think more often, "What if everybody left their trash behind?" "If I don't finish my work on time I will be slowing others down."
- Having unusual concern about social justice and the environment and expressing an unusual degree of compassion, even in childhood. "I couldn't just stand by and let that happen to her." "I was trying to get others to understand about global warming for years."

- Being easily overstimulated, and hence easily overaroused. For anyone, the more stimulation the more arousal and overarousal leads to poorer performance for anyone. But sensitive persons are overaroused sooner by less stimulation, and so report more difficulties or failures in highly stimulating situations (e.g., contests, recitals, public speaking, meeting respected strangers, being trained or under observation, timed tests, and also places that are noisy, crowded, etc.). "It's humiliating—I'm fine at practice, but terrible at the meets." "I just can't take tests."
- Being gifted, artistic, or passionate about the arts. "I've been crazy about the opera since I was five and first heard one on the radio."
- Having a strong interest in spirituality and often involved in a specific practice. "Prayer is essential to my life." "I'm a Buddhist—I meditate every day."
- Reporting a greater emotional reaction to events that evoke similar emotions in others, but less so. "I cry at the drop of a hat." "Everybody was upset, but I was devastated."
- Noticing unusual distress due to change. "I had no idea moving would be so upsetting." "I'm really having trouble adjusting to this seemingly small change in my life."
- Reporting unusually vivid dreams if asked. "I always dream in color." "My dreams seem to go on forever with a lot of details."
- Recalling any of these characteristics occurring first in childhood. "Everyone said I was really sensitive." "I liked to hide under tables and bushes or in closets and just listen to what was going on."
- Complaining about overstimulating or unaesthetic environments. "I can't stand fluorescent lights." "I had to move twice before I found a quiet apartment." (Sensitive adolescents seem to tolerate loud music, crowds, and multitasking better, but this changes in the late 20s.)
- Having physical sensitivities—faster startle response; more reactive immune system (e.g., more contact allergies; Bell, 1992)—and greater sensitivity to pain, stimulants (e.g., caffeine), and most medications (Jagiellowicz, Aron, & Aron, 2007). "I can't drink coffee—it makes me too nervous." "My doctor finds it hard to believe that I can notice anything from such a low dose, but I do, and if I take more I have all sorts of side effects."
- Speaking in a considerate, sometimes indirect way. Dropping hints. "Does it seem warm in here to you?" "I suggested to him that maybe we should go out to eat. I was too tired to cook."
- Finding that nature has an unusually healing, calming effect or being more moved by its beauty. Fond of animals, plants, and being near or in water.

THE ROLE OF THEIR GREATER EMOTIONALITY

One reason sensitive patients are so interesting and challenging to work with, and so prone to misdiagnosis, is that all sensitive persons react more deeply, albeit normally, to a given emotion-generating situation. It is a point not directly represented on the questionnaire, partly to avoid gender bias.

If a preference to process information more deeply is the underlying reason that causes the various behaviors of the highly sensitive, how does this relate to stronger emotional reactions? One might expect that this reflecting would have a calming effect, but in fact sensory processing sensitivity necessarily involves greater emotionality, for at least two reasons. First, emotion drives cognitive processing, since nothing is processed for long without an emotional evaluation that it is important or interesting. Second, processing drives emotion, in that the longer something is processed that has emotional meaning, the more emotion it will create.

This greater emotionality is related to the interaction I already described, that sensitive people who have had a troubled childhood are more vulnerable to depression, anxiety, and shyness than nonsensitive persons with the same level of distress. However, the highly sensitive are also more prone than others to have strong positive emotions (Aron & Aron, 1997), such as responding to rewards (Bar-Haim et al., 2009). To term this trait an innate "high vulnerability" or "proneness to negative affect," or, in that sense, "neuroticism," would be as narrow a definition as using "skin cancer prone" as the only term for being fair skinned. However, it remains the case that highly sensitive people have stronger emotional reactions, a significant factor for psychotherapists to keep in mind. A mild criticism can induce shame. Mild praise can produce euphoria or possibly a misunderstanding of your feelings.

Bottom Line: The highly sensitive have stronger affects, both positive and negative.

WHAT IS NOT TYPICAL OF THE HIGHLY SENSITIVE

It is also helpful to think about how people present who are not highly sensitive. Given that these are the majority of people, much can be ascertained simply by remembering what most people enjoy or are not bothered by. They are not usually bothered by noise, visual clutter, sudden change, or other aspects of an environment or experience that would be overstimulating to a sensitive person. The acceptable level of stimulation in work environments and the pleasurable level of it in recreational environments and the media evidence this very well. The nonsensitive majority mostly enjoy the rapidly shifting visual stimulation of video games, television ads, and action movies. They like street fairs, major sporting events, and shopping malls during the holidays. Many enjoy horror movies, dangerous sports, and watching dramas involving shocking violence. Nor do they ponder the future overly much until the consequences of some action are pointed out to them or become costly. For example, a large number of people fail to be tested for prostate, colon, and breast cancer.

Again, only judging from what is common behavior, the majority take risks with less extensive preparation. ("I just never expected that to happen.") The highly sensitive do take risks, but carefully. For example, in a dangerous sport, they tend to be experts on safety and are much less likely to be injured. If they fail at something, they want to try again immediately rather than reflecting on their error and changing strategies as the minority do (Patterson & Newman, 1993). The majority temperament enjoys all forms of gambling. They are less affected by actual or imagined financial or other loss or by making a mistake. They are less emotionally reactive generally. Yet they may show their emotions more, such as expressing anger about the service they are receiving, even though the public expression of anger is usually socially risky and highly stimulating. It is also normal for most persons most of the time to speak in a direct manner, with less concern about how their tone or word choice could affect the listener because they expect others to be like them, relatively imperturbable.

Many people are fond of nature, and many find comfort there. But the nonsensitive tend to see it more as a place to pursue activities and are less concerned by the suffering of animals other than their own pets. They may practice a religion, but question it less. Relatively fewer are preoccupied by spiritual matters, philosophy, or "the meaning of life." But let's return to gaining a feeling for highly sensitive people by describing one as he or she might appear in your office.

Bottom Line: It can be helpful to notice how sensitive patients do not resemble your other patients in that the latter are not easily overstimulated—bothered by noise or sudden change, for example—and are less likely to notice subtleties, such as changes in your office. Although the following is over generalizing, nonsensitive patients will be fonder of video games, crowds, team sports, and action movies; not bothered by voilence; take more risks and enjoy doing so; prepare less for activities; and speak more directly, without hints. They tent to use nature for recreation more than as a place of solace, and if spiritual, have given their beliefs less though.

A CASE ILLUSTRATION

Susan, 34, is an example of a patient who mainly needed extensive help adapting her life to her sensitivity, although she might have been assessed and treated differently by someone who did not understand her trait. She was crying as soon as she sat down for our first session. She was also experiencing "panicky feelings" at the thought of going back to work after a maternity leave, and she often imagined something happening to her 8-month-old daughter Katy. "But mostly I'm just *overwhelmed,*" she sobbed. "*I can't take it anymore.*" Then she straightened up. "But I have to and I will, of course. Don't worry about me. I'll be okay." Her tone supported that she did not wish to upset me, rather than a sudden switch to denial.

Susan had taken a new position, with a considerable raise in status and pay, but put on an open floor, to "encourage maximal communication" with those she would manage as part of the company. For her it allowed maximal chaos and constant observation by others while she was learning a new role. The CEO had instructed her to deliver on a shortened deadline, but right away she had seen signs that their product would not satisfy clients' needs in the long run. When she voiced her opinion in meetings, she was criticized for "being a Cassandra" and never signing off on anything.

There were also problems with this job and having a new baby. Susan had a very long commute, meaning having to choose between less time with her daughter or less sleep. She usually chose the latter, acknowledging that she was "pushing the envelope," but she knew many other women in similar positions who were living like she was, although seemingly more successful at it.

Susan had earned an MBA immediately after college, but since then had changed jobs frequently. I listened carefully for signs of mania, impulsivity, or stories of real or perceived victimization. But her explanations for the changes always seemed reasonable. In one case she was concerned about the ethics of a company's business practices. In another she doubted the worth of the product. Mainly she had been moving rapidly up the ladder in her field, sometimes after only a few months. She had successfully transferred her learning to whole new specialties, as she was this time.

She thought her marriage was going reasonably well, except that her husband, Phil, also had a burgeoning career. When she returned to work 5 months ago, they hired a live-in nanny. They felt they had no other option now that they were both working more than full time.

Susan described her mother fondly, as a loving parent who stayed home with her children, two daughters, until they were in school. Mother and daughter talked once a week by phone and now more often as they shared Katy's developmental milestones. Her mother did not like the idea of a nanny raising Katy, but she remained supportive of whatever the new family chose.

As for her father, she had been his favorite. He was a successful investment banker and not as available as she would have liked, so she learned to talk with him about his work. In fact, she was an investment prodigy. Her father proudly displayed in his office a graph of her gains from the stocks she had chosen and he had then bought for her. Some joked that they would rather ask Susan for tips than her father. At 12, she learned to play golf, so he could take her along when he needed to complete a foursome.

Susan was somewhat conscious that her father was the reason she was in the business world herself, aiming to be a CEO someday. He was always proud of her, although even he had noticed his daughter was looking strained and wished she would slow down a little.

Given this reasonably happy childhood, described with appropriate affect, I decided to focus on her sensitivity. She had read my book so I reminded her of some of its contents. In response she cried again as she talked about the stress she was under. Her maternal feelings were very strong and she longed to have another child, yet she loved the business world. She wanted me to explain why she could not manage the same work and family responsibilities as other women rising to the top.

"Didn't you say in your book that this sensitivity makes us more creative? If I'm so creative, why can't I find *solutions* to all of this? Instead, I'm crying all the time. Is this really what sensitivity is about? Why didn't you say that in your book?"

"I did," I said very gently. "But I think you did not want to see those parts. Understandably."

"Does this mean I have to stay home with Katy, like Mother did with us? I'd go crazy with boredom."

I asked her to look at herself as she would someone she was managing. How was she doing? She admitted she was doing badly.

"So what do you think? Does something have to change?"

She agreed, but she was still firm about wanting to succeed at this job, so we focused on new strategies. She would arrange staggered work hours, arriving and leaving early, which would shorten her commute, give her some quiet time in the office so that she was not doing work at home, and would give her more time with Katy.

We discussed her CEO's critical style and agreed he was a normal guy, just harried and nonsensitive. Susan decided she could discuss her working style with him—that she performed best when told she was on the right track, as she could overreact to criticism and alter too much. Also, since there was a surplus of conference rooms that had been converted from offices, she would like to convert one back, giving her a space where she could concentrate on this project and consult privately with individual team members.

She would withhold her skepticism about a product's design in meetings until she had convinced at least two others in private that she was right and that they should stand by her. Further, she would encourage them to make similar arguments to others, so that most were in agreement with her before the meetings began. We agreed to meet in a month, as she could not afford the time to come more often.

In our second session, she looked even more drawn. She had tried to implement our ideas, but now she was coming to work early and still leaving late, the result of the CEO's increasing respect for her work, which was leading to even more responsibilities. Her new private office meant she was being consulted even more. There was still too little time for Katy.

I pointed out that all of this was the result of her being very good at what she does, and that her sensitivity probably played a large role in that. She was the only one at work or at home who was highly sensitive. They could work 14-hour days, and they loved her for her sensitivity in the form of creativity, conscientiousness, and enthusiasm. "By the way, nonsensitive mothers hate to leave their babies, too, but on that scale, you suffer more."

A sensitive mother and child became the theme of that session. Katy was highly sensitive and Susan worried that their nanny did not understand this. Phil was not helping. "They want to push her when she holds back. That's exactly the wrong way to get her out there. They think Katy needs to be made to do what scares her, even when she's crying and pleading with them. I know what that feels like."

Her daughter had brought us to her own childhood—"Your father?"

"As far back as I can remember, he made me 'face my fears.' I learned to force myself, for him. He loved showing me off. It was so much pressure. He taught me to play golf so I could complete a foursome. I did putt well."

"That was your sensitivity, wasn't it?"

"But they called me Lost Ball Suzy."

Her first memory, always part of my history taking, was of hiding under a bush to evade her first haircut. She imagined it would hurt. When her father heard of that, he took her for the haircut and announced her fear to everyone present. "All those loud women made a huge fuss over me and I cried and cried. But he said I'd never make it in the world if I didn't learn to …"

"Face your fears. How old were you?"

"Three."

I almost gasped. "So you handle Katy's fears differently."

"It's not hard. She'll do anything if we take our time, show her the ropes, but she so much wants to please her father. I'm afraid she'll just learn to endure."

"Like you. Learning to endure, to perform beyond your limits, without protest."

She brought up her desire for another child and admitted she could not do it while working at this job. But leaving it made her "feel like a quitter."

I find it important to support both sides of an issue like this, to keep the conflict an inner one, so I suggested that we continue to explore the pros and cons of various courses of action, and we did that for the next 2 months.

Meanwhile she was slipping further—filled with self-doubt, losing weight, feeling more anxious, having difficulty focusing, and not sleeping even when she had the time to. I explained that she was simply running out of gas—neurotransmitters. After a careful discussion and her own review of the research, she decided to try an antidepressant for 6 months. (The psychiatrists to whom I refer know to begin with very low doses when prescribing for sensitive patients, as they often have more side effects or need to try several before finding the right one.)

She soon returned to her normal weight, cried less, and had better concentration. The underlying problem did not go away, but she could think about it more objectively. We explored much more deeply her imitation of her father's highly competitive attitudes. According to her father's books on how to succeed in the corporate world, you had to overcome all weakness in yourself and make use of the weaknesses of others. She could talk now about the darker side of that, both in him and herself.

From the motto of "No weakness" we hit her bedrock dislike of her sensitivity. She needed to hear many times the advantages of her trait and how others enjoyed these while criticizing what they did not like.

"They never realize it's a package deal—what they love about you goes along with what they would like to eliminate in you. The same sensitivity that made you good at putting and choosing stocks, and makes you such a good mother, also made you fail under the pressure of hitting a ball or trying to be too many things at once." Her hatred of her trait did not change immediately, but she believed she had gained enough from our work to "solve this problem on my own." I could almost hear her gritting her teeth.

A year later I received an announcement of her new business, which specialized in matching new parents in demanding careers with the highest quality professional personal assistants and childcare providers. In the margin she wrote, "I'm off the medication. And you'd be proud of me—I'm keeping this business part time and very small for now. Our new son is due in 2 months. I'm feeling as rested and ready as I'll probably ever be. I simply love being the president of my own company. I'm sure we'll go national—when *I* am ready."

SUSAN'S IMPROVEMENT

Susan was the type of sensitive patient who benefits most from grasping the full implications of her sensitivity and how it interacted with her otherwise loving, adequately functioning parents and their child-rearing philosophy. In our first session, she was highly emotional—tears and panicky feelings—so that major depression or an anxiety disorder had to be considered. Yet she seemed to be functioning well, perhaps too well, on the job. It was typical, given her good enough childhood and excellent education, that she would advance rapidly in her career, even though it may have been a poor choice. Her many job changes were also typical of sensitive persons, as I will explain in Chapter 8.

Naturally, a sensitive person with so many advantages and talents would want to enjoy all the opportunities these bestowed on her—marriage, career advancement, children. This lifestyle places heavy demands on any woman, but it can become far too much for a sensitive person of either gender without better outside support. Some of the stresses of work and family were exacerbated by her trait. I had to smile at her being called a Cassandra, since that poor woman was cursed by Apollo to always know the truth and never to be believed. Sensitive people can feel that way in business meetings.

Given the conflicts Susan faced, it is not surprising that she disliked her sensitivity. It meant she had to give up something. She had to learn to remind herself repeatedly that her trait was, as I like to describe it, a package deal. It contributed to her wealth of opportunities, but it also restricted her. Deciding what to give up leads to inner conflict, and that was intensified by her stronger emotional response due to deeper processing of what each meant to her, now and in the future. Both choices, work or motherhood, were so desired, and giving one up felt so bad.

Susan benefited from antidepressants at the point where even she could see that she needed that type of help. If I had suggested it in the first session, I am sure she would not have come for a second session.

This patient grew up with no knowledge of her trait, much less help on how to live with it. Trying to raise children with normal but extreme temperament variations often leads to misery for all involved. Parents are afraid there is something wrong with either them or their children. They force too much, protect too much, or take their children for counseling or agree to medications, all of which delivers the message to children that there is something very wrong with them.

These children need a "goodness of fit" (Kristal, 2005; Thomas & Chess, 1977), which does not mean having parents with the same temperament, but parents and teachers who structure a child's environment in a way that enhances the best aspects of his or her temperament.

Unfortunately, sensitive children tend to be so well behaved that no attempt is made to adapt to them. They adapt to others. As adults, you as their therapist must help them create "goodness of fit" for themselves. These patients must develop a new set of operating instructions, and do so without feeling this is mainly about their limitations. Alas, probably they will not do it until there is a physical or mental health crisis.

HIGH SENSITIVITY AND HIGH SENSATION SEEKING

Highly sensitive persons can also be high sensation seekers (Zuckerman, 1993). It is somewhat counterintuitive but needs to be discussed early enough for you to recognize this important variation in the trait. Susan is an example of one. These two traits, controlled by separate pathways in the brain, are independent of each other. Thus far, it is thought that sensation seeking is caused by unusually active reward areas, which are associated more with dopamine. Sensitivity is less well understood but is probably caused in part by greater activation in areas that encourage inhibition of action along with alert attention, a pattern associated with low serotonin, creating ideal conditions for processing information more deeply. Therefore, the proper interpretation of high sensitivity is not an avoidance of stimulation, even if it leads to an avoidance of overstimulation. They actually react more to success and reward than others. Rather, the fundamental motivation created by the trait is a desire to process a situation before acting, so the opposite of being highly sensitive is being impulsive.

Sensation-seeking sensitive persons are susceptible to boredom. As Susan said, she would not be a good stay-at-home mom without any other projects in her life. They will usually prefer to try new restaurants and new cuisines, not the same old haunt (unless they are feeling overstimulated). Susan liked trying new jobs. They do not like to watch the same movie twice unless it is a very good one. They may hang glide or travel to exotic places, but they are never impulsive and study the activity beforehand, doing all they can to ensure their safety. They may like novelty, but they do not like high risks or shocks. But since the dopamine-driven reward system creates a high motivation to approach or act immediately, while the purpose of the inhibition system is to do just that, to create a pause for checking things, being high on both traits can be difficult. As one person with this combination put it, "It's like living with one foot on the gas, one foot on the brakes."

Bottom Line: The highly sensitive person can also be a high sensation seeker. They are independent traits. The opposite of sensitivity is impulsivity, not necessarily a dislike of novelty.

A CASE ILLUSTRATION

Julian, 28, a freelance journalist with an otherwise normal history, came to me because of his "overreaction" due to witnessing the results of a terrorist's bombing. He and his wife were vacationing in the area, in a region where terrorist acts were least expected, so they were the only media on the scene, and only minutes after the explosion.

In the abstract, both saw it as a major journalistic opportunity. While his wife remained objective and curious, gathering details and interviewing survivors, Julian stayed very briefly. He vomited, nearly fainted, and had to retreat to a nearby hotel. He found himself crying uncontrollably for days. Images from the scene were still vivid in his memory after 6 months. He was suffering from posttraumatic stress disorder, while his high sensation–seeking, nonsensitive wife was not.

Prior to this event Julian had always thought he was perfectly suited for his career. He had loved the variety and opportunities for foreign travel, which had combined nicely with his ability to reflect, find creative angles, and write well about these. Now he doubted he was capable of any of it. He felt like a failure professionally and as a man. Although his wife insisted it was not true, he felt she had lost respect for him. It was she who had recommended he meet with me about his sensitivity, which was now obvious to her. The major part of the treatment, as with Susan, was helping him accept and appreciate the advantages of his trait.

OTHER MEANINGS OF SENSITIVITY NOT IMPLIED HERE

Again, sensitivity as defined here is not the same as introversion, simply because a third of the highly sensitive are extroverts. Nor is it about being "sensitive" in the sense of caring for and being responsive to others. Most sensitive people are usually highly motivated and skilled at showing empathy, but many nonsensitive persons are equally or more motivated and successful at being sensitive in this other sense. At the same time, sensitive persons who are overaroused can be temporarily anything but empathic, and some with personality disorders are permanently not, at least in situations they find threatening.

Sensitivity also does not refer only to being sensitive to criticism, as when someone is accused of "just being too sensitive" or "taking things too personally." Although, sensitive people as defined here do seem to process criticism more and have a stronger emotional reaction to it, that is not the essence of the trait.

Bottom Line: Sensitivity as used here should not be equated with being caring or responsive to others or only with being hypersensitive to criticism.

THE SENSITIVE PERSON VERSUS THE SENSITIVE PATIENT

The rest of this book will deal mostly with sensitive patients, so it bears repeating that sensitive nonpatients are all around you. You may be highly sensitive yourself. The highly sensitive are usually functioning quite well. I hope I do not sound too much like a rooting section, but they often need one, because mostly they adapt and are hardly noticeable. True, they generally do not like crowds. They may ask for a quiet table in a restaurant. They need a place to live that is not too noisy. Relationships have to be deep; work has to be meaningful, yet not entail long hours. They do not like fluorescent lights, but tolerate them for the sake of the environment.

On the benefits side of the ledger, they ponder matters deeply, although they may not let on that they have strong ideas about God, death, and the universe. They may fall silent in conversations about mundane matters, but if anyone asks their opinion, they often have something worthwhile to say.

They are often the ones who feel the most for what is happening on the earth and to people in distant places. They give more money to good causes and are often active in them. Frequently they are the ones who listen to you, remember you, and worry about you before anyone else notices a reason to. If you like massages or use alternative medicine, chances are the one treating you is highly sensitive.

We sense their presence among some of the wiser, quieter political and business leaders. They are often the inventors, educators, judges, scientists, historians, and general benefactors of humankind.

That does not mean they cannot be exasperating. They can be exacting, fussy, irritable when overstimulated, and critical (of themselves and others equally), even though they cannot take what they dish out. They are chronically slow to decide—although their decisions are usually right. They do not like risks, so they buy more insurance and have more savings than other people think is necessary, and they want everyone they care about to do the same.

They often take a break from answering the phone or email and say no to more invitations, or else they are slightly frazzled because they cannot. Their problem often is that most people like them very much. They do not always make good first impressions, but with time they become highly valued friends and group members.

In short, they are people well worth helping if they ask for it. They need an upbringing and environment that suits them if they are to flourish. In an experiment that could not be done with humans, Suomi (1987, 1997) took newborn monkeys who were "reactive" (another term for the trait) and cross fostered them with skilled mothers and found they grew up to be exceptionally well adapted—usually the troop leaders. Returning to humans, some (Silverman, 1994) equate the highly sensitive with the highly gifted, although that does not fit with the percentage (3%) of the population estimated to be gifted.

Sumoi's study also found that reactive monkeys raised by unskilled mothers generally had low ranks, were highly susceptible to stress, and prone to anxiety and depression, a result that mirrors those already discussed showing the interaction of sensitivity and a troubled childhood yielding more depression, anxiety, and shyness. If so much depends on upbringing and learning, then for adult sensitive patients it may depend in large part on you, their psychotherapist.

Bottom Line: Highly sensitive patients are first of all highly sensitive people, capable of making valuable contributions, but that largely depends upon the nurturing they receive.

A ROLE MODEL

My friend Jim is from a fine, upstanding, outgoing family. He was encouraged to earn his doctorate and use his learning to benefit the disadvantaged, which he does with wonderful enthusiasm. He is one of the most charming, friendly, kind, and mentally healthy persons I know, and it is also well established that he is also *not* highly sensitive. He never tires of talking and has a high enough pain threshold to endure all the various injuries that come with playing ultimate Frisbee into one's 40s.

He and his wife have two daughters. The firstborn, Betsy, is just like Jim. The second, Lily, was from the first weeks very good and quiet as long as the home was peaceful and her needs were met. Lily was also a keen observer of her world, but from Jim's point of view, a little too anxious. Still, she passed all of her early developmental milestones on time so the family did not worry.

In her second year, a worried Jim asked me to tell him more about my research. He was recognizing what I had already, that Lily was highly sensitive. Jim was relieved that she was normal, even if not like Jim's side of the family. She would have as happy a life as he, although perhaps made happy in different ways. But our discussion left Jim wondering how he could be the best possible father to his sensitive little girl.

To begin, he vowed never again to interpret his daughter's behavior as any sort of flaw, disappointment to him, or reason for anyone's concern. Neither did he want his daughter to miss out on experiences that she might actually enjoy or have her grow up afraid of meeting new people. Jim became determined to introduce her to every potentially pleasurable opportunity in life, from ocean waves, tree climbing, and new foods to family reunions, soccer, and varying her clothes rather than wearing one comfortable uniform.

In almost every instance, Lily initially thought these novel experiences were not such good ideas, and Jim *always* respected her opinion. He never forced her, although he could be very persuasive. He simply shared his view of a situation with her—the safety and pleasures involved, the similarities to other things she already liked. He would wait for that little gleam in her eye that said she wanted to join in with the others, even if she couldn't yet.

Jim always assessed these situations carefully to ensure that she would not ultimately be frightened, but rather be able to experience pleasure and success. Sometimes he held her back until she was overly ready. Above all, he kept it an internal conflict, not a conflict between him and her. He made every effort to give her time to observe, along with just a little pressure to stay in the conflict, not just back off. From his stories, I could easily imagine Jim and Lily huddled at the edge of a lake, stage, or ski slope, deep in discussion about the pros and cons of sallying forth.

In spite or because of the fact that her father generally prevailed, Lily still prefers to have her father rather than her slightly more anxious mother with her when she faces something new. And if she or anyone else comments on her quietness or hesitancy, Jim's prompt reply is, "That's just your style. Other people have different styles. But this is yours. You like to take your time and be sure."

Jim also knows that part of her style is befriending anyone whom others tease, doing careful work, noticing everything going on in the family, and being the best soccer strategist in her league. In short, he is particularly proud of his highly sensitive daughter.

Jim's story is here to provide you with a sense of what sensitive children need from their parents and what your sensitive adult patients need from you—acceptance, encouragement, and pride in their success and of the best parts of their sensitivity.

THE IMPORTANCE OF UNDERSTANDING INNATE SENSITIVITY FOR CLINICAL PRACTICE

No matter how excellent a person's upbringing, most sensitive patients did not have a parent like Jim. They may have been appreciated for being sensitive, intuitive, compassionate, creative, and conscientious. But rarely do others realize these admirable qualities are part of a package deal that also may include being overly fussy about socks, clothing tags, seams, and wool; overly upset by the slightest rebuke; or stubbornly cautious in new situations. Hence as adults they desperately need the kind of understanding Jim provides his daughter.

Said more systematically, understanding this trait is clinically valuable in a number of ways. First, even when their childhood was fine, they are more likely to need help at some point in their lives with understanding why they are different from others. Often criticisms are made by people who are concerned about their unusualness. If they receive the wrong response from you, especially if it only affirms what others have said, you will quite inadvertently do them wrong.

Second, you will benefit from an understanding of sensitivity because it makes assessment, diagnosis, and treatment planning far more accurate. You will be less likely to assume patients are like you or should be.

Third, this understanding leads to more positive outcomes because you will not be expecting a sensitive patient to become nonsensitive, moving quickly into new situations, or being more spontaneous, loudly assertive, unmoved emotionally, relaxed about feedback, and so forth. Sensitive individuals can be more spontaneous, but they will never make decisions quickly, without any worry about the consequences. They can be more assertive, but not loudly so; better regulate their emotions, but not eliminate their intensity; interpret feedback more accurately, but never relax about it.

Fourth, the therapeutic alliance is strengthened by discussing sensitivity with a patient early on and as often as needed later. Sensitive patients are usually enormously relieved to have this aspect of them recognized. It will be especially meaningful if you are the first one to provide them with the proper understanding of this difference they have always sensed and possibly saw entirely as a disadvantage.

Fifth, you may be able to avoid some kinds of impasses or dead ends, in which patients seem almost impossible to change in certain ways or complain that you just do not understand them.

Finally, your work will be more rewarding, in that you can raise the self-esteem of these patients so easily by celebrating the positive side of their sensitivity as well as alerting them to their own negative attitudes about it, acquired from the culture and those around them. Further, given the research that with the right upbringing sensitive persons can even outshine others in some regards, you may well be able to provide a partial substitute for good early parenting and see these patients improve more than you ever expected.

SUMMARY AND CONCLUSION

High sensitivity (also sensory processing sensitivity) refers to a single innate temperament trait expressed as an awareness of subtleties in stimuli as well as a potential to be overwhelmed by too much stimuli. Evidence suggests that this trait, found in about 15 to 20% of the population, is an evolved strategy of processing information deeply before acting, as opposed to acting more quickly (these two fundamental strategies are found in over 100 species).

There are as many men as women born highly sensitive. People tend to have the trait or not—that is, its distribution is usually found to be bimodal or to have a clear cut-off rather than being bell shaped. It is not the same as shyness, inhibitedness, or introversion. Indeed, about 30% are extroverts. The highly sensitive can also be high sensation seekers—these are independent innate traits. The opposite of sensitivity is impulsivity, not necessarily a dislike of novelty.

Among many characteristics that result from careful processing, the highly sensitive tend to be conscientious, creative, unusually aware of other's moods, more bothered by unpleasant stimuli, and have stronger affects, both positive and negative. One result is that they are more prone to depression, anxiety, and shyness if they have had a troubled childhood. Otherwise they are no more prone to these than the nonsensitive. Indeed, with a good environment their outcomes can exceed that of others. That is, high sensitivity is not a disorder or only a vulnerability to disorder.

The trait does have many clinical implications, much as ethnicity or gender does. Indeed, innate temperament differences may be at least as important, although easier to ignore given their invisibility. There are many sensitive people who answer yes to every item on the HSP Scale (in Appendix A), and many nonsensitive persons who answer no to every item. This is a big difference—yet those who score high must live in a world in which most score low, and therapists can help in this regard.

The concept of sensory processing sensitivity does not require clinicians to give up their current methods and theories. It simply augments these and allows them to adjust to an important individual difference. In doing so, they better serve an undoubtedly large segment of their patient population.

CHAPTER

2

Assessing for High Sensitivity

In reality, it [whether a patient is sensitive] is not a question of either one or the other [constitution or experience]. A certain innate sensitiveness produces a special prehistory, a special way of experiencing infantile events, which in their turn are not without influence on the development of the child's view of the world. Events bound up with powerful impressions can never pass off without leaving some trace on sensitive people. Some of them remain effective throughout life, and such events can have a determining influence on a person's whole mental development.

—Carl Jung, *The Collected Works of* C. G. *Jung,* **Vol. 4, 1913, para. 399**

This chapter provides guidance in assessing high sensitivity by focusing on four broad aspects of the trait, makes suggestions about questions to ask when taking a history, and discusses how to avoid false positives and false negatives. Using case illustrations, it also points out those who are more difficult to assess due to a highly adaptive persona and those who are extroverts and high sensation seekers.

The interaction of high sensitivity with life experiences to which Jung referred might seem to confuse assessment, but often it does not. The reason is that high sensitivity is a trait affecting almost every behavior. A single indicator taken one at a time, such as cautiousness or creativity, might seem to be the result of something else. But the broad pattern of characteristics generally clarifies whether this is a general style of behaving or the result of traumas, which usually affect specific behaviors. For example, a fear of criticism may be the result of a critical father and only appear around men in authority, or it may be a general fear often found in sensitive patients associated with wishing to do things right, being easily shamed, and dreading overstimulating confrontations.

Because sensitivity is an innate trait, it should have been present from birth. A key aspect of assessing for sensitivity is how parents and teachers viewed the patient in childhood. They may have used the wrong words for it—shy, fussy, or difficult. But some parents will have actually noticed their child was simply sensitive, or "overly" sensitive or "super" sensitive.

The HSP Scale (Appendix A) is intended to assess sensitivity in a research setting and should never be used alone to decide whether a particular patient has the trait. There are no norms or cutoffs, and being a self-report measure, it is always subject to some bias. For example, some, especially men, may not want to be labeled highly sensitive and others may wish to be even if they are not.

Bottom Line: Sensitivity, being an innate operating style of the nervous system, can be seen in the overall pattern of a person's style. It does not occur in only one area of life. Parents and teachers probably noted it since early childhood. The HSP Scale can help identify sensitivity but is not designed for that and should not be used alone.

FOUR INDICATORS

Again, sensitivity affects all areas of life, but grouping its signs into four categories makes it easier. If you like acronyms as mnemonic devices, the four can be remembered as DOES, standing for Depth of processing, Overarousability, Emotional intensity, and Sensory sensitivity. I will discuss each in terms of behaviors, presenting problems, history, and how it would appear in any interaction of sensitivity and a history of trauma or high stress.

Bottom Line: When you are assessing for sensitivity, you are looking for DOES, an acronym for *D*epth of processing, *O*verarousability, *E*motional intensity, and *S*ensory sensitivity.

Indicators of Depth of Processing

Depth of processing is the key trait of these patients, but it cannot be directly observed, so you will have to imagine what deep processing would result in.

Behavior

This indicator of sensitivity might appear as reflecting (*more than others would*) about the "way the world is going," the meaning of life, or of their line of work; pondering the direction a relationship is going given certain events; conjectures about how things came to be the way they are or are likely to turn out; or conscientiousness or morality that seems to arise from unusual reflection on the results of behavior rather than adherence to a code of ethics formulated by others.

To avoid hearing a merely socially desirable response ("You're right—I do think things over a lot") try something like this: "In your difficulty making this decision I hear a great deal of concern about its long-term effects on you and others. Is this a general tendency of yours? Or is this a special instance?"

Depth of processing also shows itself in deeper feelings and empathy for others. For example, most sensitive persons are unusually concerned about the suffering of others, including the suffering of animals, and about social injustices. They often work actively for some cause. These are not isolated compulsions, such as keeping dozens of rescued cats, but broader issues about which they feel passionately. How they act on their feelings usually makes sense, or at least they can explain why they feel as they do.

Sensitive persons also evidence conscientiousness about the therapeutic frame, some of which I attribute to their depth of processing. They pay promptly, come and go on time, and are respectful of all boundaries, as if they are imagining themselves in your place.

This greater depth of processing is not the strange, overly focused attention that one might find with an autism spectrum disorder, such as recognizing all types of light bulbs or moths (budding young scientists excluded, of course). It is instead a depth of processing that is connected to emotions, other people, and the world. However, much of this processing may be unconscious, so that sensitive patients often operate on hunches or "gut feelings." They also have far more vivid dreams than others.

Depth of processing may also show itself as a surprising degree of insight already gained about self and others; a sense of long-term consequences, such that there is little history of impulsivity and risk taking; or an unusually quick understanding of your interpretations or questions—a fast response of "I see what you're getting at."

Presenting Problem

A common presenting problem caused by this facet of high sensitivity is needing help to make a major decision, or feeling they have difficulty with decisions generally. As you explore this issue, see whether this is the predictable result of reflecting more deeply on a decision. For example, I might ask, half teasingly, whether their decisions are usually right. Or is this a fear of something specific happening as a result of a particular decision they are trying to make?

Regarding decisions that patients feel were wrong ones, I consider whether they actually were, given their sensitivity. For example, a highly sensitive person may decide not to take a promotion that involves a great deal of foreign travel, and then regret it because they know others would have taken the job.

The presenting problem around decisions could also be due to what I have come to call decision trauma, in that they made one terribly important decision that was unusually difficult which they later came to regret, such as marrying too early. Sensitive people strive so hard to make the right decision that the entire process, especially if it is later regretted, can become something they dread.

Depth of processing might be suggested in other presenting problems as well: feeling others do not understand them, finding most conversations or people boring, and doing poorly in knowledge areas that require one right answer.

In the History

In the first few sessions overarousal may interfere with depth of processing, so that the history given is sketchy. Equally often, however, the history may indicate deep thought about themselves, their past, their family life, choice of occupation, or the types of people chosen for close friends. Sensitivity is also indicated when patients admit to being known for making good predictions, being a "deep thinker," or showing signs of unusual creativity. Again, ask how parents and teachers viewed them. Perhaps they were remembered for asking "the most amazing questions" or making up fantastic stories; being appreciative of music or art at an early age; being happy for hours in imaginary play; having the best ideas at school or at play; being especially concerned about God, death, and why there is suffering; or when there was trouble at home, becoming very quiet and observant.

It is wise to ask about spiritual or self-help practices or anything similar that has been a major influence in their lives. Besides being informative, the question is more often answered at length by these patients. Indeed, in my interviews (Aron & Aron, 1997) it was the last question on my protocol, but it came up spontaneously before that in every case—from a strong religious faith since childhood to experiences with ghosts and angels. In one case the person expressed vehement atheism, but the arguments were cogent and went beyond the usual wondering why God lets good people suffer.

In Interaction With Formative Negative Events

Depth of processing is probably the very reason for the reported interaction that sensitive persons are more distressed than others by the same events in childhood (Aron et al., 2005; Liss et al., 2005) or adulthood (Aron et al., 2005, Study 4; Kemler, 2006, these studies used the HSP Scale but the same results have been found by many others identifying the trait in other ways, e.g., Mangelsdorg, Gunnar, Kestenbaum, Lang, & Andreas, 1990). They apparently ponder these events more deeply, developing what we might imagine as more dense emotional schemas. This pondering leads to a stronger emotional reaction and is also fed by it. We all ponder something more that has moved us emotionally. But finding that a patient has been more affected than others would have been by the same type of past or present events (criticism, for example) is in itself a good indicator of sensitivity.

These stronger effects may appear as unusually low self-esteem, extreme shyness or fear of social judgment, an insecure adult attachment style that is mainly highly anxious and preoccupied with the other, and seeing life as meaningless—that is, feeling the long-term consequences or meaning of their current distress.

Bottom Line: Depth of processing appears indirectly, as either deep thoughts or deep feelings. Examples would be a greater reflection before speaking or acting, resulting in difficulty making decisions, but generally making good ones; a quick grasp of your ideas; and a spiritual life that has arisen out of or involves considerable contemplation.

Indicators of Overarousal

High levels of stimulation lead to high levels of arousal, and very high levels of arousal cause discomfort and poor performance for everyone (Yerkes & Dodson, 1908). Cognitive capacity (how much can be held in working memory) decreases, leading to confusion, poor memory, and a paucity of thoughts or of words to express them. There is often an increase in sympathetic nervous system activation (fight or flight response)—raised heart beat, sweaty palms, churning stomach. Overarousal can affect, for example, test taking, public speaking or performance (sports, recitals, etc.), making conversation with a stranger, first dates, multitasking, being observed during training, and the way a patient behaves with you, particularly in early sessions. Patients who are easily overstimulated or overaroused in multiple situations are probably highly sensitive.

Behaviors

Temporary overarousal is often visible in the first sessions as an even greater nervousness than would be seen in others at that point. Sensitive patients may be unable to look you in your eyes, cry out of sheer nervousness, toy with a tissue, or sigh softly. They may have trouble focusing and fall into long silences. They may complain of or fear having nothing to say and solve that by coming with an agenda. While such behaviors may have many other causes, again, it will be a place to begin thinking about whether the patient is highly sensitive.

Chronic overarousal results in all the behaviors associated with chronic high levels of cortisol: trouble sleeping, loss of appetite, hypervigilance, and anxiety. After the glands producing cortisol are fatigued, there will be more sleeping than usual and probably weight gain and signs of depression.

Presenting Problems

Chronic overarousal is often the presenting problem—feeling stressed out, suffering from burnout, feeling overwhelmed, or a sense of not being able to handle any more. This will be affecting rest, health, and with time, performance on the job or in the family. Usually the highly sensitive allow their duties to be affected last—part of the problem. Hence they are in therapy because they see no options and think there is something wrong with them that they cannot handle as much as others.

Overarousal often occurs for them even more than others during important life transitions, as these usually require rapid shifts in stimuli, foci of cognition, and behaviors, while the highly sensitive by nature would prefer to reflect on what is happening. Even pleasant changes such as leaving on a vacation, moving to a new home, marrying, promotion, parenthood, or retirement will have the unpleasant side effect of making them feeling unsettled, losing sleep, and having even more emotional reactivity than usual. Often the problem can be observed in the office, at the start and end of sessions, not to mention the start and end of a longer separation from the therapist. (This would be over and above separation distress due to personal history.)

Now and then a sensitive person will describe panic attacks. Sometimes these are the result of an experience of intense overstimulation, leading to a terrifying sense of not being able to cope. These differ from more typical panic attacks in that they clear up quickly when their cause is explained and a few remedial measures have been suggested.

Another behavioral effect of overarousal is that it is simply avoided, whether knowingly or not. For almost anyone the feeling of being very overaroused is associated with failure and humiliation. It is very hard to distinguish it from fear, if there really is any difference for some patients. Many presenting problems can be related to avoiding overstimulation and overarousal—from trouble making friends (because the person never frequents unfamiliar places) to boredom.

Highly sensitive, high sensation seekers must walk a very fine line between over- and underarousal and frequently miss the mark or accept being chronically overaroused, letting the sensation seeker in them triumph over the sensitive part.

In the History

To verify a tendency to be easily overaroused I might ask: "Some people need more downtime than others after a very stimulating event—a day of sightseeing or after a big event. Would that be true of you?" This question focuses on the aftereffects, avoiding questions high sensation seekers would not agree with, like "Do you tend to avoid places that are very stimulating?" Asking about aftereffects rather than asking "Are you often overaroused?" also allows for those who have learned to avoid high levels of arousal, often true of older sensitive persons.

Ask about comments their parents might have made—that as infants they cried and fussed when they were tired or kept too long in noisy or crowded places. If a childhood memory comes up that might have resulted in or been affected by overarousal, I might ask a question such as: "So it seemed like you were more upset than other children by being away from home? Did you ever go away to camp? Do you remember how those first few days of camp were for you?" To assess specifically for overarousal in this situation, I would listen for greater than expected insomnia, upset stomach or vomiting, and memories worse than usual skill at activities requiring coordination.

Overarousal also may appear in their history as regrets about decisions made, opportunities turned down, and of course repeated inexplicable failures, in that they were thoroughly prepared yet failed under pressure. Failures and regrets can occur for many reasons. You will need to inquire gently and compassionately about the reasons an opportunity was not taken or under what circumstances the failures tended to occur. For example: "I sure hear your regret and sense of failure about having to drop out in the middle of your freshman year, but I wonder if you have some ideas now about why that happened?"

If further probing does not seem like mere suggestion, I might add: "Could it be that your freshman year was just very, very overstimulating for you in particular? Every freshman has so much to face, especially if living on their own for the first time: academic choices, studying, tests, managing money, doing laundry, meeting countless strangers, making friends, living in a small space with someone. It goes on and on, doesn't it? So much to think about and take care of at one time, and I wonder if it also felt like just too much when you took that first job and received that poor performance rating."

In Interaction With Negative Formative Events

When a patient is born with an innate tendency to be overaroused in general by stimulation, overarousal in childhood is bound to occur in stressful circumstances such as being left alone too early or too long or a divorce of parents. Sensitive children need far more reassurance in these circumstances, and in dysfunctional families they rarely receive it. The emotional schemas laid down at these times remain sources from within of high stimulation and arousal. For example, the insecure sensitive child, overaroused for years by unsupportive parenting, is more distressed by new situations and has higher cortisol levels in those situations than secure sensitive children (Nachmias, Gunnar, Mangelsdorf, Parritz, & Buss, 1996).

Bottom Line: Overarousal is indicated when patients show unusual nervousness, complain of chronic stress or trouble with transitions, report many "failures" or regrets about decisions, were remembered as fussy or awkward at team sports or unusually quiet in school, or show a general avoidance of situations that are highly stimulating. If they have a history of trauma or high stress, they also showed signs of chronic overarousal, especially in new situations or away from caregivers.

Indicators of Emotional Intensity

Strong emotional responses are easy to observe but can be more difficult to sort out from the effects of trauma or a difficult past. The difference is that sensitive persons bring more emotional reactivity to every event in life. They may be anxious when they first meet you, but if they feel you can help them, they will be unusually happy and grateful.

The traumatized nonsensitive person will mostly express negative affect. Imagine a sensitive versus an abused dog. The sensitive one will watch you from a distance, observing you closely, and show signs of wanting to approach. Once you are accepted, the dog is not likely to forget you. In contrast, an abused dog avoids your eyes and shows signs of greater conflict or agitation. The more you try to make friends, the more agitated it becomes unless you are very skilled at soothing such animals. Even then you will probably have to repeat the process many times, as the dog remembers abuse more than it remembers you. What if you are facing a sensitive abused dog? We have reached the limits of my knowledge of canine genetics and behavior interactions. In this case, it is easier to stay with humans, who can talk and tell you about their histories and what they are feeling in the moment.

Behavior

The best way to make the distinction is that the emotional reactivity is general, not specific or mainly marked by vigilance about something such as loss, betrayal, sexuality, or violence. The sensitive patient is touched by many things. Perhaps they are "sentimental" about the past or full of compassion (not just worry) about the disadvantaged. They are prone to strong positive as well as negative affects and in situations where anyone would share their feeling but perhaps less strongly. You will see that they are easily moved to tears of joy, gratitude, or relief. But those who are not too damaged are equally moved to laughter, whether by sheer silliness or subtle irony.

In the first session, they may have stronger feelings than others about simply being in your presence. In discussing their problems, they are indeed more likely to cry. To further sort out the cause, you might gently ask: "Do you cry easily? You seemed to be very deeply moved a moment ago when you said ...?" Or, "I hear that you are quite depressed right now, but I wonder if you, in the past, have also been the sort of person to feel very, very good about certain things, too?" (If you are trying to think through the relation of this trait to autism spectrum disorders, the highly sensitive often show the most emotional intensity around the social emotions such as shame, guilt, disdain, compassion, and fear of abandonment, which may seem missing or strained in a different way in those disorders.)

Another observable behavior typical of those who are highly sensitive is that, when feeling strong emotions (remember these can be positive as well), they may discuss making dramatic changes in their lives—they are ready to marry their new love or quit their job, but they usually do not actually make a sudden change. They will still ponder it a while, whereas nonsensitive patients can and do act impulsively when feeling strongly about something.

Emotional reactivity means sensitive persons also react more to the emotions of others. You may find a sensitive patient knows what you are feeling far more often than others would. This attunement occurs for all of your emotions and in most situations, not merely ones in which a history of abuse or abandonment requires the patient to be vigilant about another's negative mood.

Presenting Problems

With this aspect of sensitivity, a common presenting problem is concern about their emotional "overreactions." Other common presenting problems are diagnosable emotional disorders involving depression (not usually bipolar) and anxiety. This is because emotions such as grief or fear do lead to generalized anxiety and mood disorders if they become chronic and cannot be regulated, so when treating these problems one should look for sensitivity as well.

In the History

In childhood the highly sensitive are even more emotionally reactive, lacking affect regulation skills, although some had to learn these quickly. Sensitive men can tell you the first time they cried at school, which was often the first day, and were told to stop. Humiliated, they set out never to make that mistake again. Others were very emotionally expressive (they had tantrums when frustrated, were "moody boys" or "drama queens") and gradually learned to tone it down. Boy or girl, a sensitive patient was probably an internalizer, perhaps anxious and depressed without obvious cause. Many will have turned to the arts to express their feelings. If asked, they may want to share something from this period—for example, poetry, short stories, song lyrics, or drawings. Whatever their skill level, you will sense a depth of feeling that is unusual for the age when it was done.

They will report more emotion throughout their lives, over everything. They were distressed by fairytales, scary movies, unfairness or bullying at school, the idea of animals being killed for food, or simply being overtired or hungry. At school they were quick to befriend the underdog and responded quickly to correction but poorly to punishment. Dealing with the opposite sex was unusually difficult. Peer pressure caused greater conflict. They may tell you that they were so overwhelmed at their wedding that they hardly remember any of it. They are intensely nervous at new jobs, adoring of their children, and crushed by a friend's death.

Compare their emotional reaction to what would be typical. We expect a soldier to have posttraumatic stress disorder after 6 months in a battle zone but not after undergoing basic training. Most children fear water, yet they learn to swim by around age 10, not in high school. Most go to camp and are home sick, but some have to be sent home because of it. Some are teased a little and almost instinctively give it back, others turn away and feel it deeply.

Patients with more secure childhoods will have not just fond but ecstatic memories of family vacations, holiday traditions, or special attributes of a parent. They probably loved school and had unusually close friendships. Again, there are several lines of evidence that sensitive children are more affected by both distressing and by supportive enriched environments (Belsky et al., 2009; Ellis, Essex, & Boyce, 2005).

And of course you can ask directly: "You mention strong emotional reactions—has this always been true of you, or do you associate it with some change?"

In Interaction With Formative Negative Events

The question here is, given a negative history, is the person also highly sensitive? I would begin with the history—the degree and type of negative events—and then, again, try to gain a sense of whether this person is more distressed by the same type of events than other patients you know. Try to assess for attachment in infancy. ("Do you have the sense that your mother liked infants, especially raising them? Was she very stressed at the time you were born?") Sensitive children appear to be more affected than others by not having a secure attachment or adequate support from other caretakers (Manglesdorf et al., 1992; Nachmias et al., 1996; Pluess & Belsky, 2009).

Second, consider the breadth of their emotional reactivity. Is it high in other areas or with other emotions besides the ones you would expect, given the specifics of their negative history? For example, most sensitive patients are uncomfortable expressing anger. But if a patient does express anger, watch for intensity of other emotions, including shame when anger is expressed back toward them. Fear and sadness due to trauma could be more difficult to sort out, but watch for extremes of over- or underregulation of affect, not only in their lives but also in your office.

Internalized emotions are much more common, as the outer display of emotions is overstimulating as well as seemingly too dangerous to them. Emotions are probably surfacing, however, when these patients seem more activated, for example, talking fast, or are supplying many more details of their observations. They may sit literally on the edge of the chair or in some other uncomfortable position. In quieter moments there may be a tentative quality about them, a compulsion to be good, or a gentleness toward you that feels like timidity or submission, not simply kindness. Sensitive men with troubled histories can show tremendous emotional reserve, often evidenced by a quiet, rational tone of voice beginning with the first phone contact. But generally you will sense the overcontrol, in that there is nothing about any of this that is relaxed or casual.

Bottom Line: Emotional intensity as an indicator of high sensitivity is found with positive as well as negative emotions, in all situations for which emotion is appropriate. It can be observed in the session when the patient has more emotion than would be usual, mentions a problem of "overreacting," or appears to be at the extremes of over- or underregulation.

Indicators of Sensory Sensitivity

These are also easy to spot, but should be general, not specific to certain situations. Usually sensory sensitivity arises from the processing of stimuli, not at the sense organs themselves. A person may need glasses but still be highly observant. It is the case that sometimes the processing of one sense is keener, for example, having "perfect pitch." Sometimes sensory sensitivity manifests as a low threshold, sometimes as the ability to distinguish subtleties, and sometimes as low tolerance of high levels of sensory input. Often all three are present. This sensitivity will not be restricted to stimuli that people almost always notice—in a positive way, such as responding to perfume, or in a negative way as when reacting to feces.

Behaviors

The first cues of sensory sensitivity might come as you watch a patient react to your office the first time and then later to slight changes. Almost all sensitive persons will look around alertly or else study you. If it is a pleasant office, on the first visit or soon after they may comment on a detail others rarely notice. Or if they are studying you, you may feel scrutinized, their eyes taking you in from head to foot. If something is amiss, you will see them noticing but rarely hear them comment.

At such times you might be able to probe for this form of sensitivity by asking in a very gentle, friendly way something like "You came in looking around so observantly, like Sherlock Holmes—I couldn't help but wonder what your impressions were." However, you would need to be watchful that this does not put too much pressure on the person. Other good questions can be developed from the items on the self-test related to sensations.

Their own appearance is another cue to their sensory sensitivity. They do not generally wear flashy clothes. They may wear long sleeves or jackets when the weather is only marginally cool and say they are too hot when it is only marginally warm. They are usually neat rather than careless about their appearance and how they move into a room.

You might eventually notice comments such as "I just hate being cold" or "I have to cut all the labels out of my clothing" or "I don't know why but I just know he's mad at me" (because of having observed subtle behavioral cues). These patients may have a seeming obsession about the noise where they live or work. They may express a goal of moving to the country or leaving a job because the work environment, commute, responsibilities, or office politics are "just too much." They have more side effects to medications and in many cases need much smaller doses. If antidepressants are needed, they feel subtle, adverse side effects when given the standard starting dosage.

Sensory sensitivity also has its positive sides, expressing itself in their choice of interests or occupations that utilize it, such as art, music, healing, or living close to nature or working with animals.

In all cases when sensitivity in one situation is reported, you need to inquire more to be certain there is a general sensitivity—someone's sensory overload at work might be due to a job that would be too much for anyone, or a love of music might turn out to be a passion for hard rock played at its loudest.

Presenting Problems

Few expect a therapist to solve the problems created by their sensory sensitivity. Occasionally they will come seeking a diagnosis about it—is this normal or not? Perhaps it has created problems with others who find it annoying, think the patient is making it up, or perceive the patient's reactions as due to a weakness or psychosomatic condition. Or they may simply need you to acknowledge a form of suffering, such as an excruciating sensitivity to sound, that others do not have to deal with.

In the History

Patients usually recall sensory sensitivity in childhood. They or their parents noticed they were more bothered than other kids by new foods, foods touching, having their hair combed, wool clothing, tight clothing, shoes not fitting right, the seams in socks, the labels in clothes, having on wet or sandy clothing, the sound of fireworks, and so forth. My initial intake form not only asks about health, medications, and use of drugs or alcohol, but also about caffeine, as most sensitive persons respond more to all of these. (Caffeine use often results in symptoms that mimic or can trigger anxiety, which young sensitive persons, in particular, may not realize.) I ask about allergies, since sensitive persons have more contact allergies in particular. In their histories sensitive patients often report effects of their low pain threshold, for example during childbirth or after injuries. They may have physical disorders that could be due to stress but also might be the result of a low pain threshold. These include back and neck problems, migraines, fibromyalgia, chronic fatigue, unusual allergies, environmental sensitivities, or extreme premenstrual syndrome. (These problems can be present in the nonsensitive too, of course, especially with a history of trauma.) Finally, during intake you may hear of extensive use of alternative medicine, in part because the treatments and those offering them take sensory sensitivity more into account.

In Interaction With Formative Negative Events

It is my impression that when there has been unusual stress in the past, some of the sensory sensitivities are aggravated. It makes sense that sensitive patients would express their emotional difficulties through their sensory sensitivity. It draws their attention away from their intense emotional distress and perhaps provides a sense of identity or importance through having unusual sensing abilities or problems that compensate for very low self-esteem in other areas of life.

Again, if a patient reports a difficult or traumatic childhood, listen for whether this is expressed through sensory sensitivities, including sensitivity to bodily sensations, and whether the patient's reactions are extreme, almost as if the patient were projecting something sinister on to the source of the disturbing stimuli. One patient boarded up and sound insulated her house to keep out the noise of school children. Another built a separate shed to house his refrigerator, since even the quietest brand was too loud. (When he still thought he could hear it, he had to find another house because by then his wife wanted a divorce.) A third was involved in an ongoing lawsuit with a trucking company near his home that began its operations at 6 a.m. He could not accept that since none of his neighbors were bothered, he might have to be the one to move.

Sometimes patients are sensitive to stimuli that I do not personally sense, and I hear it more often from those with histories of trauma and abuse, but that does not mean there is nothing to their experience. One patient reported sensing where water was flowing, and since she sensed water was flowing under my office, she could not continue to see me. Some report bad reactions to electromagnetic fields, which are all around us, including from the sun itself, but are also created by appliances. More than others, they are concerned about waves in the radio wave spectrum of electronic fields, which are generated by television and radio transmissions, cell phones, and phone towers. In addition, many sensitive persons report unusual experiences that could broadly be called psychic.

The research around these unusual sensitivities is polarized by the fact that, to bother to do it, one would have to strongly want to prove or disprove their reality. Do not dismiss such sensitivities, but maintain a benign interest until you see how they fit into the overall picture.

Bottom Line: Sensory sensitivity is easy to assess by asking questions about it as well as watching the patient's reaction to your office on the first visit or after you have made changes. This sensitivity will have been present from childhood and may take an odd turn for those with a painful past.

OTHER POSSIBLE INDICATORS AND PRESENTING PROBLEMS

Besides the DOES-related issues just discussed, there are others that often indicate sensitivity because they are common problems of these patients. None of these listed below are direct results of the trait, but rather indirect ones, often having to do with a patient's culture or other individual circumstances.

Slower Development

Overall, as one hears their history, sensitive patients in an individualistic culture often seem to be lagging behind their peers in passing the major developmental milestones. They leave home later or still live at home, graduate from college only after taking time off, do not settle on a career until 30 or even later, marry and have children later, and probably retire later if they have found meaningful work. (We may even find that they die later, given their attention to preventative health practices and the findings discussed earlier, that they have fewer illnesses and injuries in normal-stress environments.)

Several Previous Therapies

When asking about previous psychotherapy, if a patient mentions many therapist changes and "failed" treatments, I do not immediately see a red flag. Like many, these patients may believe that all therapists know what they are doing, giving little thought to being a good match. They especially want to give someone a chance or become too attached to end it. I try to explore enough (or ask permission to speak to the therapists) to see if these multiple treatments could have been due to the therapist not understanding their trait. For example, these patients cannot make much progress when treated brashly or with heavy confrontations. The "failure" may come after many years, as if from a true impasse, but actually the patient should have broken away after the first session but could not bear all that that would have entailed.

The fact is, sensitive patients can be easily drawn into therapy simply in response to a therapist's initial kindness and interest. And therapists may be eager to take them on, seeing that they are bright and conscientious—an "easy patient." When therapists are unaware of the trait, they may try to eliminate its effects. When this fails, one or both may end the relationship.

Work Problems

Many sensitive patients will present having career problems. They may complain that their work is not satisfying, or it is satisfying but they are always overworked, or it would be satisfying except for intolerable physical conditions or social tensions in the workplace. Often they feel they are failing to be assertive and are underappreciated or underpaid, and this appears to you to be true. A manager may be harsh, negative, or self-serving, all of which affects a sensitive person more. Being a manager itself can be a distressing problem, in that they have to speak to nonsensitive people in ways they would never wish or need to be spoken to. In short, if they have changed jobs often the reason may be legitimate.

Relationship Problems

Patients are often highly sensitive if they have come for therapy because they are having trouble meeting anyone they like enough. This is because they are easily bored in relationships (unpublished data). Of course, more often they fear no one will like them, yet they seem to be people anyone would enjoy knowing. Because they are slow to decide rather than impulsive, sensitive patients will often be the ones seeking help to decide whether to commit to someone. If they are in a committed relationship that is not going well, they are likely to seek help deciding whether to stay in it. (Nonsensitive patients more often come after they realize they have made a mistake.)

In an ongoing relationship they frequently are, or feel they are, being taken advantage of. Conflicts over one person in a pair wanting more time alone usually means one is highly sensitive. Often they are the "identified patient" when in fact they are less disturbed than their nonsensitive spouse critic.

Patients may be highly sensitive if they say they are codependent without meeting the definition in its true sense of colluding in or enabling another's unhealthy behaviors. Rather, they feel deeply for the other person's predicament, or are not going to leave a relationship without being certain it is hopeless and having some better alternative.

Some have been told that they try to please others too much, are perfectionists, or are too sensitive to criticism. All of this may be true, but the roots may be more in their sensitivity than in their pathology. Indeed, their presenting problem may really be someone else's—others think they should be assessed because of their "strange" behaviors or feelings.

Poor Self-Care

Although many are troubled by illnesses due to the interaction of their trait with being poorly treated as children, their self-care may be even poorer than other patients'. This is in contrast to sensitive persons in general, who are very attentive to their health. These troubled ones often neglect their need for downtime, ignore their sensitivity to substances, and accept painful treatments in spite of their lower pain thresholds. They endure their symptoms almost sacrificially until they can no longer be ignored.

Dissociation

It is my impression that sensitive patients dissociate more than others, perhaps because they are more affected by trauma and more easily overwhelmed, so that very arousing experiences are never processed in memory. But they seldom are in denial, for example, about past abuse.

Low Self-Esteem

Almost all highly sensitive patients have low self-esteem, as do most patients entering therapy. For sensitive patients, however, it will in part be directly associated with their trait and feeling different. By assessing for sensitivity it may be possible to improve self-esteem, at least in this domain, quite quickly.

Bottom Line: Other possible indirect effects of sensitivity are being later than others when finding the right relationship and career, or having problems in both because of being misunderstood. Some will have seen several previous therapists for good reasons. Those who are more damaged will evidence worse self-care and more dissociation than similar nonsensitive patients.

WHEN THE PRESENTING PROBLEM IS SHYNESS

Chronic shyness or social fear can have a multitude of explanations with both the highly sensitive and the nonsensitive, and you will want to assess the cause before deciding on treatment. A common reason for the highly sensitive is that they avoid the high stimulation involved in meeting strangers and as a result become increasingly unskilled and overaroused when they do have to speak with strangers. Not behaving as well as they expected of themselves, they worry about this and are even more overaroused and inelegant the next time, so they become chronically shy.

Further, many have experienced painful rejections for being "too quiet" or "lost in thoughts," for example. They are not going to risk that rejection again. But they thoroughly enjoy being with those who accept them as they are. I always ask about a patient's various relationships, hoping to hear there are some long-standing, well-enjoyed, solid friendships. This will be more likely in sensitive patients who come for therapy describing themselves as shy.

You will want to determine whether the sensitive person has the social skills but simply lacks confidence and cannot apply them due to overarousal. This will become apparent as the two of you get to know each other better and the patient is no longer overaroused much of the time.

Remember, too, that shyness is a fear of social judgment, which is not innate but learned and present only in certain situations. Everyone feels shy at times. The patient complaining of shyness may not be shy at all, but rather just pausing to observe for a while before entering in, or turning away from a social situation because it is too overstimulating, or preferring a deeper conversation.

Sometimes patients presume they are shy when it is really a misattribution of the physical overarousal that can happen in large social gatherings. Once they call this shyness, it can become self-fulfilling. All of the above can be helpful when trying to determine shyness versus sensitivity.

Bottom Line: Shyness and sensitivity can be distinguished by assessing the frequency and causes. Shyness can be due to poor social skills; being too overaroused to use their skills; social disinterest; only seeming shy because of wanting to pause before entering in; or an unusual unwillingness to take risks, in this case of another rejection.

THE MASK IN THE FIRST SESSION

Assessment can be complicated by the fact that a few sensitive patients will appear in the first session to be functioning far better than their histories would suggest. Even if they cry, that ends soon, as they are afraid of exposing too much about their core weakness. There are some indicators of sensitivity, but the patient may seem to be reporting a troubled past just as a nonsensitive person would.

Sensitive persons can develop an exquisite adaptation to the requirements of the nonsensitive world by using their sensitivity to subtle cues about what others are feeling, what is appropriate at the moment, and what is expected of them. Further, by adopting the emotional responses of others when these are calm or socially appropriate, they have found a reliable method of affect regulation. When a sensitive child makes this adaptation, we speak of it as presenting a precocious "false self" (Winnicott, 1965). These patients have dramatically limited their psychological development and know little about their own needs and desires. Hence, they frequently harbor a deep sense of powerlessness, anxiety about being discovered as empty masks, or suppress anger at being dominated by others through having to imitate them. In an atmosphere of acceptance and emotional attunement, that chameleon-like persona will fall away, sometimes very quickly. However, it can cloud one's initial assessment of a sensitive individual, who can present as highly adapted and emotionally regulated. They are being exactly as reasonable and calm as you.

A few sensitive patients, however, wear another mask. They may overstate their difficulties or past traumas, thinking that what actually happened will not adequately justify their intense symptoms and need for treatment. They do not know that they truly do experience more distress than others to a given trauma. One patient told me initially of repeated sexual abuse by an uncle. After our work had continued for quite a while (during which I met considerable resistance if I tried to address this abuse), he finally confessed very guiltily that the sexual intrusion had occurred only once. He thought that without this exaggeration I would discount his intense reactions to what seemed to him to be a relatively normal childhood. (In fact, for a sensitive child, it was a very difficult one.)

CASE ILLUSTRATION OF A MASK COVERING DEEP DISTRESS

Anna appeared in my office looking well dressed, slim, and efficient. She reported a stable relationship and a responsible, meaningful position in a real estate office. Her only complaint was her trouble limiting her ever-expanding workload, a common problem for successful sensitive persons. When probed, she also was happy to provide an insightful, relaxed discussion of a shocking life story. Her mother was a prostitute; her biological father was never determined. Her mother not only gave Anna minimal care as an infant, but often allowed her to be in the room with her when engaged in her work. This was not done out of mere hardship or ignorance. Mother had insisted on a merger of the two of them. They shared the same bedroom, wore matching clothes, and had to feel the same things. This disastrous parenting seemed to be the result of the mother's own lack of adequate mothering, having been raised in an orphanage and a series of foster homes. Anna was filling her mother's deep attachment void.

The only bright spot in this history was Anna's college education. A number of teachers had taken an interest in her—she excelled at attracting the concern of others. In college she had developed friendships with remarkable ease and allowed these friends to take care of her in the world. In return, she was as charming as possible and did all she could to meet their needs and defend them as well as those of many other needy persons in her vicinity. There were daunting goals, and this led to the exhausting job she had when she came to see me, working in the agency that had been started by her friends.

In treatment the dissociation and survival skills that had led to her well-adapted persona soon broke down, as they needed to. Within 3 months she also lost her job and her relationship—the latest in a long series of failures she had not mentioned before. Anna developed an intense idealizing transference, which led to a deep depression and frequent anger that I could not offer her all that she needed, in particular physical comforting. Her personality disorder should have been obvious to me at the start.

Bottom Line: If a sensitive person reports considerable childhood trauma, its effects are there, whatever the presenting persona may seem.

HIGH SENSATION-SEEKING AND EXTROVERTED SENSITIVE PATIENTS

It can be difficult to recognize a highly sensitive person who is an extrovert, especially if he or she is also a high sensation seeker, because the majority of sensitive persons are not either of these. If you do not recognize this characteristic, thinking of sensitive persons as always quiet, inward, or shy, you will miss one-third of presenting sensitive patients. This third of patients are often performers of some sort (including teaching) or involved in socially highly stimulating occupations, but manage by being unusually withdrawn when away from these environments. Several celebrities come to mind who keep their private lives very private, while other celebrities, extroverted but not highly sensitive, always seem to prefer to be in the spotlight or in the company of those who admire them.

Neurotic conflict or a true diagnosable disorder can be the reason for extreme opposites of behavior, of course, but always look for the dual traits of sensitivity and sensation seeking. This may well save someone from an overdose, if a sensitive person is trying to manage an intolerable level of arousal and stimulation, because these types keep going to please others and can fall into getting themselves up with one substance and to sleep with another. Always consider this pattern when assessing substance abuse.

High sensation seeking will be innate and present from birth, so you would assess for that much as you would sensitivity. If sensitivity is also present, the best indicator of the two innate traits is a sense of very understandable conflict showing through. It is as if the patient suffers "yet keeps going back for more." One foot is on the brake, the other on the gas.

Since high sensation seeking appears to be innate, parents and teachers should have noticed it and possibly the conflict as well. ("This kid would be screaming from exhaustion, then rest a few minutes and be rushing back into the thick of it.") Another sign is that a patient insists that a new or exciting experience is truly enjoyable, yet also plans so that it is easily exited if it becomes too much. They also take extensive precautions to be sure that the activity is very safe. Indeed, they are usually the experts on safety, whether skiing or traveling to exotic places.

As for introversion and extroversion, it may seem that all sensation seekers are extroverts and there would be no difference. It is my impression, however, that introversion and extroversion are learned strategies for behaving in social situations in ways that help a person with a particular temperament fit into society. Being learned early, the two are heavily affected by family and culture. Introverted sensation seekers have adopted a strategy of seeking their novelty not through social interactions (which may seem too stimulating or dangerous for a sensitive person), but through extraordinary inner experiences and explorations—through meditation and other spiritual paths, dreams, analysis, creating or deeply enjoying art, becoming an expert in a subject that fascinated them, and so forth.

Sensitive introverted sensation seekers also engage in exciting outer activities, but alone or with one other intimate friend. I spend time at a stable that boards horses. The introverted sensation seekers ride alone, in order to explore new trails, even though that always involves a risk, so they carry their cell phones. That probably never occurs to nonsensitive introverted sensation seekers, at least to carry one for safety reasons. The sensitive introverts who are not sensation seekers join groups for the sake of safety, but are quiet or else ride in the arena where help would be available if they fell.

Extroverts, sensation seekers or not, will be talking about their many friends, their large family reunions, or the parties they give. They will tell you about the interesting stranger they met on an airplane or at the grocery store. All of this is about social stimulation, not novelty itself. If they are also high sensation seekers, you will hear about wide-ranging interests, experiences such as world travel, and all sorts of adventure. The sensitivity will probably arise due to not being able to keep up with others like them—for example, not being able to handle as much adventuring crammed into one day as others like them are able, or being more easily traumatized, as was Julian (presented in Chapter 1), the journalist, at the site of a terrorist attack. Whatever the combination of extroversion, introversion, and sensation seeking, if highly sensitive they will also need downtime away from others and recognize that need. It is the first and best indication that they are different from other extroverts who "recharge their batteries" in the presence of others. If I have heard hints of sensitivity, I might say, "I hear a lot of social activity. Do you ever get tired of it?"

Your assessment will only feel correct when you learn why your sensitive patient is an extrovert, as it may indicate extraordinary health or lack of it. Often they were raised in an extensive warm, stable family or a small community or friendly neighborhood. Highly sensitive New Yorkers, for example, seem to be more often extroverts (based on the greater number of extroverts at seminars there compared to elsewhere). Whatever is familiar is soothing, so that is where they thrive. However, they also could be in New York, acting like an extrovert, out of a desperate need to raise their self-esteem by succeeding there or identifying with that culture. If in fact they were highly sensitive and introverted, you would definitely see signs of strain, especially if they could not generate a group of supportive friends.

Some sensitive patients will have adopted an extroverted persona because they were forced by their family or life circumstances.

A CASE ILLUSTRATION

Ida would have been easy to miss had she not already gained considerable insight about herself. I interviewed Ida during my initial research (Aron & Aron 1997, Study 1). She remembered the day and hour when she became a tough extrovert. Because of a severely schizophrenic mother, she had largely raised herself, along with her younger sister, with whom she was very close. When social workers finally grasped the direness of their situation, her sister was placed in a foster home and she in a juvenile treatment facility. She was considered to be "shy," what she interpreted as introversion. She bonded closely with only one girl there, but they too were separated after a few months. Overwhelmed again by separation trauma, Ida decided not to risk intimacy again. Instead, she closely studied how others managed in the world, a task she was certain was easier due to her sensitivity.

Ida chose a loud, superficial persona and used it for years. As an adult she actually became a successful local political figure. This, too, she attributed to her sensitivity, which she said always allowed her to observe how such things were accomplished. But in her 40s her borrowed mode of emotional regulation failed her, and she had a major depressive episode that was quite severe. In psychotherapy (not with me) she realized her sensitive, introverted nature and how much of her life had been a defense against separation and abandonment. But this realization took years, and I am sure the Ida who first came to therapy was not recognized as an introvert and certainly not as someone who is highly sensitive.

Bottom Line: In assessing for sensitivity, do not forget that those who are extroverted or are sensation seekers engaged in an exciting, seemingly overstimulating life, can still be highly sensitive. They will require additional history to identify.

FALSE POSITIVES

It is possible to view someone as highly sensitive when he or she is not. This is most likely to happen when patients come for therapy already having decided they are highly sensitive. Do not accept without question a patient's self-diagnosis of sensitivity, even if it may be important for the therapeutic alliance not to be close-minded. Most of the DOES indicators should be present. If they are not, simply attend carefully to the possibility they are wrong. I am slow at making up my mind when a case is complicated. If the work proceeds well, I will have plenty of time to decide, and I may not have to make a definitive statement on the person's sensitivity for a long time, if ever.

If the patient does press you for an answer, it could indicate how important it is to the person that you see him or her in that light only. Some quite troubled persons would rather attribute their life difficulties to something innate, especially to a research-supported, relatively normal trait. It can be a flattering or at least nonpathologizing explanation, especially for those who have received a psychiatric diagnosis that they can now feel was undeserved (as is sometimes actually the case).

Bottom Line: False positives mainly occur when a patient has made a self-diagnosis for defense reasons.

FALSE NEGATIVES

The greater concern to me is the false negative—those whose high sensitivity is missed. Now that you understand the trait, you will have fewer false negatives. Still, you may see patients whom others have misdiagnosed. Even if a patient comes with information about it, some clinicians will doubt there is such a trait, not knowing the research or understanding the concept, and probably not having the trait themselves. Others will have dismissed it because they live and work among those with many of the values of sensitive persons, such as enjoying the arts and music, being conscientious, not attending loud parties, constantly searching for the meaning in their lives, being engaged in some spiritual path, having plenty of insurance, delaying gratification to achieve long-term goals, and so on. These behaviors, being normal in their subculture, or "normal for any civilized person," would seem to need no further explanation. Everyone is "highly sensitive," they would say, or at least wants to be seen that way.

However, sensitivity is broader than traits due to culture and not found in everyone. According to our random-digit-dialing phone survey (Aron & Aron 1997), 25% of the general public rate themselves as emphatically not at all sensitive. Many answer no to every question on the HSP Scale. And many sensitive persons answer yes to every item. Thus we must not lose sight of the fact that there has to be a wide range in sensitiveness among those seeking therapy.

Sometimes, due to a sense that the trait is only negative in its consequences, therapists may not want to apply such a label to patients, especially to men. Even if they see it, they may fear that using the term will do harm. I have indeed found that almost all men have a complex about sensitivity, reacting to the topic with nervous laughter, defensiveness, unusually strong attacks on the concept's validity, or withdrawal. Many determined women feel the same discomfort about the trait. Although in the past sensitivity was considered a feminine trait, in today's cultural climate it is probably not desirable in either gender. As Susan (from Chapter 1) expressed it, "I don't want to know one more reason why I can't do what I want to do." Thus, some therapists would not offer it as an explanation even if they had thought of it.

False negatives also occur, as mentioned, when extroversion or high sensation seeking hides the trait and the clinician is not able to see through to it.

Bottom Line: Assuming clinicians have heard about the trait, they may make false-negative errors because they do not understand the concept and its supporting research, are not highly sensitive themselves, see everyone as being highly sensitive and therefore do not assess for it, are afraid of stigmatizing a patient, or miss the trait in an extrovert or high sensation seeker.

SUMMARY AND CONCLUSION

In most cases it is fairly easy to spot sensitivity because it is an overall style of the nervous system, present in some way in every aspect of the sensitive person's life. It is easier to see this larger picture, however, if one breaks it down into whether or not all four broad indicators of sensitivity are found: depth of processing, overarousability, emotional intensity, and sensory sensitivity (easily remembered as DOES). These four will be found in observable behavior, the presenting problems, history, or the reaction to formative negative events in patients' lives.

There are other indicators, however, which are not innate yet direct results of the trait. For example, shyness is not innate, but many sensitive patients and those around them describe them as shy. Hence this shyness has to be assessed as to how it is explained and experienced. Eventually, you will discuss your observations and tentative thoughts with your patient. The sensitive ones will generally listen keenly, understand quickly, and appreciate the possibilities you are raising.

False positives occur in some cases, but false negatives are far more common and harmful. Having read this chapter, you are much less likely to make either of these errors.

The purpose of this chapter was to develop skills in assessing sensitivity in general, apart from the individual difficulties and history of traumas that your patients bring to you. Often assessing for sensitivity will not be your first priority. Assessing for depression, need for medications, risk of suicide, risk of violence, and so forth will take center stage. But it should be clear by now that watching for high sensitivity will be useful, even imperative, for gaining a full sense of certain patients and for planning their treatment and your relationship with them. Indeed, you have probably been thinking since you opened this book about which of your patients are highly sensitive, and those who are will already be benefiting from your assessment skills.

CHAPTER

3

Two Issues Arising From Innate Sensitivity

Being Easily Overaroused and Stronger Emotional Reactions

> It is strange to think that ... [the poet Rainer Maria Rilke] would perhaps have been broken by the circumstances in which we now live [Dutch Jews soon to be sent to Auschwitz]. Is that not further testimony that life is finely balanced? Evidence that, in peaceful times and under favorable circumstances, sensitive artists may search for the purest and most fitting expression of their deepest thoughts so that, during more turbulent and debilitating times, others can turn to them for support and a ready response to their bewildered questions? A response they are unable to formulate for themselves since all their energies are taken up in looking after the bare necessities. Sadly, in difficult times we tend to shrug off the spiritual heritage of artists from an "easier" age, with "what use is that sort of thing to us now?"
>
> —**E. Hillesum,** *An Interrupted Life, The Diaries of Etty Hillesum, 1941–1943*

This chapter transitions to treatment by discussing two potential problems for almost all sensitive persons, independent of any disorders. These, the disadvantages of two of the basic indicators discussed in the previous chapter, are being easily overaroused and having overwhelming emotional reactions.

Although in the above quote Etty Hillesum was writing about Rilke's sensitivity, she was a remarkable person in her own right, and from her diaries it would seem that she was highly sensitive. Presuming she was, Etty is a powerful example of what is possible, perhaps even easier, because of being so emotionally responsive.

Etty Hillesum was a young Jewish woman who grew up in Amsterdam in the years preceding World War II. She apparently had a good childhood as part of a gifted family that was deeply attached to one another. As one more example of the tragedies of that time and place, she was reaching adulthood when the Nazis came to power and was destined to witness her portion of the Holocaust and die at Auschwitz. Among many other things, her diaries are a testimony to how a sensitive person can manage both overwhelming levels of stimulation (constant danger, crowded living conditions, etc.) and a situation evoking the most intense emotions, although at times being completely defeated.

On November 10, 1941, Etty wrote the following: "Mortal fear in every fiber. Complete collapse. Lack of self-confidence. Aversion. Panic" (1981, p. 58). She also wrote on July 3, 1942: "Very well then, this new certainty, that what they are after is our total destruction, I accept it. … I shall not burden the others with my fears. … I shall not be bitter if others fail to grasp what is happening to us Jews. I work and continue to live with the same conviction, and I find life meaningful—yes, meaningful" (p. 161). Her diaries document day by day an intense struggle to arrive at this state of grace in spite of the sort of overarousal and intense emotional responses represented by the first quote.

She used all the usual methods of affect regulation, from distraction, seeking comfort from others, and withdrawal for time alone, to gratitude for one's blessings, helping others, and seeking a positive meaning in negative events (Larsen & Prizmic, 2004). But she did these in a gifted, masterful way. I cannot quite call her "a case illustration," but she is good to keep in mind as you observe the difficulties your patients have managing their overstimulation and emotional intensity.

AN ARBITRARY SEPARATION OF THESE TWO ASPECTS

It is not easy to separate the two aspects of sensitivity that I have called overarousal due to overstimulation and emotional reactivity. Very little overarousal occurs apart from stimulation related to or caused by emotions. The exceptions are when overarousal is due to substances such as caffeine, physical exertion, or stimulation that is entirely physical, such as howling high winds or flood warnings, and when we have exceeded our cognitive capacity, which is our ability to hold what we need to in working memory. Even these usually lead to emotion, however. For example, too much caffeine can lead to euphoria and have a stronger effect in a sensitive person, or perhaps a sensitive person would notice a racing heart and worry more about a coffee addiction, while cognitive overload can lead to frustration and fears of failure. Further, stimulation comes from within as well as without, and much of that is due to the perception of bodily reactions resulting from emotions. However, I will continue to divide them, rather arbitrarily, into how to help patients deal with overstimulation due to outer stimuli and helping them regulate their affects in the way they wish.

SIMPLY DISCUSSING SENSITIVITY CAN CAUSE OR MITIGATE THESE TWO ASPECTS

You can use the information in this chapter in the straightforward way it is written or in a more gradual, indirect fashion, suited to a psychodynamic or relational approach. All of these issues will eventually surface without you needing to bring them up beforehand. Indeed, I would recommend a gradual approach even in the briefest therapy. If you are going to discuss in detail the five problems discussed in this chapter and the next, explore one per session so that you do not overload the patient with information or emotions.

Emotional overload is a particularly significant problem when discussing this material. These patients may be flooded at any time with feelings of profound relief, gratitude, grief, or anger as they realize the implications of what they are learning. Readers of *The Highly Sensitive Person* (Aron, 1996) have often commented that they cried much of the time while reading it, and either devoured it in one sitting or had to space reading it over months. Although you will become habituated to the term and its implications, patients new to it may feel as if they were "coming out." They have been keeping secret all these separate embarrassing problems without ever knowing the scope or the value of what they were hiding or that there were others like them. Having the complete picture can be quite profound.

For each of the aspects of the trait discussed in this chapter and the next, I begin with a review of information you can share with your patient and then provide a list of specific suggestions.

OVERAROUSAL

Overarousal was discussed in the previous chapter as one indicator to watch for when assessing for sensitivity. Another way to think of it is having too much to process.

General Thoughts

Stimulation becomes overarousing when fatigue sets in. Fatigue arises because the processing of stimulation requires nervous system arousal and attention. Further, the highly sensitive are usually being additionally fatigued due to inhibition of their behavioral response, which they do to a greater degree than others in order to process stimuli more thoroughly. That requires self-control, which is specifically known to be physical work with physical limits, even though it is psychological in nature (Muraven, Tice, & Baumeister, 1998).

The Many Sources of Stimulation

Patients need to realize that overstimulation has many faces. It can be due to having to deal with extremes—high intensity (e.g., loud, bright, rough to touch) or very low intensity (e.g., subtle differences in pitch, subtle variations in a pattern). Some stimulation can be managed for a while, but it becomes overstimulating if it goes on too long (a car security alarm going on for hours, a project requiring intense focus for weeks). Overstimulation due to complexity is often missed (e.g., too many brands of jam to choose from, someone speaking to you in a crowded train station while you search for your train and try to listen to an announcement being made about track assignments). Overstimulation can also arise due to novelty (e.g., meeting a stranger, reading about a new idea) or suddenness (a horn honk, a dropped pan). Often environments we are in almost every day, a grocery store or public transportation, involve all of these.

Social stimulation—being observed, praised, criticized, loved, or hassled, for example—is some of the most intense. We are social animals designed to notice every subtlety about facial expression, posture, tone of voice, and physical attributes such as age or height as well as the possible meanings of vocalizations. Remaining a respected or loved part of a dyad or group is essential to survival, so a great deal of anyone's brain activity is devoted to interpreting these, but this is even more true for sensitive persons. Perhaps the worst is intense stimulation forced on a person against his or her will—for example, an older sibling holding a sensitive child down to tickle him or her, or someone refusing to turn down his or her music when you request it.

Stimulation inside the body also has to be processed—hunger, muscle spasms, a discomfort that requires a change of position. Even if the reaction is automatic, such as walking, it still requires processing stimulation as to one's position in space, for example. This is part of why when we have lost something it works better to sit, calm down, and think rather than search more and more frantically. Closing the eyes reduces another large proportion of stimulation, as does going to a quiet room. Without such measures, the brain cannot stop processing what it sees or hears.

Appreciating the breadth of sources of stimulation helps sensitive patients realize how much is impinging on them during normal activities such as going to the grocery store or watching television. You might not want to emphasize this, however, to patients who have withdrawn too much.

Overarousal's Effect on Comfort and Performance

In listening to evaluate the sheer amount of overstimulation, it is also important to notice how being overaroused affects the patient's self-esteem and what coping strategies he or she typically adopts to deal with it. As I emphasized in the previous chapter, overarousal in anyone reduces both comfort and performance on any task. For the highly sensitive, that means many failures in the very situations that matter most to them, and they will have coped with this in many ways. Social situations, again, are highly stimulating and if also unfamiliar, such as when meeting strangers, the resulting overarousal contributes enormously to being less confident and effective.

Bottom Line: Overarousal is generally due to overstimulation. Stimuli have a number of aspects that can make them more arousing, and stimuli come from everywhere—from inside as well as outside and can be social as well as purely sensory. Overarousal causes discomfort and poor performance and is a major factor in the mental health of sensitive persons.

A CASE ILLUSTRATION

Christina was a highly sensitive Olympic-level athlete who broke several world records at small qualifying meets, but at the larger events she could not even place. Her coaches and a sports psychologist were trying to help her, but their imaging exercises and self-affirmation strategies were making the problem worse because she was failing at these as well. Without an explanation for her problem beyond performance anxiety, focusing on it only increased her own arousal. So we talked about the impact of the high level of stimulation at these meets and how she might reduce her exposure or even habituate to some of it by, for example, going to the site the day before. We also discussed ways her sensitivity had made her a better athlete, which allowed her to accept without shame that it was hindering her at the very stimulating larger meets.

In the end, one conclusion we arrived at together was that the true function of the Olympic games was not merely to identify the best athletes, but rather to identify the best athletes under pressure. These conversations substantially improved her performance, although she eventually decided not to pursue her dream of performing at the Olympics.

Suggestions Regarding Managing Overarousal

These suggestions have been gleaned from years of listening to and advising the highly sensitive, so the list is somewhat lengthy.

Reassure Them

Being easily overaroused is the most distressing part of being highly sensitive, and being distressed about it only increases their overarousal. Patients need to feel positively about their sensitivity if they are going to take the steps they need to take, rather than deny its reality. For example, if they have been out with friends all day sightseeing and in the evening the plan is to go to a party and then stop at a club for some jazz, sensitive persons will almost surely recognize from past experience that this is not for them. But to leave the group and go home is difficult for many reasons and harder still if you are ashamed of your sensitivity.

Take patients back to the neutral nature of their innate strategy. Sometimes it is an advantage, sometimes not. Sensitive animals prosper when noticing subtleties is most important. If they were a deer, they would live longer when predators were a special danger, even if their alertness to every tiny stimulus meant hesitating to enter a safe place and getting less to eat than less cautious deer. But they would need to rest from their alertness, or suffer stress.

Another neutral metaphor is to think of the way oranges are sorted into sizes: They roll along, falling into small, medium, and large slots according to where they fit. The small ones fall into the first slot while the others fall into later ones. But if finer sorting were needed and there were 15 slots, the oranges would pile up into a terrible jumble if the conveyer belt was not slowed down. The same happens to a sensitive nervous system—it does a great job with subtle differences, but cannot handle too much at once.

Continue to assert the value of their sensitivity and the "package deal" idea. In the museum, weren't they the ones to point out subtleties others missed? Don't people often praise them for good judgment or intuition? A great deal of stimulation is processed unconsciously, which is called implicit learning. In everyday language, they have good intuition, which they will readily agree to and which everyone admires. Throughout society, everyone benefits from the highly sensitive person's awareness of subtleties. For example, I am certain that annoyance about secondhand smoke was first voiced by sensitive persons.

Assess the Current Overall Level of Self-Protection

A place to begin is to help patients assess whether they are "too in" or "too out." (I wrote about this in *The Highly Sensitive Person* [Aron, 1996] and *The Highly Sensitive Person's Workbook* [Aron, 1999] and these could be good resources for patients.) Even though all patients will have to deal with overstimulation in certain situations, some will be protecting themselves too much. The reasons for this will differ. They may have already experienced failures and want to avoid more. They may have been abused and feel victimized by the stimulation created by others or separated themselves from the world for some other dysfunctional reason. Hence, they are not tempted out by the possibility of pleasure, companionship, or self-expression. As you work on the causes for this, you can also discuss the need to maintain an optimal level of stimulation. They do not need to avoid overstimulation, but being on the low side can also cause discomfort, such as boredom, lack of self-expansion, a sense that their life has no meaning or purpose, and the lack of any opportunities to have positive experiences. We need stimulation the same as we need food and water, and prolonged, complete isolation does strange things to people—this is why it is among the most dreaded forms of torture.

Most patients, however will be too overexposed to stimulation, mistakenly living a lifestyle suited to the nonsensitive. Often they are trying to overcompensate for or eliminate what they see as a weakness, their sensitivity. The too-out need educating about the risks of chronic overarousal. Most of what follows applies to the overexposed patient, but these suggestions also can help the underexposed to feel safer when they begin to move out into the world.

Help Them Be Creative in Overstimulating Situations

After Christina had seen just how much stimulation she was taking in at the large Olympic trials, she could avoid or alter aspects she had control over. For example, she did not have to stay on the field and watch other competitors, although she should not automatically avoid watching either. In some cases it might actually reduce her anxiety, but she needed to weigh the advantages of going or staying. Encourage them to experiment.

Help Them Learn to Say No

Most therapists are familiar with ways to develop assertiveness (as much as can be done, given other forces in the personality). It helps to appreciate that sensitive persons come into the world with thinner personal boundaries. They sense all too well the feelings of others, including the other's needs, desires, and disappointments. They also fear being criticized for failing to do what is needed or expected. It is important not to shame sensitive people for their natural difficulty at being assertive, but to encourage valuing themselves and respecting their own needs to keep stimulation within bounds.

One woman patient was invited to a retreat being held by an ongoing women's group. She knew the person slightly who had extended the invitation, but no one else. As a popular artist, she would be the honored guest at what was advertised as an intimate, "full and fulfilling" summer solstice weekend. I knew her to be a very private, introverted person who was also in the midst of some intense personal work with me, so I was not surprised that she was worried about going. I had to agree that the weekend sounded like hell! Yet she could not say no. We explored her other options, such as doing a 2-hour presentation of her own work and leaving, but also why her feelings about going were her least consideration.

First, I described a scale. One side was how much would the group suffer due to her absence, and on the other, how much she would suffer going. Which way did the scale tip? What helped most, I think, was my story of a prominent academic colleague who had told me that the secret of his having accomplished so much was that he always delegated what he could to others. Further, he always chose the person already overworked, knowing he or she could not say no. My patient finally saw how unkind it was to her sensitive self simply to do something because someone had asked her to, without checking in with herself first.

She finally told them she was not able to come. I tell patients they do not need to make elaborate, contrived excuses, as if their sensitivity was a shameful burden to others or that something else is the problem instead, like being sick. Others can accept a simple, "It just isn't going to work for me." The group was not happy with her, but it seemed that this only increased her desirability, in that she received many more invitations after that to speak to large groups. Generally she turned them down.

Develop Methods of Self-Soothing

Patients should learn to use self-soothing whenever they are anticipating, enduring, or recovering from overstimulation. The key here is "whatever works." For some, prayer or thinking of a loved one is self-soothing. You might help them develop an inner safe place using guided imagery. Transitional objects are also helpful. Whatever soothes is "transitional." The "soothing maternal primary presence through the transitional act may actually make the most frightening, painful, and destructive realities tolerable" (Horton, 1981, p. 153). Anything can become a transitional act or object in this sense, including special objects, but also pets, being immersed in satisfying work, special places such as one's childhood home, religious beliefs or texts, and of course comforting foods. Some patients have had such empty childhoods that they never had a transitional object, so they will need to learn from experience that "reliable relief from pain through transitional activity is always available" (p. 151).

Suggest Meditation

I place meditation in a separate category of transitional acts, as it can have quick and dramatic physical results (Beauchamp-Turner & Levinson, 1992). Methods of meditation vary in their effects much as medications do. I like transcendental meditation for this purpose because it is truly effortless and emphasizes how you feel afterward rather than achieving specific states during the meditation. Whatever the method, it should be practiced daily as much as possible so that the physiological relaxation response is automatic. After 35 years of meditating twice a day, I can count on the process to lower my arousal in any overstimulating situation. As an example, I was once on a crowded subway stalled beneath Manhattan with increasingly agitated passengers. I closed my eyes and meditated, standing up. I immediately felt calmer and it seemed that others did too.

Some patients will say they have tried to meditate and could not. Their mind was too restless. The problem is the form of meditation or how it was taught. Again, it should be effortless and practiced for its results, not for achieving some special state, so that neither the person meditating nor the particular meditation session is ever a failure. It will feel different each day, just as the body and brain differ in small ways every day. If you are under stress, it will reflect that. The mind will wander more or stay focused on some external problem or idea. But this is just as when you take a bath—the water is dirtier the more you needed to bathe. The dirt reflects success, not failure.

Meditation does not require a quiet, nonstimulating environment, but does feel different in a highly stimulating place. If you sit down and close your eyes and simply intend to meditate, it is always useful for reducing arousal. I describe to patients a scale from zero, which is no arousal ("no thoughts, pure awareness") to 10, high arousal. A good meditation at home might take you from 3 to 1. But out on the tarmac in an overheated plane delayed 5 hours and full of angry passengers, a meditation might go from 10 to 7, yet be far more useful than what was achieved at home, regardless of whether it feels like it was unsuccessful as a meditation. Even when you are listening to talking around you, the attempt or intention to meditate re-creates some of the needed physiological changes.

Emphasize Being Rested and Healthy

Handling a highly stimulating environment takes energy. If you are sick and tired, you have to reduce your exposure to stimulation. Patients should learn to monitor their bodies and notice its ups and downs. If they have a choice, they should be patient and wait until they are at their best before facing anything very difficult. For example, schedule interviews in the morning, while fresh; allow time to recover from jet lag before beginning to tour a city. If you feel run down or sick, wait until you are feeling better. Again, this may require being able to say no, even when it inconveniences or disappoints someone.

Encourage Being Fully Prepared

For my dissertation defense, I rehearsed many hours, long past my just "having it down." Understanding my sensitivity, I knew I needed my thoughts to be so automatic that I could discuss almost anything related to my topic, in spite of my predictable high, high arousal. I also rehearsed with an audience, having them increase the skepticism of their questions. Knowing I was so well prepared helped reduce the arousal that was due to fear.

Perhaps equally important, I anticipated my worst fears. What if a criticism was made that I had never thought of and was completely right? I had to decide that there was nothing that could completely destroy my arguments, given the facts, but I could still say, "That's an excellent point—I will have to think about it and get back to you." Dwelling on negative possibilities is probably not helpful for the nonsensitive patient, but the highly sensitive are imagining these anyway. Better to make the worst explicit, even to the point of black comedy. I still remember my plan for "What if someone says this is so bad they are going to vomit, and do?"

Finally, I countered the perfectionism inherent in the sensitive individual's strategy of "do it once and do it right" by expecting at least two things to go wrong that I had not prepared for, which they did. I merely thought, "There's number one," and later, "There's number two." If there had been a third, I would have shrugged at that too. By the end I was actually enjoying myself in this very overstimulating situation.

Make Success Likely

In Chapter 1 I described my friend Jim, who saw to it that his daughter Lily would almost always succeed at what he was urging her to try. That is the spirit in which sensitive patients need to think of themselves, even if others do not. Christina's coach, who was very proud of her, made the mistake of sending her to meets when it was not clear she was ready. He was counting on what he loved about her—how hard she would always try. But one failure took away most of her confidence. Once she was anxious, the feeling stayed with her at future meets.

Focus on the Familiar

One quality of stimulation that can be reduced is novelty. The more exposure ahead of time, the less stimulation there will be. For my dissertation defense I reminded myself that I have given many successful talks before and answered many questions on my topic in conversations. What may have helped the most was that I did a dress rehearsal in the room where I could present the next day, even choosing the same time of day so that the lighting would be familiar. In addition, it is important to help patients focus on the familiar behaviors they will use or the people who will be present.

Teach "Pace Yourself"

Another aspect of stimulation that can be controlled is the length that it continues. Almost anything can be handled if one takes breaks *before* one has reached *over*arousal. Taking breaks runs the gamut from simply closing one's eyes a moment and taking a deep, abdominal breath to vacations and sabbaticals. The ideal break during a long task would be a minimum of 20 minutes.

Encourage Nature Breaks

It seems that the highly sensitive are especially responsive to nature. If your patient is, encourage it. Remind them that a "nature break" is better than standing in the coffee room. Perhaps they can only go outdoors and look at the sky or lovingly consider a tree. Pets are another form of nature known to reduce arousal. They might simply bring a goldfish to work, to watch it gliding about or restfully floating inside a bowl on their desk, among a bit of green water grass—nothing plastic. If they exercise, they should do it outdoors instead of on indoor equipment, and for purposes of recovering from overstimulation it is best that it is rhythmic motion and certainly should not be competitive.

Emphasize Social Support

Most mammals are calmed in potentially overwhelming situations by the presence of a familiar, supportive other from their group or family. Taking a friend into a highly stimulating situation always helps, as does thinking of someone who loves them, whatever they do. So often patients do not take advantage of social support, thinking they must go it alone or do not want anyone to see them struggling. Admittedly for some patients the lack of social support is the problem in itself. Other sensitive patients could have support if they used their sensitivity to notice when another person is glad to help. Remind them that friendships are only strengthened by giving and receiving real help; they need more than lunch now and then.

Eliminating Extraneous Stimulation

Sometimes it is possible to eliminate extraneous stimulation by, for example, closing one's eyes and only listening to someone talk; asking that the radio be turned off during a medical procedure; not carrying on a conversation while driving in heavy traffic; or relaxing parts of the body that do not need to be tensed.

Planning for Rest and Recovery Time

After returning from a trip, the sensitive person needs a day to recover, or even longer if jet lag is involved. When a project ends, there should be some easy work for a while and extra rest at home. A vacation to recover from stress should not require getting up early for a bicycle trip into a volcano, or getting up early for anything. Sensitive patients who are also high sensation seekers especially need to hear this.

EXAMPLE DIALOGUE

Sometimes after making all sorts of good suggestions, I have a dialogue much like this.

Patient: I want to learn how to cope with being highly sensitive.
Therapist: Hmm. I thought we were doing that. Perhaps all these suggestions I make are not quite meeting your needs—your real needs.
Patient: You're right. I still don't know how to cope with it.
Therapist: After a while I think that with your good intuition and basic knowledge of what you need to do and what you need to avoid—you'll come up with your own creative solutions.
Patient: I just want you to tell me how to cope with this!
Therapist: Perhaps we have a different idea about what it means to cope with it.
Patient: Well, like not have it affect me so much.
Therapist: Like get over it?
Patient: Yeah. I know you say being sensitive has advantages and all that, but I'd like the advantages without all these disadvantages.
Therapist: Something like, it's nice to live in the country except it's so far from town?
Patient: You mean I'm being unreasonable. But this affects everything. I have to prepare so much. I have to think ahead about so much. I ought to meditate, take more time to recover. Other people don't have to do all that. I want to be, well, "normal."
Therapist: So it sounds like there might be something to grieve here. Seeing what you gain from being sensitive does not change the fact that you are learning that certain things are not ever going to be easy for you.
Patient: That's right. I guess it's sad.
Therapist: It is. But you know, even if we're moving from a crummy hut to a beautiful palace, it's human nature to grieve the hut. It's gone forever—you might miss it a lot.
Patient: Miss the nonsensitive version of me that I thought I was but wasn't.
Therapist: I'm remembering a quote about that. "Every change is a loss, every loss must be grieved."

STRONGER EMOTIONAL REACTIONS

Most of psychotherapy is about managing emotions: helping patients know what they are actually feeling, using feelings to develop the therapeutic alliance, educating about emotions, and so forth. The focus here is on methods that work especially well with the highly sensitive.

General Comments

These patients need to realize that they came into life with stronger emotional responses, for better and for worse. (As infants they are often termed "negative" because of their strong reactions to unpleasant stimuli.) They will stay emotional. Compared to others in the same situations, they will be, for example, sadder, happier, more irritated, afraid, curious, or ashamed, and wanting more than others to be very close. Their stronger emotions need not always be expressed, but they want to be aware of them rather than fear them.

If you sense hidden emotions, or emotions that ought to be there given the situation, try to focus on allying with who or what within the patient is feeling these hidden emotions. This will help the patient know more about what is happening inside of him or her.

You cannot turn a race horse into a turtle nor a sensitive person into a perfectly emotionally regulated human being. The task is helping them live with this aspect of their trait and tilting the balance so that they are enjoying more than before the benefits of their strong positive emotions. These will show up, even if patients have come to you because they are feeling too much sadness, fear, shame, or disappointment with someone. Remind them that good feelings, strong ones, are also a part of their emotional repertoire.

My own overriding sense of sensitive patients is that they have spent a lifetime wrestling with their intense emotions. Sometimes the intense emotions have won, in that they are jerked every which way by their affect, and sometimes the individual has won a dubious victory. Affect regulation, however, does not mean victory over emotion. It means in a given situation having the right emotion and expressing that to others in the right degree. It requires a negotiated peace followed by a steady alliance. It is no victory to suppress or dissociate emotions to the point of having no idea what is happening inside. Rather, highly sensitive patients need to become emotional experts. Their sensitivity can detect what they are feeling as well as what others are feeling. They can become experts easily, once they make it a goal.

Bottom Line: Sensitive persons have stronger positive as well as negative situations. They have already developed their own ways of dealing with them and should be helped to become more expert at this.

Suggestions for Teaching How to Cope With Intense Emotions

Most of the suggestions below are about teaching your patients to be the experts. As you work with their emotions, teach your patients how to work with them. You want to back off when you sense overarousal, but teach your patients to tell you when this is happening so they know the signs themselves. Once the emotions have settled down, rather than you providing an interpretation of what has happened, the two of you can search together for the cause for that particular sense of being overwhelmed. Again, that way patients learn to do it for themselves.

Inventory Their Emotions

After you have a good alliance with your patients and they are at least as interested as scared of their affects, go over the basic emotions with them: fear, anxiety, worry; irritation, anger, disappointment; sadness, grief, depression; curiosity, interest; joy, contentment, satisfaction. Go separately through the social emotions: attraction, loneliness, pride, guilt, and shame. Have them identify which ones they feel often and which ones they never feel. You can add your own observations from the sessions. Pay special attention to shame, the feeling of one's core self being worthless, as this emotion is feared so much that it is usually hidden behind numerous defenses: blaming, projecting, minimizing, denial, overachievement, social avoidance, and of course narcissism. Explore why some emotions are favored and whether these are sometimes substituted for the others. Usually these emotional habits were learned at home. The forbidden emotions need encouragement. You can both do that.

Remind Them of the Advantages

Help patients remind themselves of the many wonderfully powerful good feelings that they have known and that many people do not feel things as deeply as they do. In my interviews I found that their strong feelings were what many sensitive persons valued most. One recounted his very first memory of lying under beautiful swaying vines, experiencing pure beauty. He also remembered hearing his first opera at age 5. He was "transported into bliss"—what he still feels when hearing opera. He flies all over the country to hear performances of Wagner. This same man described with rich detail his emotions the day before our interview, while watching the setting sun reflect on the windows of a skyscraper. I can still "see" the evening he described.

He told me these experiences in order to explain why he found his sensitivity to be such an asset. He affirmed this in spite of the pain he had experienced as a sensitive child—allergic to hay, no less, and adopted into a tough farm family. He was teased and shamed for only being good for "women's work." It was a family and home that he knew he would have to leave as soon as possible, and he did. He said he was basically homeless for a long time afterward, until he found other sensitive people to live with. He loves them, deeply.

Another advantage to these innately strong emotional reactions is that they allow patients to exhibit "emotional leadership." After seeing a sensitive person's response, others often become aware of what they are feeling or should be feeling. We all have been helped at one time or another by the first one to cry at a memorial service or the first one to be shocked into coming to the aid of a victim, so that we can join in.

Discuss Anticipatory Emotions

Because these patients look ahead to the likely outcome of things, they often react and feel ahead of time an anticipated loss, separation, joy, unpleasant event like a medical or dental procedure, or even an accomplishment, long before it occurs. The nonsensitive might view this as a strange waste of energy or not "living in the present," but it fits with that basic strategy of reflecting before acting and anticipating how things will turn out.

If a patient is upset without knowing why, I ask about what might be coming up for them. "Could this possibly have anything to do with my upcoming vacation?" Or, "I wonder if this anxiety is about the move you are planning?"

One patient had a 9-year-old niece coming to visit for the summer. Around the first of the year, the patient, childless herself, began going through anticipatory emotions of anxiety (all sorts, from what to feed her niece to being rejected by her), joy, curiosity, anger about things she imagined her niece might do (break a beloved vase), and the desperate sadness and loneliness she might feel when alone again after 3 months of having someone else in her home. What surprised us both was that by the time the niece came, the patient was quite calm. All of her fears had been worked through well in advance.

You will have your own approach to such seemingly premature emotions, but do not call them irrational. Rather, point out their relationship to the patient's trait. By the way, my own approach to worry is to tell myself I will wait to worry until it really happens, or if I know when it will happen, I tell myself I will begin worrying at such-and-such hour or day, not long before the feared event.

Teach Them How to Handle Change

Younger sensitive persons especially will take a job in a new city as they see their peers doing, and then be amazed by how difficult the transition proves to be. The new job by itself gives rise to strong feelings, involving as it does meeting new people, learning their way around an office, and adapting their skills to a new situation. They are anxious about doing well enough. Plus they are adapting to a new community, living space, and natural environment, usually with less social support than where they moved from and missing where they came from much more than they expected. As I said in the dialogue above, every change involves a loss and every loss leads to negative affect, and this is even truer for the sensitive person. A sensitive person must have time to process this loss as well as the gains experienced or still hoped for in the new situation. Very often even the most emotionally skilled will be surprised by how long it takes them to feel as settled after a move.

Stay alert for patients planning major events, whether a happy one like marriage or a sad one like going home to sort out a deceased parent's household and finances. Help them realize how much they will feel and to plan for that. A small wedding may be a far better idea for them. Sorting out the parent's personal effects should be done in slow stages, with supportive others around if possible. They should anticipate, too, how others in the family may behave under the emotional stress of their loss or the excitement of a wedding.

When adapting to a new situation, the old familiar ones should be kept alive in memory rather than banished out of the fear of being overwhelmed by grief. Help them learn that grief, even their especially intense form of it, can be survived. A sensitive person benefits from returning often to the old community, coming home often from college, going by the old house, or calling a friend "lost" through moving. This reinforces in the emotional mind that the beloved places are still there and continued contact is possible, and at the same time that the change and thus the loss is real.

Discuss Social Support

Mammals generally live in groups of at least two and use each other to provide affect regulation (Lewis, Amini, & Lannon, 2000). Even though being around others can be highly stimulating for sensitive people, it is also innately soothing. Listen for whether these patients are underusing social support or driving others off by burdening them too much. If they underuse social support, discuss why. They may fear bothering others. It can help to ask them to put themselves in their friend's position and realize that they would be glad to help their friend, so why not the other way around.

Those who, rightly or not, have become a burden to their friends need to learn how to check in with others before expressing their feelings, seek a little social support from several people rather than relying on one, and have some highly sensitive friends who will not tell them they are overreacting.

For many patients the lack of human relationships or relatedness makes this form of affect regulation impossible and is a large part of their problem, in that they lack relationships because of their poor affect regulation—a vicious circle. In that case, you may be their only social-emotional support and a very important one. Since they pick up on subtle cues as to what others feel, consider what emotions you want them to sense in you during their emotional crisis. Will it help them to see that you feel calm, safe, and secure? Can you help them learn how to be in a relationship at such times, what to expect from the other, how to ask for what they need, and how to accept what they receive?

Discuss Their Emotional Schemas

Emotional schemas, otherwise known as complexes, are the set of memories, emotions, assumptions, and defenses (ways of surviving) that are associated with an overwhelming experience or repeated experiences, especially traumatic ones. These schemas are dissociated and autonomous, having their own function, to protect you from a repeat experience. They come to life when triggered by anything that resembles the original situation. Most of us have, to some degree, an emotional schema around jealousy, for example, and the expectation of betrayal; around money and the fear of not having enough or what it means when someone has a lot of it; and around food, that it may be unclean or unhealthy, or that being fed delicious food by others in a lovely setting is the perfect source of pleasure. Perhaps the "mother of them all" is the negative mother complex, the fear of separation and loss because the person you need most is indifferent, preoccupied, or dislikes you, which leads to a state of feeling hopeless and worthless. This state is often well hidden, but if it is a large part of a person's experience, it is easily triggered. Some of the signs of a triggered complex are that you feel no longer present as an individual but only as a part in a script the other has written ("I know you don't like me"). Argument is futile ("You're just saying that—you can't really mean it") and emotions are intense (the voice is louder or very soft, the speech peppered with "always" and "never").

Because the highly sensitive have intense reactions to events, they have more complicated, easily triggered complexes. The good news is that I have found that they quickly grasp the idea in general and their emotional schemas in particular. When sensitive patients are overwhelmed again and again by certain feelings, such as fear of being alone in public or finding it unbearable when their therapist is on vacation, it often helps to discuss the underlying schema and what triggers it for them, as well as help them develop a new reaction. They also need to know that one never is completely free of a schema. The goal is to spend less time in it.

To spend less time caught up in a schema, a sensitive patient needs to and will go into it again and again, returning to the core trauma or issue and then having with you a new, better experience around it. I suggest that you supply that through your feelings for the patient as expressed in your words and presence—your understanding, acceptance, empathy, compassion. Most important, you replay it as it should have been, without the too harsh punishment, the betrayal, neglect, or whatever happened. You can say what you would have done if you were there.

These patients will need this rewriting of their emotional schemas more often than others because their greater reaction to the original situation has made the schema more deeply elaborated. At the same time, that reaction also created exceptionally strong defenses that prohibit this reexperiencing. Hence, these revisions of the past and new perspectives on the present will not hold very long. It is important that you not lose hope in this process. Again, an offsetting plus is that often these patients quickly see what is happening and can observe what has triggered their schema. They grasp that when seeing life from the schema's perspective, it seems to be the only way to view everything, yet there are other times when they are not in it at all. This type of self-understanding helps them to contain the schema better.

When people emerge from their complex, they often want to forget about it, as if it never happened. Often they feel intense shame about what they said or did. A discussion of what happens needs to take place, but with great delicacy, especially with sensitive patients.

EXAMPLE DIALOGUE

The following is an example of a dialogue that might take place when a patient is struggling with a complex.

Patient [has begun to cry for no apparent reason]: I guess I've been depressed and didn't realize it. Nothing seems worthwhile.

Therapist: Things seem pretty hopeless to you. [Pause.] Do you have a hunch what this might be about?

Patient: No. Not a clue.

Therapist: Can you recall when you were not feeling this way and then it changed?

Patient: No. Well, I recall thinking about next week, how bleak it is going to be, not coming here.

Therapist: Not being able to come here because I will be on vacation.

Patient: Yes.

Therapist: Sounds like you will miss me?

Patient: I guess so. More than I thought.

Therapist: When you are as intimate with someone as you and I have been—I think you'd agree that I probably know more about you right now than anyone else in your life—it's pretty expectable that you would miss me.

Patient: But will you miss me?

Therapist: That's the crucial question for you, isn't it? [At this point sensitive patients especially will feel ashamed of their abandonment complex, and deny it.]

Patient: I don't expect you to miss me. You have lots of patients. You want to go on vacation, get away from them. Me. That's completely understandable.

Therapist: But this question of will I miss you, that would surely be predictable given your childhood, and you knew the answer pretty well from how your mother acted when you came home from camp that time. You were so excited to see her, and she said she was sorry you were back because she had not gotten enough work done while you were away.

Patient: I don't want to be someone who gets depressed because their therapist doesn't miss them. As if I didn't want you to have a good time or something.

Therapist: You were very affected by your mother's absences and not wanting you around. It would have played havoc with anyone's emotions, but being highly sensitive, it was worse for you. Now you are also feeling ashamed, I think. That you would be someone whose needs caused them to make demands, and now it seems even less likely that I would miss you. This is tough. Can you give yourself a break here? That you will not be missed, not even wanted—that's a pretty awful way to experience a separation. You feel that you aren't interesting enough, much less lovable enough—even to your own mother—to draw her away from her almighty work.

Patient: It's that complex again, isn't it? About the mother who didn't love me.

Therapist: That complex can sure kill hope for any human connection. And without that, life can seem pretty bad. Like not just the next two weeks, but all of the rest of your life.

Patient: Yeah. That's it.

Therapist: We're almost out of time, but I look forward to going on with this when I am back. And by the way, I *will* miss you. When I am working I look forward to my vacation, but when I am on vacation, I honestly miss my work, and you are an important part of that. When I think of returning and going back to this work I enjoy, I know I will think specifically of returning to our work together.

The therapist linked the complex to its cause, provided a new experience of being left by someone the patient needed, addressed the role of sensitivity and of shame, and in the end did address frankly the question, "Will you miss me?" This was the final act in making the question a reasonable thing for this patient to ask, given his background, and an easy one for the therapist to answer. The complex was reexperienced and altered, even if only slightly.

Make Important Subtle Distinctions

Sensitive patients can easily mistake overarousal for anxiety or shyness, and their natural caution for fear. Which one is experienced will be determined by how cues from the environment are interpreted. For example, a study by Brodt and Zimbardo (1981) found that when normally very shy women were asked to chat with a handsome male confederate in a very noisy room, if they were told it was the noise that was causing their pounding heart and sweaty palms, they had no trouble conversing to mere overarousal and they did not feel shy at all. Those in the experimental condition, in which subjects were not given another explanation of their bodily sensations of nervousness, felt shy.

Patients need to learn that overarousal is a likely explanation for their feelings and that a break from the stimulation can allow them to reexamine what seemed like a threatening situation. For example, a sensitive chef in a noisy restaurant came to see that she was not becoming increasingly anxious at work, but increasingly overstimulated. She eventually found a quieter kitchen and did not have to give up the work she enjoyed because she thought it made her too anxious.

A cautious *attitude* is part of the sensitive person's innate life strategy. Chronic anxiety or excessive fears are not. Fears are learned (except for a few specific fears that can be innate, such as a fear of heights, snakes, or blood). They arise in specific situations similar to what was frightening in the past. Caution, on the other hand, precedes learning that a situation is dangerous rather than following from it. For example, a sensitive patient was afraid to commit to taking a job in a city where she had never lived. She took this as another example of her fears holding her back, but I pointed out that this seemed like a natural, healthy caution until she determined if she liked the city, what the cost of living would be there, and so forth. This interpretation changed her view of herself, from a person with too many fears to one who made good decisions.

Use Dreams to Monitor Emotions

Sensitive persons have unusually vivid dreams, as well as disturbing nightmares, that they may not mention unless asked. Even if you use dreams in no other way, the amount and type of emotion felt in a dream is roughly equivalent to what needs to be expressed in an overcontrolled sensitive patient. Paying attention to intense dreams for this purpose, with or without consideration of their symbolic meaning, can fit into most approaches.

Help Them Express Appropriate Anger

Sensitive patients often have a history of hiding their anger so that others are not disturbed by it and potential dangerous responses are averted. Frequently they say anger is never an appropriate response, and in a sense this is true. But anger is a way of raising the volume when others are not getting the sensitive person's hint. Further, a lack of all anger is easily interpreted as meekness or weakness.

My research found no difference between the sensitive and nonsensitive on self-reported proneness to anger. Indeed, highly sensitive persons with naturally strong tempers seem better off in that they speak up more readily when something is too much for them. Hence these patients can and should develop their expression of anger at least as a resource when they need to get a point across.

Therapy is often a good place to begin practicing the expression of anger. Watch for errors you may have made and point out that the patient rightfully might be feeling anger and can express it without harming the relationship. Even the tiniest complaint or hint of a different way to see something other than your way should be welcomed. (When the therapist admits to an error it also provides the opportunity to role model acknowledging a mistake without being plunged into shame.)

EXAMPLE DIALOGUE

When Julia, 20, came to me she rarely expressed anger. She was "all sweetness and light," believing that it is always possible to say things kindly. But in fact she harbored tremendous rage toward her father and stepmother, and this anger leaked out toward others in various situations, usually in a passive-aggressive form that was very damaging to her relationships with friends and at work.

Finally she admitted to being angry with me about something. It was at the end of a session. She had come wanting to talk about a serious financial problem and felt I had made too many suggestions when she merely wanted a space to reflect on her own about it.

Julia: The session's almost over and I guess I'm still feeling pretty bad.
Me: It hasn't been very helpful for making you feel better about this. Maybe you needed something else?
Julia: Oh, it was okay.
Me: But just okay. What would have made it better?
Julia: I don't want to be critical.
Me: Yet I want to be as useful and helpful as possible to you, so I need feedback. What didn't help?
Julia: I think, I don't think I needed so many suggestions.
Me: You could have got those from your friends.
Julia: Yeah, there really wasn't much new there.
Me: So naturally you feel angry about not getting what you needed.
Julia: Not angry.
Me: Irritated?
Julia: Maybe frustrated.
Me: I wonder why not really angry? You felt terrible and really needed help with that, not what I gave you.

Julia: I don't want to be angry, not with you.

Me: Not with anyone, as I remember. But we've known each other a while now. It's not going to change our relationship, not in the long run. Might even make it better. Not saying you're angry, that could be not so good for our relationship. Maybe you would tell yourself, "Well, she makes too many suggestions, but better not tell her. She makes a lot of these kinds of mistakes, but she's okay." I'd rather it be, "She made a lot of suggestions today but I told her so that she knows and it's all fine now." If saying something angry is too hard, perhaps you could just check out inside if you are angry, then tell me or not.

Julia: I was angry.

Me: Not now?

Julia: Well, maybe a little is left.

Me: Could you just say the words, "I am angry with you for all those suggestions that took up so much time?"

She repeated the words; then cried. We talked about this moment several times over the next few sessions. She acknowledged the value of expressing her dislikes as well as her likes to those who wanted to meet her needs.

I have also seen a few sensitive patients having problems with strong, unregulated anger. With them it was indicative of a deeper issue, the need to ward off unbearable shame or to avoid intimacy. In these cases I try to be attuned to the underlying feeling rather than the anger.

Whether anger is being over- or undercontrolled, I explain to sensitive patients that their goal is not to express as much anger as others might, but to learn to know when they are feeling it and then express it as a tool, strategically, so that it helps to meet their needs rather than frustrating them. For example, patients can mobilize anger to set proper boundaries with others and "get through" to nonsensitive persons when simply asking has failed. But it has to be done skillfully.

I use the example of volume control and explain to patients that to have a nonsensitive person understand, for example, that you need them to make more of an effort on the job, you do not begin with a hint that "it would be nice if ..." That would be a 1 on a 1-to-10 scale of volume, something only you in their position would hear. Receiving no reaction from your nonsensitive worker, you do not stew a while because you have seen no change and then blast the person with a 10. You turn up the volume to a 5, then a 6, and when that fails, rethink what is going on. You can spare yourself all of this by starting with a clear 5—"I need you to do better in this area in these ways ..." Never mind how painful it might be for the patient in that position to be told so directly.

SUMMARY AND CONCLUSION

Being easily overaroused and having strong emotional reactions are two facts of the sensitive person's life and of the therapy treatment. These will not change. Patients can benefit a great deal, however, by learning more about regulating stimulation, arousal, and emotion. Thus your goal is to teach them about managing these, so that they can recognize and adapt as well or better than you can.

Patients often feel shame as they discuss their "failures" due to overarousal in important situations, they will feel even more shame as they reveal their strong feelings, especially if these are based on emotional schemas and, therefore, distorted and especially intense and inappropriate. You will always have to be careful not to shame these patients, but in these situations especially. They may not need your interpretations of the cause of their failures, intense emotional reactions, or poor emotional regulation. Above all, do not discourage them. Although greater emotional reactivity and the tendency to be easily overstimulated are innate and also even more problematic when patients had a painful childhood, many sensitive patients can change through psychotherapy from being overaroused, anxious, and depressed to being mostly happy, optimistic, confident, and content. That is a wonderful fact.

CHAPTER

4

Three Common Problems

Low Self-Esteem, the Wrong Lifestyle, and Overreactions to Criticism

> A sensitive and somewhat unbalanced person, as a neurotic always is, will meet with special difficulties and perhaps with more unusual tasks in life than a normal individual, who as a rule has only to follow the well-worn path of an ordinary existence. For the neurotic there is no established way of life, because his aims and tasks are apt to be of a highly individual character. He tries to go the more or less uncontrolled and half conscious way of normal people, not realizing that his own critical and very different nature demands of him more effort than the normal person is required to exert.
>
> **—Carl Jung (*Collected Works*, 4, para. 572)**

This chapter continues to look at the five problems most sensitive patients face. In the previous chapter, we considered two arising from the trait itself. This chapter looks at three indirect results of it that are experienced by most sensitive persons: low self-esteem, trying to live like nonsensitive persons, and being unusually distressed by criticism. Suggestions are made for working with each problem. The second half of the chapter discusses the interaction of the trait with gender, age, and ethnicity.

Carl Jung wrote extensively about sensitivity in his early work and concluded that neuroticism as known in his day was the result of environment plus a sensitive temperament. Fitting into this category himself, you can always hear his ambivalence about it. To him it was a weakness, yet it also made one extraordinary—"highly individual" with "more unusual tasks in life." He thought, as do I, that self-reflection with the support of an analyst or therapist was what their "different nature demands." This is part of the greater "effort than the normal person is required to make." Central to this effort is the work they will do with you as their therapist, which necessarily involves your helping them to appreciate themselves in the three ways discussed in this chapter and that Jung touches on in the above quote: the general need to value themselves differently (overcome low self-esteem), to stop thinking they are like "ordinary" people, and to be less open to criticism from the majority, which can hinder them from pursuing their unique "aims and tasks."

LOWER SELF-ESTEEM

The third problem (two were discussed in the previous chapter) common to almost every highly sensitive person is low self-esteem. As in the previous chapter, I begin with general comments and then provide suggestions. We all have ways of improving self-esteem, so these suggestions are additional points to remember when working specifically with highly sensitive patients.

General Comments

I know the ubiquity of this problem both from my own experience as a therapist and from some of my unpublished data, in which the highly sensitive were significantly less likely to answer yes to the single question "Do you feel good about yourself?" This was true even when measures of negative affect and childhood were separated out. Since this negative sense of self is not found in every culture, or was not (this may be changing), it is not innate. It is not even found in every individual in the current culture, as some families give high praise to sensitive behavior and the adults I have met with such backgrounds were confident high achievers.

Noticeable personality differences are always given some subtle or not-so-subtle value in a given culture. Margaret Mead (1935) was perhaps the first to appreciate that children are born with a wide variety of innate traits, but only a few are part of a culture's ideal man or woman. Ideas about the perfect personality are inserted into "every thread of the social fabric—in the care of the young child, the games the children play, the songs the people sing, the political organization, the religious observance, the art and the philosophy" (p. 284). Traits not idealized are mostly ignored.

Some entire cultures, particularly older ones—Europe, China, Japan, and India—value the highly sensitive a little more than other cultures do, although that may be changing. For example, Chen, Rubin, and Sun (1992) compared the popularity of 480 school children in Shanghai to 296 in Canada and found that those rated by others as sensitive, quiet, and shy were among the most popular in China and the least popular in Canada. In Mandarin, shy or quiet means "good" or "well behaved," and sensitive can be translated as "having understanding," another term of high praise. In younger, immigrant cultures—North and South America, Australia, and New Zealand—bold decisiveness, high sociability, stress tolerance, and low emotionality are all idealized. The same would be true of any highly competitive, fast-paced culture, a style now circling the globe. Indeed, Chen, He, Cen, and Li (2005) found that, while the above was true in 1990, it was not true in 1998, and in 2002 shyness was associated with peer rejection, school problems, and depression. This is not good news for the self-esteem of those who are pausing before acting, aware of the subtle, easily overstimulated, and slow to make decisions.

Families, being the first influence, are the main force in transmitting culture, and families have their own cultures as well, offshoots from the main trunk. The suppression of undesired traits usually begins with selective misattunement of emotions by caregivers (Stern, 1985/2000). A sensitive infant's distress when being tossed in the air might be ignored or greeted with only mild sympathy, but curiosity or rapid approach might be met with high enthusiasm. A less-than-ideal trait is also given names that emphasize its disadvantages or expected negative outcomes—in the case of sensitivity, we know these are words like shy, inhibited, unsociable, neurotic, overly sensitive, indecisive, fussy, moody, being a "drama queen," or simply difficult. School children have their own terms for aspects of the trait. Some of these labels might be sissy, cry baby, teacher's pet, goody-goody, or nerd. Hence sensitive people learn to hide their trait and view themselves as flawed.

This sense of being flawed because of their trait interacts in various ways with the other difficulties of sensitive patients. For example, if a situation was traumatic for them but not for others, they can see that they reacted more—that is, they "overreacted." All children who have been mistreated tend to feel that it was somehow their fault, but this core sense of being at fault will naturally be far stronger and harder to overcome in someone feeling deeply flawed already due to being "different." It may feel to them as if they were marked by fate to suffer.

Bottom Line: Low self-esteem in the highly sensitive is probably due to it being a less-than-ideal trait in families and entire cultures, so that the trait in combination with negative childhood events leads to even lower self-esteem.

Suggestions for Improving Self-Esteem

Realistic self-esteem, like affect regulation, is a major goal of all the varied forms of psychotherapy, but again, some additional points can be made for working with these patients.

Discuss the Impact of Culture

Make the impact of culture vivid for them by encouraging them to see it in their own experiences. Point out the specific ways that their unique social environment views sensitivity and how it influences them. Most patients will immediately relate to this and spontaneously begin to reframe their past in ways that raise self-esteem.

Identify the Source of Negative Self-Statements

Explore their history to identify the persons who ignored, criticized, or shamed them about their sensitivity. Remind them often that this is not about blaming others, but about gaining a more realistic self-understanding.

Help Them Reframe Their Past

Reframing should not be left to chance. Most persons with low self-esteem can recall countless incidents of what in their minds were serious failures, regrettable decisions, justifiable rejections, and other proofs of their core worthlessness. When their sensitivity was a factor, these incidents need to be gradually or systematically reassessed.

For example, poor academic performance can almost always be traced back to overarousal during timed tests, work at the blackboard, or being shamed by a particular teacher for being slow to respond. Choosing not to commit to a relationship or someone else choosing not to commit is often the result of sensing a mismatch in temperament. And sensitive persons often reject a promotion or are not considered for one that requires frequent travel, managing of others, public speaking, or long hours. (This does not mean that sensitive persons are unable to do these—I will discuss these issues in Chapter 8.)

Reframing cannot be rushed, however. Even if it is entirely accurate, anyone with low self-esteem will mistrust what they perceive as distortions of the truth about themselves said only to make them feel better.

Encourage Them to Meet Other Sensitive Persons

I have been present at a number of seminars, lecturers, and weekend events for highly sensitive persons. Over and over I hear how life-changing it was for the participants. Not only do they receive support and a sense of normalcy, but they notice the positive aspects of the trait in others. There are ways they can do this connecting with others online as well as in person.

Help Them Learn How to Discuss Their Trait

Teaching is often the best way to learn—certainly if they cannot explain the trait in a positive light to others, they cannot do so to themselves. When they want to discuss their sensitivity with others, they must of course take into account the available time and the other's interest and role in their life. This can be good therapy in itself, as it involves important social skills and insights. Most patients do try to discuss their sensitivity with others, but may do it in ways that do not help them gain the support they expected. Some therapists might want to use role playing or rehearsals to address this. Later chapters describe how to handle some specific situations, but the following are a few examples. If someone is called shy or unsociable, he or she might say, "I don't think of myself that way so much—to me it is more like wanting to observe before entering in. And I am certainly social in that I do thoroughly enjoy a good one-on-one conversation, probably more than parties like this where I don't know anyone yet."

If someone is told he or she is overly emotional, the person can say, "I appreciate your concern, but most of the time I am glad to have my strong feelings. Many of them are good feelings in situations that maybe others would miss. So it balances out."

Before a medical procedure a sensitive person might say: "I'm sure you know this—people vary widely in how sensitive they are to pain. I'm one of those with a very low pain threshold."

When being observed or performing and one's nervousness has become obvious, the person might say: "It usually takes me a little while to get used to being watched. I'll be fine soon."

During a lesson a sensitive person might say: "Even more than other people, I respond better to praise." Or, "I know myself—I'm learning even if it isn't showing yet."

Often it helps to remind others that they have encountered sensitivity before—it is normal. "I'll bet I'm not the first person to complain about the noise. Lots of people are sensitive to sound."

Encourage Reading About the Trait

Reading is another reality check that can stabilize the aspect of self-esteem affected by their trait. There are scientific articles for those who would appreciate them as well as books and newsletters. However, these must be well chosen because the concept has been taken up by a wide range of persons with various skills and education who wish to make a career of helping the highly sensitive. Many have shifted the meaning of sensitive slightly. For example, some equate it with being disabled or else with extraordinary psychic powers. Of course, I think my Web site (hsperson.com) is a reliable resource.

Bring Up the Benefits Often

When clients are distressed about some aspect of their sensitivity, bring up the positive side of that same aspect and how easy it is to forget that this trait is a package deal. For example, at work a patient may be praised for "foresighted quality control" one week and the next criticized for being "obsessive compulsive." Link the two as sides of the same coin. Patients may pride themselves on their financial security; then later criticize themselves for being misers. At some point I often learn that my sensitive patients have literally saved a life, or at least a project or business, because of what on most days they see as their deepest flaw.

Your Attitude Is Decisive

Whatever else you say, patients will sense your attitude about sensitivity. None will believe their trait is something to be cherished if secretly you do not, a strong possibility given our culture. This is not about respecting your patients in spite of their sensitivity or because of how well they have endured it. Even when therapists are themselves highly sensitive, they may have a subtle negative feeling about it, especially if they are men. If they are women, they may have a bias about sensitive men. Just as you would with any other prejudice, you must look carefully for it in yourself and offset it as best you can.

Example Dialogue

The following is a typical dialogue a low self-esteem sensitive patient might have with a therapist.

Patient: I'm in a pretty bad mood again today. She told me again the other day that I'm too sensitive. You say I'm not, but she's the one I have to live with.

Therapist: I guess you're saying your bad mood is related?

Patient: Sure. I feel crummy about myself.

Therapist: Hmm. What are the things she does like about you? Why did she start dating you?

Patient: I get it. Yeah, she said I was so creative, and listened so well to her. She liked how concerned I was about the environment. I was the first guy who really liked her cats ...

Therapist: Sometimes it happens that the very thing we like most about someone at the outset becomes the thing we like least as time goes on. Anything you aren't liking so much about her these days?

Patient: Well, her bluntness. Like when she said that to me about my being too sensitive.

Therapist: You mean what you've also called her honesty?

Patient: She could have thought about it a little, how it would upset me.

Therapist: So her spontaneity is also a problem? Looks more like "impulsive" to you now?

Patient: I get it. I liked it well enough when she flat out told me she loved me after knowing me 2 weeks. So what if she doesn't always think before she says something. She's worth it. If she doesn't like who I am, better for her to decide that now.

IMITATING THE NONSENSITIVE LIFESTYLE

It is natural, especially for young adults, to behave like your peers. But when the sensitive live their lives like the nonsensitive, they are failing to take into account their different physiology.

General Comments

The physiology of those who are sensitive means that, compared to others, they need more downtime to process the stimulation they have taken in and to reflect carefully on its meaning to them. They are more sensitive to all sorts of things, often including caffeine and alcohol. They do not really thrive in noise and chaos. They do not do well multitasking. To ignore all of this would be like owning a Porsche, but operating it according to the owner's manual for a Chevy truck.

This failing to appreciate their difference is especially likely because it is invisible, so it is rarely acknowledged by the nonsensitive people whom they interact with on a daily basis. Often those who care about them most are the ones trying to help them fit in, get along, and toughen up. Being sensitive makes the imitation of others far easier and more exact. It is almost second nature to the sensitive minority to fit in with the majority. But one can always appeal to their conscientiousness: Besides the problems of dealing with their own well-being, others also benefit from the sensitive people around them feeling their best, arriving at their own conclusions, and having their own responses to a situation rather than the majority. For example, a sensitive person may provide an unusual creative solution or complain about a noise level that is harmful to others' ears even if these others do not know it. When the noise goes down everyone is better off.

Bottom Line: Sensitive patients need help recognizing that they cannot live like the nonsensitive, given that invisible individual differences are hard for others to acknowledge and that the highly sensitive are so well designed to adapt to others.

Suggestions for Adjusting Lifestyle

I do not usually suggest to my patients what specific changes are needed—the choice is the patient's. Nor do I expect a change like taking more time off to be permanent at first. Often facing the truth of the necessity is very painful and the change is difficult to carry out, but there are ways you can help.

Help Them Face Reality, but With Pride

No one wants to see their limitations. In addition, sensitive people often feel ashamed that they cannot live as others do. Point out that they actually can live any way they wish—in a noisy fraternity, drinking six cups of coffee a day, or working 14-hour days. If you can say it truthfully, tell them that you think they can accomplish almost any goal if they want it enough—large family, a demanding career, frequent world travel, intense competition. But they do need to recognize that these choices may come at a high cost to them, given the experiences of other highly sensitive persons you have known. Other joys in life might have to be sacrificed. Make use of whatever advantages to being highly sensitive that they have acknowledged and enjoyed—point out the package deal and that no one gets everything in life.

Another way to open up alternatives is to ask patients to think about or even list and weigh their values and resulting priorities, then consider together whether those priorities are actually coming first. Often a priority for them is to be happy, content, or at peace, yet they are pushing themselves constantly. If their goal is to help others, can they be effective while stressed out by fatigue? They need to see how their current choices fit with their values.

Often a particular patient is clearly not suited or able to achieve certain goals or endure certain lifestyles, yet is very reluctant to give them up. If you comment on the cost of their choices, you may hear an angry defense of them, as these may relate to fundamental ways they view themselves. As often happens when an emotional schema has been triggered, the patient will feel you are greatly misattuned. Try saying, "I agree—I haven't fully understood how much you want to be …" It is important to acknowledge your misattunement, but you can also stand by your own view of it and demonstrate that people can disagree on their perception of something without it ruining their relationship.

When the emotional schema that created this anger has passed, go back to why they feel so strongly about it. Whatever it is that they cannot give up, what does it mean to them? What dream would be lost if they could not be a rock star? Who would they disappoint if they did not go to law school? How would they see themselves if they no longer lived in a loft with 10 others?

Time is on your side. Eventually they will see, as Susan did (in Chapter 1), that they cannot live as they are now. It is true of all of us that we often do not make changes until we have "hit bottom."

Encourage Them to Look for Fresh Possibilities

Once sensitive patients can accept that it could be good to stop trying to be like others, they can think about the pleasure they might find in other goals or in taking more time for rest, reflection, creativity, or service. They might actually find the meaningful work they have longed for, or the inner peace that the nonsensitive say they seek but do not stop long enough to find. Most will become creative about their options once they face the consequences of not doing so. For example, Susan (in Chapter 1) was so angry about having any physical limits due to her sensitivity, but when she was over that, she chose to start her own business, one that gave her a better lifestyle by harnessing her immediate interest and knowledge of childcare for career women.

Some will not be at liberty to change much of their lifestyle, but help them explore smaller creative solutions. If they feel generally hopeless and trapped, it is probably better to address that before working on solutions. It is possible they are not yet at that place of acceptance or able to see themselves what they need.

Discuss How They Make Lifestyle Choices

How objectively can your sensitive patients see themselves? How much can they advocate for themselves within their family, at work, or against inner critical voices? And about a specific choice, why was it made? Was it even a choice, or just going along with the others? Was it out of simple ignorance of the nature of their difference? Was there a fear of the deeper implications of their seeming limitations, such as financial "failure" as measured by the majority? Or is this a persistent imitation of the least sensitive, most risk-taking, flamboyant people in society, perhaps as a compensation for feeling flawed?

Example Dialogue

The following is a sample dialogue a therapist might have with a highly sensitive patient who is struggling with lifestyle issues.

Patient: So you think I made a mistake choosing emergency room medicine as my specialty?

Therapist: Pardon me if I smile a little bit, but to start with, isn't it just about the most grueling residency? And you want to start a family. Rough one.

Patient: I can do it.

Therapist: I imagine you can. I've met a few emergency room workers who were highly sensitive. They're great at it. They have thought through every horrible problem ahead of time. They rarely make mistakes. But they really have to harden themselves to it, and they don't have any other life. Dedicated.

Patient: That's how I imagine myself being. I'll use my sensitivity to save lives, not be stopped by it.

Therapist: I'm curious. How did you choose emergency medicine? Was it your favorite rotation?

Patient: My father did it, and his father. I know what you're thinking. But it was my own choice. Nobody pushed me.

Therapist: So it has nothing to do with what you were telling me a month or so ago, that your father brooks no questioning.

Patient: When I was a child. I can stand up to him now.

Therapist: And you are pretty sure the child in you did not fear him when you made this choice?

Patient: I can't change now. I'm already admitted. To change I'd have to wait a year and go through the whole process again.

Therapist: So you've thought of changing.

Patient: Only since I've been seeing you.

Therapist: Hmm. I don't think we've ever discussed it, beyond your fear that you were so stressed already that you worried about starting your residency. The lack of sleep and all. Your "presenting problem" was what you called "a mysterious acute anxiety." Could we be solving the mystery?

Patient: I don't like the way this is going. You're against my doing what I want to do.

Therapist: I hope I haven't said that. I think I'm *for* using this time to see if you feel any inner conflict about this choice. As you know, inner conflict is often the cause of anxiety.

Patient: Of neurotic anxiety. I don't like the way this is going.

Therapist: Okay. I can appreciate that. You feel the choice is made. No conflict, except between us.

Patient: That's right. I need a therapist who will support me, not question my choices.

From this dialogue, it is clear this patient is not ready to look at his choice. The approach was probably too forceful. This work will take some time, even if it means a crisis when his residency begins.

STRONGER REACTION TO CRITICISM

Life is full of dangers and problems if we are overwhelmed by shame when told we have made a mistake or may be flawed in our approach. Yet this is the world, dangerous and problematic, in which most highly sensitive patients live.

General Comments

If highly sensitive persons follow an innate strategy of avoiding mistakes, of "doing it once and doing it right," then it would follow that they would be more affected by criticism, whether by simply seeing the poor outcome or by receiving feedback from others. Feedback is the essence of trial-and-error learning, aiming toward no errors. To be oriented to feedback in this very sensitive way, one would need a strong motivation to get it right and not do it wrong. Strong motivations lead to strong emotions about outcomes.

Partly to check that assumption, in a study already described, Aron et al. (2005) randomly assigned students to receive positive or negative feedback on an aptitude test, after which they filled out a mood checklist (designed to seem unrelated to the test) and were then debriefed. Students scoring high on the HSP Scale had stronger emotional reactions to both kinds of feedback than the nonsensitive students, who had almost no reaction to either.

Their strong reaction to criticism affects therapy as well. I sometimes tell patients that therapy requires that they accept a paradox, that they are truly good, valuable, and deserving of love, and that they need help with a serious problem. As therapists we work on a continuum, one end being the providing support and reassurance and the other being discussing problems in depth. With sensitive patients one can become stuck at the support end because these patients hear anything else as criticism or simply that there is something wrong with them, even if this something was caused by others. Thus working on their reaction to criticism is central for therapy that is not strictly supportive.

What you must think about and teach is how a pervasive strategy of adapting one's behavior after receiving negative feedback, and even having a strong emotional reaction to it, need not mean being completely derailed by criticism. An individual's experience with criticism and general self-esteem will be the deciding factors. But all too often sensitive patients are either crushed, become highly defensive, and blame the one doing the criticism, or resort to extreme compensatory behaviors. They may become true perfectionists, not just careful workers. They may far exceed expectations in order to avoid the slightest error. With you they will try to be the good patient, finely tuning their behavior to the subtle cues they pick up from you. The result is that both of you are happy and happy with each other. But is there growth?

Meanwhile, they are avoiding situations in which criticism might occur, such as any work in which they might grow through learning, or avoiding contact with any but the most supportive, familiar others or those clearly inferior to them in some important way. Others wanting or needing to be around them learn to avoid giving them feedback or criticism or to express irritation. This leaves patients in a false and confusing world where they are not being given the feedback they need or are receiving mixed messages, since they are sensitive enough to know something is wrong. People seem to like them, yet never call them back; supervisors say their work is fine, but they are not promoted.

Bottom Line: Sensitivity to criticism results from the combination of an innate attention to feedback, in order to "do it once and do it right," and low self-esteem, which together can make a patient ashamed or defensive when receiving anything but perfectly positive feedback. This hinders them in nearly every aspect of life, including therapy.

Suggestions for Sensitivity to Criticism

Stay Neutral in a Caring Way

Therapists are always hampered by not knowing what actually occurred in an interaction outside of therapy. You may strongly suspect the feedback was invalid and want to support the patient. Or you may be equally sure that an emotional schema that is all too familiar to you was triggered. Perhaps the patient lacked the knowledge or skill required. It can be so difficult to know. Very often I have thought I was hearing the perfect moment to help someone see his or her unhelpful pattern and then later, after listening more, have decided I was wrong about who was at fault. The patient had every right to be defensive or hurt.

However, if the emotions are still raw, which they will almost certainly be whether sensitive patients know it or not, the therapist must wait to figure out whether the criticism was valid. Help them recover their basic self-esteem first, so that they can reflect on the criticism from a calm, more rational place. First providing solace helps with self-esteem because it demonstrates that you value them for who they are enough to care how they feel. You do not have to agree or disagree with the criticism, but reflect that you see how badly it has made them feel. If they need to know if you are taking their side, say you are eager to hear the whole story, but want to return to how they are feeling. This teaches them the necessary affect regulation: Of course they are upset at first, but they can set aside the issue itself until they are calmer. I sometimes tell them that I have learned from experience that when I receive editing comments that upset me, even enrage me, I always wait 24 hours before deciding the validity of the suggestions. That gives me time to cool down.

Help Them Decide if the Criticism Was Valid

Because they react so quickly and thoroughly to feedback, they need to be able to see when the source was a good one, when it was distorting the situation but partly right, or when it was just plain wrong. There is always a message in any feedback, at the very least that someone was noticing and had the reaction he or she has expressed in the feedback.

But that may be a message the patient needs to learn to ignore—people are often noticing and expressing themselves, for any number of reasons. The content of the feedback has to be considered. Was it actually negative, was it helpful, and was it valid in the sense that the person was in a position to know? Was it based on a simple misunderstanding? And the motivation for the criticism has to be considered, as that also affects content and the tone of the feedback: Was the other trying to be helpful or was the reason for the feedback centered entirely in the other's needs or state of mind? Was the person just tired that day? Does the other have a particular reason to be jealous, offended, or defensive? (Sensitive patients often cannot imagine being a threat to others.) Does the person criticize almost everyone?

Sensitive patients need to be skilled amateur psychologists. Given their innate ability to sense what is going on, they can easily learn to understand when and why some people are especially sharp, blunt, rude, or even cruel. For example, the other may be power hungry and willing to say anything to undermine another's confidence or reputation. The critic's emotional schema may have been triggered so that he or she is for the moment or quite often out of touch with reality. People can be disturbed in various ways—narcissistic, borderline, sociopathic, unable to judge another's emotional response (an autism spectrum disorder), and so forth. These people are out in the world interacting with all of us, and it is valuable to be able to recognize them.

Observe How Your Criticisms Are Received

Many sensitive patients are overly open to criticism—I find that if there is a problem between us, they feel it is always their fault, not mine. They are quick to feel shame and often hear criticism when it is not there. This gives you a glimpse of how they might be responding to others. At the other extreme are those who become extremely defensive or distraught if they are offered any comment that strays from pure support. These are the most difficult to treat, as they cannot bear to hear what needs to change. Of course there are individual issues that trigger patients as well. When observing, keep in mind that your own style could be to make comments that seem like criticism. You might normally ask directly, without any softening of it, "Why did you do that?" The question can sound like either interest or criticism. To you and to most people you know it would not be heard as criticism, but if your patient hears it that way, that tells you how much he or she can feel criticized by comments of nonsensitive persons who speak more directly or briskly. You can help them interpret comments like this by telling them to check with you any time they think you are being critical and to bring in comments others have made that they were unsure about so the two of you together can decide what messages they might contain.

Help Them to Receive Your Feedback Better

Explain to these sensitive patients, again, that it is natural for them to be more sensitive to criticism than others. Talk openly about the problem of shame—that your comments might be focused on change but that does not mean the person is intrinsically flawed. It does not alter your basic respect for them. Sensitive patients may need to hear this often, but do not give up on them, opting for supportive work only because they are "just too sensitive." The right support can be the basis for change. Instead, discuss what in their histories adds to their natural sensitivity to criticism and what emotional schemas are triggered by it. For example, do you sound like their critical parent? Or is shame easily triggered due to bed wetting as a child? Talk about how much better their lives would be if they could control some of their natural-for-them reaction to criticism.

Sometimes it helps to say gently, "I know you came here wanting my help in changing some things. We have to agree what those things are, because every change requires first knowing and accepting where you are starting from, and there's certainly nothing shameful about wanting to improve yourself in some way." And I might add, "You are so hard on yourself—it would help if you could hold back a little on your certainty that I think you are a bad person. If you already feel shame, for example, could you be kind to yourself by not also feeling ashamed of being ashamed?" When they are able to do this, you can generalize these attitudes to other criticism. "Looking ahead, do you think this feedback is going to turn out to be helpful?" And, "You do feel criticized, but I think you are learning to be kinder to yourself—not to attack yourself just for making a mistake—and this might be a good time for that kindness."

Help Them Recover When the Fault Was Theirs

For sensitive patients to tolerate having made a mistake they need to know they can survive the momentary bad feelings they will have, which will be stronger for them. Their first defense may be their knowing you think well of them, whatever their mistakes. I have various other thoughts I might share with a patient. One is from the character Jean-Luc Picard, captain of the Starship *Enterprise* in the *Star Trek* series, who was modeled after C. S. Forester's Captain Horatio Hornblower. Both men were depicted as heroic and also highly sensitive. Basically, the quote is "Well, I've made some *fine* mistakes in my lifetime," and by implication, I'm no less of a person for admitting so.

I tell patients that I expect to make at least one mistake a day, whether it is forgetting to put money in a parking meter or not thanking someone who should have been thanked. When it happens, I just say, "There's today's." And I always ask myself whether I really could have done it much differently, given the information I had at the time or the state of mind I was in. Some days I am just not going to handle details, or people, well. I may be rushed, stressed, tired, angry, or distracted. I also just may not even be very good at certain things. Again, "no one is perfect." It is okay. Tomorrow or a year from now it will not matter.

Role Model How to Take Criticism

Your mistakes as a therapist are the perfect opportunity to role model how to take criticism or admit to error. Hopefully, you react without shame (i.e., not from a place of feeling like a worthless person), but rather with genuine gratitude and willingness to explore the issue, accept blame when you are wrong, and move from a question of blame to what the two of you need to attend to I as a team. When you cannot quite manage that high ideal, you can at least control your defensiveness or not appear too shaken. You have your peers and consultants to take these issues to.

An early mentor helped me with blaming myself: The mistake is not the problem, but what we do with our mistakes. Can we admit to them, talk about them, and grow due to them? The same is true for our patients—it is how they handle their mistakes that matters in the long run.

Limit Generalizations From the Criticism

Globalization is always a cognitive problem to watch for, but it is particularly true of the highly sensitive. Being even more motivated to avoid all mistakes and therefore to take things to their ultimate logical conclusion, they can decide, "The whole thing has to be done over" or "I'm just no good at this." If it is only a way to express strong feeling, let it go. But watch that they do not act on such conclusions.

Example Dialogue

The following patient had several good friends. This may be a typical dialogue for someone who overreacts to criticism.

Patient: I was a complete wallflower last night. No wonder I have so few friends. It's a wonder that anyone likes me the way I blend into the background. What a bore.

Therapist: Sounds like it was an awful night. Pretty hard on your self-image.

Patient: Hard on it but correct. My friends summed it up well. I'm "ridiculously shy."

Therapist: Ridiculously shy? So last night feels like the real you?

Patient: What are you getting at? That I'm exaggerating?

Therapist: I think you are having a natural reaction for any sensitive person. You're looking at the long-term consequences of being shy, of fearing being judged by others. It's a real problem for everyone at times. You are seeing something you don't like about yourself. That's the first step toward getting it more the way you want to be. But you have to be clear about what that is.

Patient: You know what they meant. A hopeless case. I've tried all my life to change this. I've always been afraid of people. Everybody says it.

Therapist: Everybody? Or only those who are so *un*shy that they have no hesitation to tell others they should be exactly like them.

Patient: Well, aren't people with social skills the best ones to tell me how I need to change?

Therapist: Maybe. If we are really talking about social skills. Do you think they necessarily are defined by how you respond at large parties full of strangers? Maybe some of what you need to change is what you expect of yourself. Maybe you don't have to be good at everything. Your specialty is something more intimate. For an introvert, you appear to have just about the right number of friends. Pretty loyal ones too, from what I hear, even if they do call you "ridiculously shy."

Patient: I guess. Yeah. But it's still true that it's hard for me to be around strangers.

Therapist: Yes, that sounds true, and I can appreciate wanting to change that. We always need to add a few new friends to replace the ones we lose for various reasons. We can work on it.

THE IMPACT OF GENDER

One could say there are really four genders: sensitive men and women and nonsensitive men and women. Your intention should be to open up space for the first two to be acceptable versions of their gender. Men especially need this space.

Although there are as many sensitive males as females born, their style is not the ideal. They represent half of an impossible idea. Men should be bold, decisive, winners in every competition, undaunted by stress, in control of all emotions *and* tender, sensitive, wise, above the fray, and prepared for anything—a combination of nonsensitive and sensitive that only occurs in romantic novels. Temperament does not work that way.

Likewise, women are supposed to be sensitive, but only in the social sense. In particular, they should be outgoing and especially fond of relating to other women. Sensitive women can feel they are not real women when they need extra time alone or prefer deep intellectual or artistic pursuits over chatting, shopping, or even being a mother. Many sensitive women think twice before having a child or at least a second child, knowing that parenting can be overwhelming for anyone at times, but especially for them. Does that mean she is not a "real" woman?

Still, of the "four" genders, anyone can see that in our culture sensitive men have the most difficult time. Most of the gender-related problems of sensitive women are those of all women—discrimination in the workplace, having equal power in relationships, having to choose among too many roles, and feeling demeaned by men seeing them only as sexual objects. Indeed, many sensitive men might recognize this list as well. Small surprise that psychological data on sensitive men and on all women are often similar—for example, those three "genders" are more impacted by childhood problems (Aron & Aron, 1997). This actually makes nonsensitive men the anomalies. Given that they are the dominant gender of the four, this is another reason why special attention should be given to empowering sensitive men—it might make for a better world.

Bottom Line: Sensitive men have particular difficulties.

Men: Three Cases

James was a tall, slim midwesterner who directed a West Coast theological seminary until his recent death. James was famous for his sensitivity, in all the DOES (as presented in Chapter 2) senses of the term. Everyone noticed his sensitivity and liked him for it. He was soft-spoken, gentle, attentive, and private about his personal life. One sensed he would also keep private anything you told him. He seldom gave advice, yet most people who talked with him felt they had received wisdom. He seldom entered into battles, yet usually had his way eventually, simply because he was right. His patience was legendary, but so was his anger, seen only a few times when he felt someone needed straightening out.

This all sounds a bit like a halo around a dead man, but I knew him well enough to say it was true, and that he also had his faults—he could be fussy, a bit pedantic when his intellect took over, and very slow to take action. Some called him the Mr. Rogers of academe.

How did James come to make such fine use of his sensitivity? He was raised on a farm by parents who were well and widely read. They were as pleased with their eldest son's interest in music, art, and philosophy as they were of his brothers' athletic skills or stamina under stress. Given that he had two nonsensitive brothers, James had to learn how to handle himself in a fight or a rough-and-tumble game. He just never liked it.

His parents wisely encouraged him to attend a small Christian college nearby, followed by graduate studies farther away from home. He moved smoothly into his chosen academic career in philosophy, to which he later added a degree in counseling psychology. He began teaching pastoral counseling and is fondly remembered by interns as being able to conduct group supervision in such a gentle way that no one felt criticized, but rather fully supported. Yet his style, values, and expertise were mysteriously absorbed, so that his ex-students were particularly esteemed.

In his role as director of the seminary, James found creative ways to protect himself from the demands of his job. If he was walking on roundabout paths across campus, everyone knew he was not to be disturbed. The same was true if he was heard playing the piano in his office. When it was 5 o'clock, he was gone. He gave the world two evenings a week of himself, no more. He was a man who had never seen his sensitivity as a serious limitation, but rather as a tremendous asset. He never doubted he was a real man.

Kevin, my second example, happened to have the athletic good looks of a Greek god and a talent for sports. Still, he harbored serious doubts about his manhood, partly because of his father's rejection of him for his sensitive and partly because throughout his childhood his mother preferred him over his older sisters, using him as a confidante. Being home schooled as well and not allowed to watch television or play with guns, other boys found him odd. Fortunately, all of this ended as he neared puberty and went to public school. He was able to capitalize on his athletic talents and became very popular both with the boys and the girls.

He still felt he was too feminine underneath, even though it was easy to make friends and date women. His friends never guessed that he was especially sensitive about anything, but the nonsensitive, showy women who dated him for his looks were not so easily fooled. They expected him to be more aggressive sexually as well as more decisive, assertive, and fond of loud parties. He came to expect their eventual rejection of him, mirroring the rejection by his father and childhood peers. When he came to see me, Kevin had no idea that he was "highly sensitive," but the news was little comfort at first. It only added to the reasons for feeling he was not acceptable as a man.

Tom, in contrast, was short and very thin, with a face marred by a chronic unhappiness. When we first began to meet, Tom was 42 and desperate to marry. He was glad to hear about the assets associated with his trait, but it was no magic cure for his predicament. His was a classic case of women wanting him as a friend but not for a date. Throughout his life he had been perceived as feminine and sometimes homosexual, although he fervently denied being gay, and I never saw the opportunity to pursue it without distressing him. As a child, he had been the subject of considerable bullying. His parents and teachers took the old-fashioned attitude that it was up to him to learn to be more aggressive. As a result he experienced repeated traumas, some sexual, in back alleys and behind the gym.

Tom focused on college and becoming an accountant. As soon as he was established professionally, he set out to find a wife—someone attractive, warm, and not like himself. After reading books by dating experts, he decided to cover up his gentle, conservative style with something more aggressive. He learned to speed date and "market himself," to speak only of his strengths, to tease and be cynical. Sometimes women would go out with him, but never more than twice. I suspected that the less authentic he was, the less attractive he was. I certainly felt that in our sessions—as soon as he would switch to this persona—I would have trouble staying focused.

A few relationships lasted longer, when he changed tactics and began seeking out sensitive women. The major breakthrough, however, came from a different direction, when he received a huge promotion because of his many creative ideas combined with his careful work. I pointed out the probable role of his sensitivity, and at last he saw it as a true asset, even a financial one. He used the resulting income to buy an expensive albeit practical car and a new home with an ocean view. He decided to enjoy his life as it was and forget about finding the right woman, although they were finally coming to him, and not just for friendship.

The Sensitive Male Body and Father

I have observed no tendency for sensitive men to have a particular body type, but it does make a critical difference, as it did for these three, in that Kevin was spared Tom's experience because Kevin had the ideal male body. Even James might have recalled a harder life if he had been short. Like almost all sensitive men, all three had low pain thresholds and early memories of being hurt in some playground or neighborhood accident and openly crying. James was told to "act like a man." Kevin of course was terrified when he was told "don't be a mama's boy." Tom heard "you sound like a girl."

An important difference among them was their fathers, as is usually the case for sensitive persons. Fathers, like all men, tend to have intense, confused feelings about sensitivity in anyone. Sensitive daughters are usually much easier for fathers to accept. Sensitive sons can pose a threat to a father's own masculinity. James's father, however, was delighted by his son's sensitivity. Kevin hardly knew his father, who was almost surely also highly sensitive. Kevin remembered having to be quiet when his father came home and went straight to his study, rarely coming out before Kevin went to bed. Whether it was for that or other reasons, this father took the path of many and left his irritatingly sensitive son to be raised by women.

Tom's father was the most damaging in that he tried relentlessly to turn his son into a "real man." When he failed, he wrote him off and teased him as a "hopeless case." Some fathers even try to beat the sensitivity out of a son, hoping their son will eventually toughen up and rebel.

The strategies sensitive men take in adulthood usually reflect how their fathers viewed them as sons. Some, like James, know they are different and are happy about it. Some, like Kevin, set out to hide their trait and to a great extent succeed at it, in some cases hiding it even from themselves. They become as unlike the man they fear they are as they can possibly manage. Finally, some approach life as Tom did, expecting to be bullied and finding themselves friends with women, who as a group have also suffered due to male aggression.

At least 100 men in the media have interviewed me about my research. I would say that all but a handful were highly sensitive high sensation seekers. Almost all admitted it to me in a private way. About a third openly discussed their sensitivity. Most made flippant jokes, appeared personally disinterested, questioned my reasoning at length, or attacked my science. (My response was to talk about my observations of male interviewers when discussing the subject of sensitivity—if we were on the air, it certainly enlivened the show.) I saw some of the deep roots of these culturally based fears when I was interviewed by two men on a supposedly Christian station. They insisted that the Bible intended that women be sensitive but never men, and that my ideas were deeply anti-Christian. Male patients who come from such a background have a great deal to overcome.

The relation of sensitivity and men to homosexuality always lurks in the background. I have no statistics on it, but I have discussed it with gay men, who observe, as I have, that there is about the same percentage of sensitive gay men as sensitive men in general. That is, the majority of gay men are not highly sensitive—many very obviously not. However, theirs is a culture in which some aspects of sensitivity are encouraged, so that sensitive men can feel more welcome and willing to come out. Given that the gay subculture partly defines itself by defying gender stereotypes, some nonsensitive gay men enjoy being more sensitive in specific ways than the average male.

Bottom Line: Body type and the father's attitudes toward sensitivity are important factors to consider during treatment of sensitive male patients. Most men struggle with the very concept of sensitivity, a conflict reflected in our culture as well.

Suggestions for Working With Sensitive Men

Offer Role Models of Sensitive Men Who Are Thriving

If you are not a sensitive man, at least describe those you have known who are successful in various ways because of their trait, not in spite of it. Some sensitive men will have found role models on their own. You can mention my observation that traditionally sensitive men have assumed, among other roles, those of shaman, healer, artist, strategist, negotiator, lawmakers, judges, teachers, and keen observers of nature or science.

Discuss the Culture Problem

Explain how much culture shapes us all, and the importance of their countering their own antisensitive attitudes. In part, older and more evolved cultures are more appreciative of a man who is artistic, reflective, philosophic, scientific, or strategic. Immigrant cultures have less use for these qualities. They appreciate quick action and toughness over other virtues or refinements. In fact, this is true whenever brute strength is more important to a group's survival than more reflective qualities, but in the long run no group survives without a balance of these two types of men.

Make Explicit a Sensitive Man's Advantages

The advantages of being sensitive can be general—the ones already discussed—as well as those of the patient in particular. Help them see how much the world needs them and their type.

Help Them Prove Their Manhood in Their Own Way

Young men of all temperaments need to prove themselves, but too many sensitive men feel they have nothing to prove, only something to hide. It can be helpful to encourage whatever might be for them a heroic journey, whether it is a solitary bicycle trip across the country or delving into their inner life. If the man is older and this has already occurred, identify this for him. Otherwise, perhaps they need to identify what does, or would, prove their masculinity to themselves and those who know them well.

Discuss Competition

Men are expected to be aggressively, even ruthlessly, competitive, to relish it, and to win. Sensitive men generally do not like competition and mix that up with not being competitive in the sense of being good at something. You will need to end that confusion. They are usually at the top in something, such as being a successful healer or counselor, but do not see healing or counseling as examples of competition in the sense of being mainly about validating their superiority.

They do not like competition in part because they do not like being aggressive and the cause of others feeling inferior, which many people, if not all, would see as a virtue. In part, they simply do not like to take risks, so they often do not compete unless they know they can win. To be in that position, they train or make elaborate preparations. For example, at work they may do their job so well that there is no question about a competitor. Then they think it was not a true competition because no one could compete with them. Help them appreciate that in a sense they held the competition ahead of time, in their imagination, until they could be sure of success.

The need to appear competitive extends to dating and romantic relationships. Men are expected to be the aggressor, to be decisive about what the two will do and always be sexually ready. But sensitive men do not want to risk harming others by controlling them or angering others by not consulting them. Most men will brag about their exploits or discuss women as trophies, but sensitive men generally do not. Some have so absorbed vicariously the suffering of women that they are more cautious about a woman's rights and feelings than is even necessary. Meanwhile, many women equate masculinity with being overtly competitive, partly as a sign that a man is strong enough to protect them. Point out that sensitive men are often the winners as protectors, too—they do not assume that nothing bad will ever happen, and so they prepare more than others for danger. They have thought through what action they would take and are faster to recognize signs that the time has come for action. Finally, they are more troubled by another's predicament and are more likely to put another's needs first.

Help Them With Their Relationship With Their Mothers

All men are shaped by their relationships with their mothers, but sensitive men often have had unusual relationships—for example, they may have been Mother's confidant or her little helper. For being so sensitive and caring, these boys may have won the oedipal competition, with all the attendant anxiety about being punished in some way for this wrong. On the other hand, a mother can also fail to respect her sensitive son because she feels he is not a "real" boy. Sometimes all of this occurs at once or at different times in a boy's development. These dynamics will have done harm in various ways and certainly affect their relations with women. They may be too submissive, fear being controlled, doubt their masculinity, or be so angry that they cannot do anything but hurt or reject one woman after another.

A sensitive man may not even have had a problematic mother, but carry some fear or anger toward women because sensitive men sense more than others the power to punish or reject that every mother has over her son, including the power his mother had over him.

In these cases you need to develop insight about emotional schemas relating to Mother, but also provide an experience of a maternal presence (whether you are a man or woman) that is loving and supportive of your patient's sensitivity while maintaining respectful boundaries.

Sensitive Women

As already suggested, sensitive women tend to have fewer problems with their trait (even though they may be more affected by the problems of women generally). Being sensitive and being a woman have even been equated, in the sense that women are sensitive to the needs of others. But that sensitivity has been expected to exist along with almost unlimited energy and resilience. That is true today more than ever. Susan (in Chapter 1) is a prime example.

Still, if women avoid entering into the world, they will feel less shame about it than men will. Men may be drawn to such women in order to enjoy the feeling of protecting them, and this can be flattering to a young woman. They move from home to marriage without ever having lived alone or supported themselves.

As with sensitive men, I find that their father's role in their lives was crucial. In some archetypal sense, fathers tend to teach children how to be in the world. In this regard, some fathers ignore their sensitive daughters as the least interesting or likely to accomplish anything important. Some see sensitivity as a dangerous flaw, perhaps even more dangerous in a woman because she might be taken advantage of or not be able to support herself. These fathers try to toughen up their daughters to overcome their weakness, exactly as they would with a son. Some, like my friend Jim (in Chapter 1), do it right—they accept a daughter's sensitivity, but expect her to be in the world and successful in it, on her terms.

Bottom Line: Sensitive women need to avoid the stereotype that they are mainly sensitive to the needs of others and have unlimited energy to give. They are often drawn into an early marriage and are as affected as men by how their fathers handled their sensitivity.

Suggestions for Working With Sensitive Women

Encourage Interdependence

As a therapist, support a sensitive woman who has decided to live on her own or with other women before marrying or living with a man. Otherwise, her more intense emotional reactions—fear, loneliness, times when she feels very down or hurt—may give her the impression that she cannot manage on her own. However, help her to see that no one is truly independent. We are all interdependent, even if in separate rooms or houses. She will not be alone, but will have friends and family to turn to, and you. In addition, when she does meet potential partners, she should be looking for someone who appreciates interdependence.

Many sensitive women patients will still be emotionally unable to live alone, however. Fear or loneliness due to past insecurities would overwhelm them. When you discover that a woman cannot live alone, be careful not to make her feel ashamed of this. Make it normal given the interaction of her trait with her life experiences. If she wishes, living alone can be a goal. If she has never been alone and is in a reasonably equitable relationship, especially one that is providing the resources needed for therapy, be grateful for that. In that case, help her to appreciate what she contributes and how she and her partner are interdependent and both better off for being together.

Explore Their Sexuality

Sensitive women (and men) patients may be reticent about their sexuality, but as their therapist you need to bring it up anyway, in a gentle way. Wait until it is present, through her comments or dreams. Watch for sexual experiences that have affected her more than they would have others. Encourage her own sexual style, which will be different from a nonsensitive woman's in some of the ways described in Chapter 8. I listen for shame when they talk about sexuality and try to role model more openness. I also listen for how they view men and sex—whether they can trust some deeply but are not indiscriminately sensitive to every man's needs.

Guide Them Regarding Stress

Many sensitive women will be like Susan (in Chapter 1)—trying to do too much and torn by love and duty or a desire to prove their competence in a male world. They may appear to be managing, but watch for signs of too much stress and do not forget that being overwhelmed and chronically overaroused can be the underlying cause of many mood and anxiety disorders as well as relationship problems, parenting problems, and seemingly unrelated health issues. Your job as a therapist is to make the connection between stress and other difficulties, if it is there, and stay grounded in the reality that something has to change. You will have to point out that they are different and more vulnerable in this particular sense. They are not failing as a woman or a person. They are simply highly sensitive. This makes them strong, but in different ways.

Bottom Line: Sensitive women should be encouraged to live on their own for a time to know that they can do it, but to live interdependently. Do not force the issue, however. Initiate, gently, open discussions of sexuality and watch for being overwhelmed by work and home life.

DEVELOPMENTAL STAGE

Therapists who work with sensitive patients have sometimes observed that these patients pass through the developmental stages more slowly. As children they were slower to give up transitional objects or lose interest in toys. They were slow to develop sexuality, left home later, married at an older age, and took longer to settle into a self-supporting career. There is no single explanation for this, except that perhaps they are again observing before moving on and probably gaining more from each developmental period. There are exceptions, of course, especially sensitive children who develop a precocious false self that seems extremely adult, even middle aged, while their age is still in the single digits. However, when they reach adulthood they are often the most stalled, as they sense they are not truly prepared for life, especially a life of adapting to a nonsensitive world.

I am not a developmental psychologist, but I did venture to write a book about rearing sensitive children, *The Highly Sensitive Child* (Aron, 2002), with the consultation of temperament Jan Kristal. I also highly recommend her book, *The Temperament Perspective* (Kristal, 2005), which is written for professionals working with children as well as for parents. Given that these books are full of parenting advice, I will not give much of that here. Mainly you as a therapist need to be aware that temperament plays a major role in developmental problems, and before assuming a child or family has a serious problem, consider whether the child's environment is a "good fit" for his or her temperament and what might be done if it is not. Thinking first about temperament is especially important with sensitive children, who if rushed to therapy will immediately sense that important adults think there is something wrong with them. *The Highly Sensitive Child* has a questionnaire to help parents and others assess a child's sensitivity or it can be found on my Web site.

Infancy

If we begin at birth, sensitive infants can be identified at least by 5 months, although some will be noticeably sensitive from birth in that they seem to do better with less stimulation around them. Realizing a newborn infant might be highly sensitive can help parent and child bond more easily. Some parents seem to sense sensitivity in their infants and begin to respond to it very early and not always wisely. One parent complained that her newborn would never stop crying. He was "too fussy." Then she confessed that she was trying to prepare her son for a world of high stimulation right from the start by moving him from room to room, having him sleep in different places, and even in different kinds of bedding. Once she stopped the rotations and reduced the stimulation, her baby relaxed. The problem remained of helping her to accept her child's temperament.

School-Aged Children

At this age goodness of fit extends to play groups and school. Most sensitive children are slow to warm up so they need to be encouraged socially. At the same time, they need more downtime than other children and will not thrive on an endless round of soccer practices, gymnastic lessons, and play dates, followed by television or family activities when they come home. Sensitive children should have their own room if at all possible. Many are gifted (Silverman, 1994) and need to have that fostered so they are not bored or held back. Giftedness, in turn, can mean being ostracized unless their school is, again, a good fit for them.

Adolescence

Adolescence is the age when sensitivity to physical stimulation is at its lowest ebb. Some of their tolerance for loud music, bright lights, and all the rest is because they are still strongly influenced by their peers, who are mostly nonsensitive. It also seems to be part of the nature of the adolescent nervous system. Many sensitive youths will study with music or television playing, behaviors they will stop by age 30. This reduced sensitivity certainly helps them enter the world and may even serve that function.

If you consider how rapidly children become adults and how complicated adulthood is, it comes as no surprise that the highly sensitive do not usually have all of this in place before turning 30. Most have a serious crisis at the time of graduation from high school, college, graduate school, or whenever they must seriously face earning a living. During these transitions they can become anxious, depressed, or physically ill even if they never were before. They are looking ahead, as is their innate strategy, and seeing how difficult adulthood is for everyone, but especially how difficult it will be for them.

It is important to disabuse them of the idea that they must rush this process in order to be considered successful. Parents and therapists need to help sensitive adolescents take successful steps into their future. If they choose to make those steps small, such as going to a local college and living at home, they should be praised for it. They are doing what is right for them, which is especially difficult if they have the opportunity to go to a university far from home. If they have a choice among schools, point out some of the advantages of choosing one close to relatives, that a close friend will attend, or that is known to keep a close watch on them.

Dating and sexual experimentation may also lag, and that lag also should probably be encouraged. Peer pressure is very strong, however, and sometimes parents contribute to the pressure, worrying if their child is not dating someone or still a virgin at 20. In my survey of sexuality, sensitive women waited longer to have sex, were more cautious about who they had it with (usually chose sexual partners they loved), and not surprisingly, had fewer bad experiences. Many, however, added optional comments about having been more sexually active than they had wanted to be while young and regretting it later. Sensitive adolescent patients should be encouraged to discuss their sexuality and particularly the role of peer pressure and how active they truly wish to be. Above all, they need to feel supported at home or by you, so it does not feel to them that that closeness and nurturing can only be found in exchange for sex.

On the whole, sensitive adolescents are the easiest to raise. They usually experiment less with drugs and take fewer risks of all sorts. They are more conscientious. They are usually the best students. They are often the easiest patients to help as well.

Parenthood and Maturity

Sensitive people make wonderful parents. However, they need help with their worrying and with being easily overwhelmed. Above all, they need to have different expectations of themselves than those fostered in the media. Having a baby, like having a wedding, easily falls into the hands of commercial interests who convince their customers that they do not know what they are doing without outside help. But this advice is always one-size-fits-all and can leave sensitive parents feeling there is something wrong with them because they are not having the normative experience. Yet these parents also feel the most obliged to read all the parenting books they can. As their therapist you can help them sort out some of the information and encourage them to use their intuition, based on the solid knowledge of their child and themselves.

Regarding the older sensitive person, they are usually best adjusted to their sensitivity, having had so much experience with their uniqueness. Perhaps because of this, they also seem less stressed and to age slower, passing this developmental stage later as well. In part, they are probably more conscientious about preventative health practices, yet less distressed by the aging process, because they have anticipated rather than denied it. They have learned to be more focused on their inner life and on self-expression through the arts or their careers, which are ageless endeavors. Few people care about the age of a writer or a scientist. At the same time, sensitive persons never stop thinking about death. It has been with them since childhood. They have been preparing for it, too, all their lives and have well-developed spiritual or philosophical ideas to support them.

On the other hand, those who come as patients may be evidencing more distress than others by the decline due to aging and by losses because of their stronger emotional response generally and their greater fear of loss in particular. Again, your role as their therapist will be to help them understand that their strong reactions are normal, and then to teach, role model, or in this case perhaps only witness how best to find one's way along this passage.

Bottom Line: Age makes a difference with highly sensitive patients. In particular, they will be least sensitive as adolescents and slower than others to mature. As parents, they mostly need reassurance, and their response to aging will probably be at the positive and negative extremes.

Helping Sensitive Patients Stalled on the Way to Adulthood

Lagging behind their cohorts on the path to adulthood is often the main characteristic noticed by therapists when working with sensitive patients. Why does this patient still live with her mother? Why is he still at such a menial job? When is she going to stop dressing like a teenager? Why is this patient still thinking like a child?

The resolution of this lagging behind will be unique to each patient, and slow. Lecturing them generally accomplishes nothing, as they already know all too well that they are not keeping pace with their peers. The reason is usually fear—fears that they are ashamed even to admit, such as the fear of making even a single mistake and having someone mad at them. Some know about these fears, others will have a million other excuses: "Nobody goes to college these days—they make their living on the Internet." "Having a family is too much work." "I want to live in the moment, not planning my whole life like my parents did." Sometimes these are sheltered children, who up till now, simply have had no incentive to mature and know, consciously or not, that they have not been prepared. Others have had a traumatic failure—were fired from a job, had to drop out of school because of depression or anxiety, had a long-term romantic relationship fail, or saw a parent suffer through such a failure.

Sometimes there is a parent more directly behind the stall, offering help, usually unconsciously, just at the moment when their adult child is ready to act independently. Mother offers to pay the rent or to make the down payment on the house (but she picks the house). Father employs his child in his office or rationalizes that "He's just having a good time before settling down, like I never did." The following are suggestions for these stalled patients.

Reduce Shame and Build Self-Esteem

Since low self-esteem is mainly the cause of their hesitancy, be especially careful about shaming these patients for being stuck. They already feel ashamed about not keeping up. Explain their situation, to yourself and them, by turning to their learning experiences and resultant fears. Demonstrate that you value them at this moment, whatever they do or do not do in the future.

Be Patient

Everyone around a stuck young adult wants quick results, but the patient may be afraid to admit to being stuck and try to seem happy or to have chosen this situation. Nothing can happen until they admit to being unhappy with the lack of progress. This will not occur until they are sure you care about them, again, whether they are stuck or not. Those moments of their own dissatisfaction must be kept in mind, but not leapt upon.

Keep the Conflict Inside the Patient

Try to avoid becoming the representative of adulthood, reason, or moderation, while the patient takes the other side of it. Try to keep the conflict inside of them. "You say I want you to stop drinking. I don't recall exactly saying that. I do recall repeating what you had said—that sometimes after the surfer in you drinks too much you feel rotten, and that you often worry that all of this hanging out at the beach and drinking is just an escape. You also seem to thoroughly enjoy it, and something keeps you returning to it. That's a really difficult conflict to be in." An excellent stance to take is "I'm confident that in the end you will make the best decision you can."

The inner conflict has its own voices. Instead of wondering "What is keeping you from getting a job?" try "Who inside of you is keeping you from getting a job?" Speaking of parts reduces shame. Sometimes the patient can actually give that part a voice. I may imagine what that part would say and wait for the patient, or rather that part of the patient, to correct me. I might try, "I suppose it would tell us that it's afraid." The stuck part of the patient may respond with "just wants to be taken care of."

Let in the Child Wanting to Stay a Child

Very often the desire to escape adulthood is present, and it must be allowed in so that the patient can hear what he or she is up against. I encourage that part to speak, often learning from it a great deal about the problems in childhood and still present that keep it from growing. The more it is welcomed, the more it reveals. None of this should be used against the patient later: "I guess that's that childish part of you that just wants to be taken care of." Rather, I might ask to speak with that part again, to learn how it is evolving and what new fears it faces.

See the Future Through Their Eyes

The highly sensitive do look ahead and see consequences, but sometimes they are stuck on proximate problems that are paralyzing them or a depressing image of themselves as adults—worried, burdened with responsibility, living only to please others. Who would choose that? The long-run view must be brightened by their being able to be more creative than that. They do not have to be like others. Even if the short-term situation has to be nothing but overwork and facing down obstacles, help them take at least a few steps right now to follow their preferred path. Yes, they should earn their PhD before trying their hand at writing a novel, but they can write short stories now. You might say something like: "What I would do is think ahead 10 years and look at the different trajectories if you do or don't write the dissertation. If you don't, I guess you'd be an ABD, All But Dissertation. They can usually do adjunct teaching, although the pay is poor. But that might be fine for you. You could always afford to rent a room in town and continue your novel. Perhaps do some technical writing on the side. The good news is that either way, 10 years from now you won't be writing long papers. But on this PhD trajectory, writing those papers is the worst part for you. Thankfully, 10 years from now it won't matter what you wrote. Just that you wrote something. You've done the research. You know you write well. If you could just get around your perfectionism. And your fear of your adviser. I wonder if you could get him to look at what you would call a very rough draft of the first chapter to see if you are on track." Be very careful not to push too hard if you know this patient cannot do it through will power alone. You will only create another failure.

ETHNICITY

Assuming there are roughly as many sensitive persons born in every race and country, the question is how the trait is viewed. Is it honored, accepted, ignored, or rejected? Generally Europe and Asia are a little more appreciative of sensitivity than the Americas and Australia, although this too may be changing.

In the United States, I have observed the responses of various ethnic groups to sensitivity, although it is terribly difficult to make generalizations. Among African Americans the trait seems outside of the self-concept for most. I suspect that during and after slavery (or immigration), most of those with the trait did not survive or did but had to adapt to such an extent that they were unaware of it. Yet I also suspect that some of the most important African American political and spiritual leaders have been highly sensitive extroverts. Unless I have a wealth of facts to back me up, I generally avoid guessing about historical figures being highly sensitive because they are not here to agree or disagree. However, it seems that African Americans who were highly sensitive would have been among the most distressed by what was happening, most prone to have a vision of change, and most creative in their leadership.

The African Americans who have offered their thoughts to me on the subject note that women of their race are supposed to be invariably strong, and men have enough problems with their self-concept without adding the label of sensitive. Yet many are sensitive and find it a source of extra pain as well as sustenance. Some feel the plight of their people and themselves so deeply that it is almost paralyzing, but most have found creative ways to alleviate that plight. Some also have used their sensitivity to adapt to the white majority so thoroughly that they have been able to dissociate the damage to them done by prejudice. Perhaps some of them have healed it, or escaped it entirely, but usually I assume they only wish they would have.

As for those from Spanish-speaking countries, the response to sensitivity seems more varied according to the family. I suspect that the highly sensitive from those cultures are more often extroverted, given that family and community life are generally a source of such support. I wish I had more to say on the subject of ethnicity, but perhaps with time more voices will be heard on the subject from the highly sensitive themselves.

Bottom Line: Each ethnic group and family within it will have its own view of sensitivity as a trait, and that greatly influences how patients of that ethnicity grasp hold of their temperament and understand it.

SUMMARY AND CONCLUSION

This chapter has discussed three issues—low self-esteem, trying to live like the nonsensitive, and being overly bothered by criticism. It has also explored some specific issues around gender, ethnicity, and age.

The problems discussed in this chapter are largely the result of sensitive persons being a minority rather than due to the trait itself, so that many of their problems can be seen as the result of negative stereotyping. That is, they are another minority facing prejudice, in this case due to their temperament. This prejudice is surprisingly blatant, from the schoolyard and school classroom to the corporate office and their doctor's office. Like others who have experienced prejudice, they have come to feel bad about themselves. They want to suppress their trait and behave like those around them even when it does not suit them. They have come to expect negative feedback and take it to mean they are deeply flawed. The results of this prejudice have been the focus of this chapter.

As with any victims of prejudice, clinicians must make a special effort to appreciate the highly sensitive and deal with them fairly, which is their best hope of overcoming the damage done to them. We want to give them the experience of full acceptance while helping them identify how the culture's prejudices have affected them personally, perhaps in ways they are not aware of. This righting of a wrong can be very gratifying work.

CHAPTER

5

Adapting Treatment to the Highly Sensitive Patient

> The truly creative mind in any field is no more than this: A human creature born abnormally, inhumanly sensitive. To him … a touch is a blow, a sound is a noise, a misfortune is a tragedy, a joy is an ecstasy, a friend is a lover, a lover is a god, and failure is death. Add to this cruelly delicate organism the overpowering necessity to create, create, create—so that without the creating of music or poetry or books or buildings or something of meaning, his very breath is cut off from him. He must create, must pour out creation. By some strange, unknown, inward urgency he is not really alive unless he is creating.
>
> **—Pearl S. Buck, novelist, Nobel laureate**

This chapter addresses ways that therapists can adapt their practice of psychotherapy in order to better suit their highly sensitive patients (including adaptations when the therapist is not highly sensitive). These methods are considered by returning to the acronym adopted in Chapter 2, DOES, *for recalling the four basic characteristics of the trait: depth of processing, overarousability, emotional intensity, and sensory sensitivity.*

To serve the many highly sensitive persons who come for psychotherapy, we want to suit them well. A place to begin is to return to the concept of goodness of fit, from the child temperament literature (Kristal, 2005; Thomas & Chess, 1977). This does not mean that therapist and patient must have the same temperament. Rather, it refers to the therapist's task of adapting the therapy environment and experience so that these create a good fit for sensitive patients, physically, socially, and emotionally. Fortunately the therapist, setting, and frame can all be readily "tweaked" to achieve that end. As with children, adapting to their temperament improve outcomes. Hence it is well worth the attention of the therapist.

You might think, "But they are adults—they have to learn to adapt." True, when children grow up, they must do the adapting or search out people and places that are a good fit for them. Your sensitive patients, too, are adults mostly adapting to their nonsensitive world. But it may be best not to force them to do that in your office, given the evidence already presented (Bakermans-Kranenburg, Belsky, & van Ijendoom 2007; Ellis et al., 2005; Pluess & Belsky, 2009) that sensitive and difficult children generally are unusually well off if they had the right parenting and environment in childhood. Surely encouraging sensitive adults to be themselves while you provide the good fit seems very likely to lead to better than average outcomes for them.

The quote above by Pearl S. Buck is a bit dramatic, but it is offered here to remind you that sensitivity is very real for your patient, whether it is for you or not. Further, it is safe to say that every sensitive person is unusually creative, even if it is going unexpressed or there is no particular, exceptional talent present. But your sensitive patients may be so beaten down by life that the inward urgency that Buck says would normally keep them alive is simply too deadened, and part of what you are doing is bringing it back to life.

WHAT ABOUT YOUR OWN TEMPERAMENT?

Although therapists do not need to have the same temperament as their patients in order to provide a good fit, they will need to stay aware of the effect of their own sensitivity or lack of it.

If the Therapist Is Not Highly Sensitive

Therapists should read this section even if they are highly sensitive, since even a sensitive therapist may not feel or be as sensitive as a particular patient.

Assets Nonsensitive Therapists Offer

Again, it does not require an innately highly sensitive parent to raise a sensitive child. It requires skill, however. (Remember Suomi [1997] who cross-fostered "reactive" monkeys, and only those raised by skilled foster mothers avoided being shy, depressed, and anxious.) With it you can use your temperament difference to sensitive patients' advantage. For example, the nonsensitive therapist's respect and admiration are even more meaningful. There will be moments when you spontaneously defend your sensitive patient's right to express needs that differ from the majority.

You will easily role model how to turn up the "volume," the intensity of speech in all ways, when sensitive patients need to do that in order to be heard by others like yourself. Also, when you are inevitably too blunt or ask questions in a way that sensitive patients find threatening, you are providing the chance to learn how to handle such communications and find out what was the actual intention behind the volume. You provide a close-up experience of how the majority think, experience them, and in general what can and cannot be expected from those without the trait.

When sensitive patients are overwhelmed, you might be calmer and more soothing than a highly sensitive therapist would be, and your patients will internalize this calmer response. Finally, since you probably tend to speak and act more freely, you provide a role model for being more spontaneous.

Dangers of Being Different

Beware of making the common human assumption that others are like you, and that all patients' difficulties or differences are due to a trauma that has to be uncovered and healed, or to a thought process that has to be corrected. The fact is, some aspects of highly sensitive patients will never change. It is not a case of unconscious resistance, nor does it indicate that the therapy has failed.

The advice I give to couples in which one is sensitive and the other is not also fits the therapy dyad. The very first step is accepting the difference and perhaps even grieving it. If you are very fond of someone, you want him or her to be like you. It makes the two of you closer. It also seems at first that the one you care about would be happier if he or she were not sensitive and could be more like you and other people.

In all honesty, however, you may not be thrilled to have to adapt your own ways to serve the other's "fussy" sensitivities. Like a nonsensitive spouse, nonsensitive therapists have to accept and even grieve their sensitive patients' differentness. Only then can the two engage in problem solving in creative ways to adapt to each other. Before that there will always be the "Yes, buts." "Yes, but don't you think you could get used to ...?" Or, "Yes, but try it this one time and just see...."

Suggestions are perfectly appropriate once you fully accept your patient's sensitivity. You can encourage sensitive patients just as my friend Jim encouraged his daughter Lily (in Chapter 1). You do not always have to take no for an answer when you think a patient can do something and will be better for it. Often these patients have experienced people giving up on them too soon, out of exasperation. Since the patient wants to succeed, this respectful confidence is extremely hopeful.

The slowness of the entire process can be frustrating, however. You may not like having to do everything so cautiously. You will need patience, and your consolation is that patience is a good virtue to develop. You could also be bored more than a therapist who is highly sensitive. Sensitive patients may have strange, deep, and often humorous insights, but these surface slowly. When they are silent and you know they are thinking, it is tempting to finish their idea for them or do "multiple choice." "It seems like you're finding it hard to speak your thoughts—are you afraid of my reaction or your own?" A better solution is something like: "I notice you seem to be having trouble putting your thoughts into words—is this true? Is this more so than usual? [If so] I wonder why that might be."

Nonsensitive therapists can be dismayed to find they have very unintentionally hurt a patient's feelings. Or they only find it out when the patient discontinues treatment. To avoid this, therapists must try to turn down the "volume"—the forcefulness of their words. Everyone tends to put their thoughts into words with the same intensity as is required for others to get through to them. The highly sensitive, however, only need hints, gestures, glances, nuances, and tones of voice, and that is what they usually give out. The nonsensitive therapist's suggestions may seem like strong orders to be obeyed invariably. "Don't leave a message after nine at night" might only mean that you often do not check for messages after nine, but can be heard as do not be a nuisance and bother me after nine. Questions can sound like attacks ("Why did you do that?"). Interpretations can come down as judgments about the integrity of their intentions ("Maybe the real reason you bring me these gifts is that you're afraid I would reject you if you didn't?").

The therapist must tread with especially great care when the highly sensitive are cautiously uncovering their subtle feelings. These feelings are like sea creatures brought up from great depths and barely able to survive in full sunlight. Your smile or digression may simply seem too irreverent, so that they will not share that type of material again, even though it is central to their lives. As one patient put it, "It's as though I was in a dark, candlelit room praying, and then you came in, turned on the overhead light, and asked me what I was doing."

Of course, these patients can learn to adapt to a nonsensitive volume—many have already—and may gain so much from that or from you in other ways that it ceases to trouble them. But the danger with high volume is that you will be having too much influence. The patient may say nothing about it, and possibly not even know about it, being so used to being overruled.

Then there are the sensitive patients who have learned to dish it out with the best, but they definitely cannot take what they give.

Case Illustration

Josh was a short, slim, highly intelligent, and very sensitive teenager who grew up mostly with nannies and in boarding schools. Being invariably the smallest in his class, he had developed an attacking, mocking defense that covered an acute fear of rejection. This defense was especially brutal in the boarding schools, where most of his fellow students were feeling the same rejection by their parents and venting their rage on one another.

He came to therapy during a summer vacation after he had received a DUI, which then revealed his multiple substance addictions and self-destructive behaviors. Being young and having the best legal defense his parents could buy, he was sentenced only to substance abuse treatment followed by a year of therapy. Again his parents bought the best, and of course Josh used his boarding school defenses with his therapists. The first two returned it in style if not content, probably thinking they were attuning themselves to a tough young man. The third tried reflective listening, which only got him stony silence. Josh refused to continue with any of them, calling them incompetents. The fourth, a colleague of mine, was not fooled. He was not highly sensitive himself, but he had a daughter who was. She had developed a similar tough style to deal with the "back stabbing" girls in her high school.

My colleague started by slipping up on Josh as one might a shy horse—he looked over Josh's intake and began to muse out loud to himself about the conflict in our culture, about whether it was "all right to get high." Josh's anger burst out, but not at this therapist, who remained as calm, attentive, present, and nonaroused as possible. Rather, Josh was talking about how abused and rejected he felt by the courts, his parents, and, above all, the previous three therapists. Two of the three he felt had attacked him and the third treated him "like a child." In many ways, these three attempts at therapy turned out to be some of the most upsetting events in his young life. He felt that these professionals, who should really know, had validated how unlovable and disturbed he really was.

Little by little, Josh began to reveal more of his sensitivity, which the therapist used as an early focal point of the therapy. Indeed, together they decided that his drug use was not for thrills, to go along with others, or even to gain his parents' attention, but simply to self-medicate his overarousal at school and his wildly swinging emotions. As he understood more of why he was in this predicament and that it was not his fault, he accepted taking medication to contain himself for now. Once Josh took into account his sensitivity (along with his insecure attachment), he found it possible to give up what was illegal, with the support of a relationship with his therapist, and enjoy in moderation what was legal. What took longer was for him to allow his defensive tone to settle into something more representative of his true feelings and nature.

When the Therapist Is Also Highly Sensitive

The advantages of a "matched pair" should be obvious. The two understand each other immediately. The patient feels comfortable, well heard, and has the role model of another sensitive person who is coping relatively well in life. The therapist has real experience coping with overarousal, intense emotions, and other problems universally associated with sensitivity. The therapist is not thrown off by or made envious of the depth and wide-ranging intuition of the patient. Above all, just by being themselves, sensitive therapists improve the self-esteem of their sensitive patients.

In short, there would seem to be little adaptation needed. However, even when sensitive therapists are at home with their trait, there are pitfalls here. One is assuming the patient is similar in other ways as well. For example, I tend to expect highly sensitive patients to be introverts like me, but some are not. I may ask them to remind me when I am assuming it, and I have to adapt myself to sensitive extroverts' ways of thinking. I may also assume a sensitive patient has the same limitations and preferences I have. I am careful to hide my dismay if a sensitive patient takes up hang gliding or aims to run for public office, goals I would neither have nor feel I could achieve.

In addition, when discussing the patient's other relationships, especially marriage to a nonsensitive person, both you and the patient can forget the nonsensitive person's perspective. It helps if therapists have significant others in their lives who are also not highly sensitive. If you don't, try to develop a friendship with one.

Sensitive therapists may also have issues that would impact all patients, but perhaps sensitive ones more. For example, having been the target of negative stereotyping yourself, you may have come to feel flawed and tend to submit in a conflict. Thus you may have difficulty being assertive about your needs, such as proper compensation or undisturbed down time. You need to call on your conscientiousness and remember that these behaviors are role modeling poor boundaries, the last thing sensitive patients need. Watch whether you postpone a difficult confrontation, take the blame too quickly in an interaction, or even feel deeply guilty or ashamed at times, all without considering whether these feelings might be due to unconscious pressure from the patient that you submit to his or her will. As a highly sensitive person yourself, you can understand highly sensitive patients' needs better, but that does not mean you have to fulfill them.

Adapting to the needs of the sensitive patient can lead to a satisfying professional success, but if it requires that you first work on your own issues about your sensitivity, you have the opportunity for a satisfying personal success as well.

Bottom Line: If you as a therapist are not highly sensitive, you have much to offer a sensitive patient: the special meaning of your appreciation of the trait; experience communicating effectively with a nonsensitive person; your calm during intense, potentially threatening emotional moments; and your firm encouragement. But you will have to be more patient and adjust your "volume" so that you do not hurt these patients' feelings or have so much influence that patients lose sight of their own views. If you are yourself highly sensitive, you have the advantage of understanding the patient and being able to role model how you adapt, but you may assume the patient is like you in other ways, misjudge the feelings of nonsensitive persons in the patient's life, and have your own unresolved issues about your trait that affect your work.

DEPTH OF PROCESSING AND STAYING ATTUNED TO ITS PRODUCTS

Returning to DOES (presented in Chapter 2), how can a therapist adapt to highly sensitive patients' depth of processing?

We can begin with the silences it causes. Because they are processing so much, they are certain to have difficulty putting very many of their thoughts into words during a session. In addition, their feelings may be so intense that no words seem adequate to describe them. Further, they will be censoring vast amounts of what has come into their minds and could be discussed. This is not just due to their personal defenses—with sensitive patients it is also their innate style to reflect longer than others and choose the most important of their thoughts before speaking.

Staying Attuned During Silences

One result of deep processing will be your own uncertainty during long silences. Because so much is happening inside, much of it unsaid and difficult for the highly sensitive to put into words, it is a challenge to stay attuned to these patients, especially the introverts. You simply do not know for certain what is going on and neither wish to foreclose a profitable inner exploration nor leave patients in a silence that is leading to further distress.

You will have to use all of your skills at reading nonverbal cues and intuition about what might be going on now, given what has just happened or what might be coming next. The bottom line is to speak or not to speak. And if so, what to say? It all depends on the silence.

Silences You Cannot Tell About

These are often the most common, especially in the beginning. With sensitive patients, who may be thinking almost anything and perhaps for too long, I just go ahead and interrupt if I do not know what is happening. I might ask, "I'm wondering if this is a helpful silence, one that you need. If so, take all the time you want. But tell me if it shifts to something that might be helped by sharing your thoughts."

Some will be grateful for the interruption; some will lose their train of thought. You can apologize for your miscue, but do not let it keep you from interrupting in the future. Most of the time in life and in therapy a pair of people will be slightly or enormously misattuned. Risking that is all right—patients learn from this, too. A misattunement often leads to patients becoming clearer about their states of mind and their needs.

Silences Arising From or Leading to Overarousal

These are the ones I want to catch. Sometimes the tension is palpable. The patient is almost frozen by fear or overarousal. If not interrupted, the arousal only goes higher as the silence lengthens and the thoughts are less and less likely to be helpful.

Silence Guarding Uncomfortable Thoughts

Of course, some silences happen in order to avoid a thought that has arisen but that patients do not want to discuss. Having heard many answers to my probes into silences, I have found that long, moderately tense ones are often about me or the therapy—thoughts that sensitive patients are very hesitant to share because of their concern for my feelings or fear of the long-term consequences of expressing these thoughts. This requires some intuition as to how the relationship stands, but I almost always probe these slightly tense silences, as they can provide important breakthroughs. "Could it be that you were thinking about us, how we are getting along?" Or "I wonder if you were thinking something about what just happened?" Again, what is often then divulged is very important for improving the therapeutic relationship. When a patient processes deeply, it is only to be expected that what surfaces may be too difficult to reveal without your help.

Peaceful, Deep Silence

In other silences, you will gain a sense of peace or alrightness. These do not need to be probed. They are being used by the patient to calm down, notice deeper feelings, recall something important, or just savor the moment.

Shared Silences

Some silences have the potential to be deeply meaningful moments in which the two of you are sharing feelings that are ineffable, beyond words. If the patient tries to speak and feels frustrated or inadequate, I might make just that comment, that some feelings can be almost too deep for words. Sensitive patients are often especially relieved to hear this. Still, later it is valuable to talk about it, with some reverence about what has happened, in order to reiterate how deep the connection can be between two people, especially if the patient has rarely experienced this.

Attunement During Long Speeches

Equally common, however, are those times, when due to their depth of processing, sensitive patients are racing through material. Sometimes this seamless thread is meant to hide a few important feelings they cannot bear to focus on. To stay attuned to these hints requires a kind of bookmarking or moving an idea you want to come back to from short-term to long-term memory. Hopefully the few you can remember are the secret messages. If you miss them, however, they will return, rest assured. This may have been only a trial run, and if the feeling failed to be heard and was not too frightening to voice, the volume will be turned up on it next time.

Most of the time, however, the rapid train of thought is due to their processing so much that there is not enough time in a session to express even a little of it. The problem is often intensified after a break, when there is so much news to report, plus all the processing of it, along with the overstimulation coming from being back in the office together.

If the patient can afford meeting more often, that is the best solution to the pressure of content. A scattering of double sessions is also possible, but usually these are too draining for both. Some sensitive patients will spontaneously keep a journal of their thoughts between sessions, just to try to contain their processing. An extraordinary amount of important additional material may be there. Yet how can all of this from outside the session be absorbed together when so much is also arising in the moment? Even if you read it and charge for your time, will what you read take you away from what should be discussed?

A further complication is that often journaling contains thoughts too uncomfortable to express to you directly. Thus I think it is best that if patients want this outside writing to be read at all, you should only offer to read it in their presence. This keeps patients aware of the boundaries of the work and of life, in which, in the end, they will have to be selective about what line of thinking to pursue. They must learn to be decisive according to an inner compass and intuition about what is needed in the moment. So I usually let the patient choose what to read, although I will point out if it seems to be interfering with being present. Their notes, after an especially difficult session, are probably most useful.

Sensitive Patients Miss Very Little

With their depth of processing, not only do you occasionally have to read the minds of sensitive patients during their silences or long speeches, but they will occasionally seem to be reading yours, although possibly it is a wrong reading. For example, they may see a look or gesture as disapproval or wandering attention. They miss very little, although quite possibly they will be equally careful about mentioning what they have observed. If you have said anything that could possibly be upsetting, such as a mere comment that they are "overemotional" or that they "ruminate too much," they have heard the innuendo and you have almost certainly hurt their feelings. If you find yourself sitting with your arms folded or glance at the clock or at something behind them, they have noticed. Even blowing your nose could be felt as a moment of painful inattention.

This does not mean you should not say or do such things, but you should know you have had an effect. Usually you will not be told about it, or not until the feeling caused becomes impossible to contain. It is often very worthwhile to work hard to help sensitive patients lose their fear of saying what they notice or what does not work for them in a close relationship such as therapy.

A more serious case of their missing very little is when the sum of their observations becomes a negative evaluation of you or the therapy. Sensitive persons tend to be highly critical of themselves and everyone else. They often harbor doubts for a long time before these thoughts erupt in fully elaborated but usually distorted forms. (On the other hand, they could be quite correct and provide you with a better direction to take.) It is best to inquire frequently how the work is going—and when you do, ask several times in different ways—in order to elicit these types of comments. It is important to welcome them without defensiveness, but also not always to take them at face value. In particular, patients critical of you are probably even more critical of themselves, and equally inaccurate.

When checking in about the therapy, if I hear comments about being pleased with the progress, I store these mentally so that I can mention them when darker comments surface. I assure them when I resurrect their positive comments that this is not to prove them wrong, but only to maintain some perspective and avoid precipitous changes.

Aspects of the therapeutic frame receive the same scrutiny. Some will raise astute questions about your particular procedures or boundaries. Sensitive patients are highly aware of lateness in beginning or ending. They cannot help watching for their therapist's other patients. Seeing one arriving or leaving always stirs feelings. Fees are a delicate topic for all the usual reasons, but more so.

Case Illustration

Betsy, an extremely conscientious, highly sensitive patient, was paying a reduced fee because she was a student. When she graduated and took a job, I waited a few months and then asked if she could now afford a higher fee. She was horrified that she had forgotten to offer that herself. She had planned to speak to me about it, but had forgotten. After that session she had a dream that I was a prostitute, furious with her for not paying. This opened up the issue raised for her (and most patients) about "having to pay for love and attention."

Bottom Line: Patients' depth of processing can lead to long silences, and some of these are probably best interrupted. On the other hand, they may run on or speak rapidly. If this is not defensive, it may signal a need for more sessions. Sensitive patients may write material outside of the session, and you may want to read this with the patient present. Their deep processing of even your minor comments means they may hear things you did not intend, so check in frequently about how the work is going and expect reactions to any changes in the frame (your coming late, ending late, raising fees, changing amount of contact between sessions, etc.).

OVERAROUSAL IN THE OFFICE

How might a therapist adapt to sensitive patients' tendency to be easily overstimulated, leading to being overaroused? Some of the signs of overarousal are trouble concentrating, not remembering what they wanted to say, not grasping a rather simple interpretation or suggestion, or seeming a little dazed or confused. Arousal also accompanies any emotion, and besides the effect of the emotion, there is the effect of it pushing the patient into overarousal. Fear or anxiety is the most common arouser. The patient avoids eye contact, which both reduces arousal and is the instinctual posture of submission. The patient may make repetitive nervous gestures such as twisting a tissue, sit in a stiff or uncomfortable posture (because the body is being ignored), and generally look anxious or miserable. Patients may say they are nervous or even quite anxious, and of course could be feeling that for reasons unrelated to their sensitivity—for example, fear of telling you something. Arousal is further complicated by nervousness or anxiety anyway, because when anyone is overaroused, the person knows he or she will be less effective and fears it. So it is worth thinking in terms of overarousal as well as anxiety because overarousal is having a separate, multiplicative effect.

In the First Sessions

There are a number of ways to ease this overarousal and anxiety in the first sessions.

Phone Interviews Before the First Session

Consider using the first phone contact for more than arranging an appointment. Phone time has financial costs, of course, and not knowing at first if a patient is sensitive, you would probably be deciding to do this for all new patients who sounded anxious or sensitive. However, being a little familiar with each other and with the patient's goals makes the first minutes face to face far easier.

Be Casual in the First Few Minutes

Even if this is not your usual style, consider being light while you observe the patient for overarousal and anxiety. Do not ask questions, but rather make comments, such as you are glad he or she was able to find the office. Stay aware of whether more or less of this will be needed to reach the patient's optimal level of arousal. Remember that optimal is not the same as low arousal or complete relaxation, although it could be a good place to start.

Normalize Nervousness

When a patient complains of or is embarrassed by nervousness, it could help any patient to discriminate among feelings by saying something like: "Of course you are a little nervous. It's our first session. You've got a lot to take in at once. That makes it harder to think, and that feels strange, and so here you are—feeling nervous, or at least overloaded. If you want, we could just ignore this kind of nervousness for now. Once things start to feel familiar after a time or two, then we can think more about whatever is causing the nervousness that remains."

Case Illustration

Tess was one of my most anxious patients in the first session. Her anxiety manifested as trouble thinking and a long silence before she spoke. When I relaxed her a little, she would launch into pressured speech, as if to compensate. Near the end she remarked on how much it helped that I had ended her silence. She told me about a previous experience in what was apparently very classical psychodynamic therapy. The therapist, who happened to be a man, took her basic information and then settled into silence. Tess was already nervous and had no idea what to say. She asked him how she should proceed and he only said, "What do you think about it?" This sounded to her like a test and made her even more nervous.

That session had passed in almost complete silence, as did the next two, before Tess simply could not bring herself to return. It was an especially unfortunate way to begin her first therapy experience because this very sensitive woman had never been able to hold her father's attention, as a child or as an adult. One thing he had not liked about her was her "weird nervousness" around him. She would be unable to think of anything to say when with him. He would say he found her boring and turn away, or they would play ball and she would drop it and annoy him with her clumsiness, or she would keep her head down, her long hair hiding her face, and he would declare her unattractive.

Optimal Arousal in General During Sessions

Suggestions or interpretations made when a patient is overaroused are often forgotten, and these sessions will usually be unpleasant for the patient and perhaps even retraumatizing. The same signs of overarousal discussed above can warn the therapist that things may need to cool down. Reducing overarousal never means moving to underarousal by being too casual or reassuring. It can be very appropriate and necessary for patients to feel on the alert, excited, distressed, wary, or anxious. The level of arousal simply should not be so high that the session is a waste of time for both of you.

Maintaining an optimal level also does not mean that overarousal should never occur. Overarousal and overwhelming emotion are almost inevitable in effective psychotherapy and in my view can be invaluable. Besides offering the opportunity to see how readily and in what situations the patient is overwhelmed, they provide the therapist with the opportunity to help the patient regulate these overwhelming affects. But in general the patient will gain more from a session if you can prevent overarousal.

Listen to the Hints

Some will learn to say when they want the therapist to slow down. Others will learn, consciously or unconsciously, to signal this, even if they cannot say it. One patient always became dizzy at the moment when I was opening up too much emotion. Another developed a headache or nausea. Another would come late or not come at all to the next session. With each I was eventually able to discuss these defenses so that we could note progress by how much less often they needed to give this type of signal.

Restore Calm

There are many ways to calm a patient, and some will work better with a particular one than others. You can drift off into something a bit mundane or connected to the outer world. Sensitive patients may well know what you are doing, but you can discuss what you did and why. You might ask them to look around, ask what they think of some change in the office. You might ask them to notice what is going on in their bodies. This may intensify the problem, but if it works, will not require leaving the topic altogether. The same is true of talking about the overarousal itself and why it may have come up, perhaps using the past tense to suggest it is going or gone.

Help Them Learn From the Experience

When arousal is back in the optimum range, in that session or later, acknowledge what caused the sense of being overwhelmed and compare this to other experiences in therapy and elsewhere. The goal is to add to the patient's repertoire of affect regulation.

When Overarousal Remains

Sometimes patients will leave the session still feeling overwhelmed. You might want to ask them to call and leave a message as to how they are doing, including if they would like you to call them back (some will find actually speaking to you overarousing). You also might allow them to wait in the waiting room or encourage them to stay in the parking lot until they have calmed down. At the next session, it is important to inquire as to how the patient weathered this emotional storm and perhaps offer more help with how this might be done in the future. If they made use of calling you, discuss how that worked for them. Meanwhile, make note of what was the trigger and revisit it when the patient is in an especially optimal state.

Such "digesting" sessions are often calmer and may seem less productive, but patients should see that all types of sessions have value—indeed, even the disappointing ones. Exploring what happened in a session from the point of view of both of you also helps the patient see that he or she shares control over the pace at which things proceed.

Underarousal and Sensitive Patients

It is highly unpleasant to be overaroused, especially when it is due to frightening thoughts or overwhelming emotions. Hence it is no surprise that some sensitive patients have developed elaborate defenses against having such states ever again. This is particularly true of men, since our culture's masculine image includes being imperturbable. So they keep you and them underaroused by embarking on long, distracting digressions. If you use active, behavioral approaches anyway, you will interrupt these.

Otherwise, you can listen for the symbolic content. For example, consider this chitchat. "I didn't go to work today. I felt too sick. My friend called, but she is such a bother—always trying to get me to go to her doctor and find out why I get sick so often. I don't want to talk about my illnesses all the time. Not with her or with you either." This could be a statement of her feelings today about the therapy today as well. To raise her arousal, all the therapist needs to do is suggest that possibility.

It is not always wise to explore the symbolism in digressions. That could be shaming or dismantle a needed defense. In any case, you first must delicately explore whether the actual content is in fact an important subject to the patient, in which case remaining attuned to it is essential, even if it seems to be about something else or bores you a little. A big event to a sensitive person might not be one to you. To put it in other terms, just because you are underaroused does not mean the patient is.

On the other hand, an indicator of a defensive digression is often that you feel profoundly underaroused—bored, sleepy. This might be a time to "just check in" to see if what is happening in today's session is what the patient intended. Will the patient leave the session satisfied or wish he or she had said something more? Or you might ask what is going on right now, what the patient is feeling in this moment, perhaps a bodily state. Is there anything the therapist had not noticed?

In my own counseling, some sensitive patients have stayed on a bland topic because I seemed interested—I kept asking questions and seemed to be listening attentively. They wanted to drop the subject but thought I was the one interested in it. Others have learned enough about these defenses to ask me to stop them when they stray off. They are excited to be able to share the details of their complex observations, but they also want to be doing something more connected to me and their goals. That is, they would like to be more aroused.

Bottom Line: An optimal level of arousal—not under or over—best facilitates change, so it is worthwhile to observe and manage a patient's arousal, which is especially high in the initial sessions (although it is not possible or desirable always to avoid over arousal).

EMOTIONAL INTENSITY: ADAPTATIONS THAT SUPPORT AFFECT REGULATION

Chapter 3 presented some adaptations you can make to sensitive patients' stronger emotional reactions. I emphasized there what you can teach patients in order to make them experts in regulating their own reactions. There are also other steps you will want to consider.

Sensitive patients usually very much appreciate any help with overwhelming feelings. They tend to give all sessions considerable thought, but especially these. If these painful sessions are not discussed, they can arrive at extreme ideas about what their emotional outburst meant or how you felt about it. Most sensitive patients are ashamed of their strong feelings and fear that you, like others, will find them too intense. This is an invaluable time to provide reassurance, build trust, and educate about strong emotions by exploring what precipitated them and how, when appropriately expressed, these often impact a close relationship for the better.

Your Office

You can use your office environment to signal your views about emotions, because your office will be filled with cues about that which your sensitive patients will sense whether consciously or not. You may obviously be saying you encourage the expression of emotions with pillows to pound or teddy bears to hug. The presence of these may actually be upsetting or embarrassing to sensitive patients at first. You may not want to display these and bring them out with great care. But art materials, sand tray materials, a discreet blanket, and a place to lie down would still signal that your office is a place where feelings can be expressed.

You will send a different message than patients will read if you have firm, business-like chairs and décor, more like a doctor's office, perhaps with a desk you sit behind. The books visible on shelves will send messages as well as the lighting—soft or bright. Of course decorations and what is hanging on the walls send a strong message. Diplomas mean one thing, mandalas another. If your office is furnished in an expensive way, the message is that you have more status, meaning you may look down on those who cannot control their emotions, or be a strong force in regulating them. Some sensitive patients will see too much luxury as a signal that you lack concern for social justice.

Even the make, model, color, condition, and visible contents of the therapist's car, once seen by the patient, will suggest your personality and emotional style. The point is, none of these details will be missed by sensitive patients and will suggest how their feelings will be received. I think there is an environment that says emotions are welcome yet can be contained, and that is perhaps a calm office with emotionally moving but "quiet" décor, and of course a therapist in it who welcomes emotions without being frightened that negative emotions will take over everything.

Medications

Naturally intense emotional reactions, especially negative ones, bring to mind the need for medication. Compared to others, highly sensitive patients can be far more resistant to medications, or at least need longer to decide about it. They worry about the long-term consequences, of course. They feel ashamed that they cannot control themselves on their own, especially because prior to therapy they may have been able to do this, so now you are seeing them at their worst. They may fear that medication will change them so much that they will no longer be their real selves. They will now be bland, insensitive, domineering, or whatever. Even after they have agreed to take medication, they may be afraid to take the first dose and may very well feel its effects at the time and later more than other patients. This is not about being a nuisance somaticizer or "poor responder." They actually do feel these things, and alas, they usually have more side effects.

Keep Explaining the Reason

Make it clear that when patients do good work in therapy—being honest and focused—it often makes them feel worse before they feel better. Medication provides a safety net so that they will not get so very, very low or anxious, but it does not stop their inner work. There will still be a need for therapy, but the medication will help as they will be a little more buffered from the intense feelings that are being generated. They may want to see or hear about the research that finds medication and therapy work better together.

Discuss Medication in Light of Sensitivity

Bringing up medication may seem to signal that you now think something is wrong with them, something more than just being highly sensitive, or that sensitivity is really a disorder after all. Emphasize that sensitivity is not a disorder and the medication will not and is not meant to take away their sensitivity. Discuss the difficulties and traumas in their histories and explain that their sensitivity has made them more vulnerable. It may also mean they will benefit more from psychotherapy.

Prepare Thoroughly

Go ahead and discuss any potential negative side effects or potential long-term problems. Do not worry about suggesting a negative outcome—sensitive patients will read the fine print that comes with the medication anyway. So I balance any as-yet-unknown risks with the many known long-term dangers of untreated depression. If they later gain weight or lose their sexual interest, they will not feel betrayed that you knew this all along and did not tell them.

If a person is deeply depressed, however, I do less discussing and come closer to deciding for them. I may emphasize the harm that could be done to their brain, their heart and other organs, their relationships, and the therapy itself if they do not try to treat the depression, and that after one untreated depression the risk of a recurrence increases. Do not paint such a grim picture, however, that it will be distressing if the medication is not effective or they have to stop due to side effects.

See that they start on a low dosage and do not increase the dosage past where they feel adequate benefit, whatever is the supposed correct clinical dosage. I have seen many patients improve on a very low dosage and some develop unpleasant side effects at a dosage closer to "normal." Tell them they will feel different, but they have experienced other things that have altered their mood yet have not felt they have lost their basic self. Women understand this if you remind them that hormones, produced inside of them, alter their mood in major ways, yet they still keep their sense of a unitary identity. On the day they take their first dose, tell them you will be available if they need to talk about their experience.

Rest assured, however, that most sensitive patients who decide to take medication encounter few problems and are happy with the results.

Case Illustration

When Ann passed through a deep stage of grief that began to turn into true depression, she agreed with enormous reluctance to try an antidepressant. I had suggested she research the medication using trustworthy Web sites, watching especially for any health risk for not treating depression. She saw that the medication might help her and agreed to try it. But the morning after she had taken the first dose she told me that she was awake all night watching "the forces of darkness combating the forces of light." Every time she drifted toward sleep she felt the good side of her was finally losing and dying. She left me a tearful message vowing never to take that medication again. In the light of day we were able to review why she was taking the antidepressant and what was actually happening in her brain. She tried a different drug and this time was able to weather the changes she felt.

She felt better in 10 days at a very low dose, but had been told to increase it after 2 weeks. At the higher dose, she began to notice a low "sizzling" in her nervous system. She was aware of it day and night, and it was making it difficult to sleep. She reduced her dose but she said it was still there. She was given another medication, and then another, but the sizzling remained. When an antipsychotic was suggested and she read about these, she decided she would prefer to be depressed. Later she found an alternative treatment plus meditation helped her more than her brief good experience on an antidepressant. I never questioned her experiences, but supported her through them, and happily she did find a solution eventually.

Bottom Line: The environment in which therapy takes place gives the sensitive patient cues about your orientation toward emotions as well as creating a place where emotion can be more readily experienced, more readily controlled, or both. When it seems that a patient's intense negative emotions could be helped with medication, prepare the patient, keep the dosage low and increase slowly, support the validity of the patient's experiences no matter how strange, and be prepared for the possibility that medication may not work.

SENSORY SENSITIVITY: A CHANCE TO SHOW CARING

Sensory sensitivity is an important aspect of adapting the work to these patients, even if they do not complain about your choices. But do remember that they are paying in part for you to supply a space that is as right for them as possible. Attention to these details is one of the best ways to show respect and caring within the appropriate boundaries of the relationship.

The following are suggestions for adapting to all sensitive patients. You will need to decide your attitude regarding specific needs as well as what will be best for each patient. I try to adjust to patients' specific needs because I know everyone has different sensitivities—what is nothing to me may really bother someone else. If someone finds the glare from the windows hurts their eyes, I make a note to adjust the blinds before they arrive. I do the same if patients always place a certain pillow behind them in the chair—I have it sitting in the chair before they come. I want them to feel that this is one place where their sensitivity to physical stimulation will be fully accepted. Of course there are a few patients who, for me, are expecting too much or seem to feel entitled. If I find myself balking at meeting their needs (e.g., that other patients should be asked not to wear chemical perfumes; that there be no sources of electromagnetic radiation in the building), I do not cater to them because I know I will resent it. Since these usually come up early, I suggest they find a therapist with similar sensitivities, perhaps through support groups, chat rooms, or the Internet, and I will try to help with that.

The Sense of Smell

I air out my office between patients, as one can habituate to odors that those entering will notice immediately. I try not to eat in my office for the same reason. Flowers or plants that give off pleasant scents can be nice. If someone is allergic to them, they can be set outside and the office aired.

Vision

I have no clutter in my office and keep my personal belongings mostly out of sight. I like to have flowers and plenty of light, but nothing glaring such as old-fashioned ceiling fixtures. Décor can be well considered and unobtrusive, from carpets to clocks. Objects and art works that are beautiful or meaningful to me seem to be well received.

Sound

I have a white noise producer outside the door and turn off any potential ringers or buzzers. I have avoided having an office on a busy street or near any other predictable source of noise. Consider carefully any music in the waiting room and do not play a radio there.

Touch

Furniture needs to be covered in something soft and comfortable. Bare legs can stick to leather. It is best to have enough time between patients that the furniture is not warm from the previous patient. Soft carpets are nice to walk on. Throws or blankets can have wonderful textures and comforting weight. Things are arranged the same each time and I try not to make changes in the office without warning patients ahead of time.

Taste

Some therapists serve coffee and tea, perhaps in the waiting area. Most sensitive patients will want tea, especially several interesting herbal varieties.

Temperature

Certain patients may be by nature easily chilled or overheated (usually chilled) and I can adjust the temperature before they arrive. I always inquire if I see patients trying to adjust on their own by adding or removing clothing, as they will rarely ask for an adjustment of an environment that they assume suits you best.

Bottom Line: Adjust the physical environment to better accommodate patients with sensory sensitivity. Thinking about how each sense impacts them is one way to consider the entire office systematically.

SUMMARY AND CONCLUSION

Adapting to sensitive patients does not require being highly sensitive yourself. There are numerous ways to make sensitive patients welcome and improve their outcome, which can be roughly grouped into methods for maintaining an optimal level of arousal; attuning to their thoughts and feelings, which are frequently deeper than those of other patients; working with their especially intense emotions; and accommodating when possible to their sensory sensitivity.

When classroom teachers are asked to take individual temperaments into account, their first response is usually that they do not have the time to adapt their teaching to each individual. If they try it, however, and do accommodate the needs of those students with extreme temperaments, they usually report that it saves time in the long run. The entire classroom becomes easier to manage and students learn faster. This is especially true when teachers adapt by sending very active children on errands around the school, or give persistent children a warning that it will soon be time to stop. Highly sensitive children are often so good that they receive no special treatment at school, even though it means that their joy in learning is sacrificed.

In therapy, however, the value of accommodating the needs of highly sensitive patients is much clearer. It leads to their staying in treatment, feeling cared for, and overall progressing faster. Further, surprising them by taking the trouble to accommodate their needs and desires without hesitation is probably one of the easiest and most rewarding efforts you can make.

CHAPTER

6

Helping Them Establish Relationships

Meeting Others, Shyness, and Fears of Commitment

> The word "sensitive" was applied to me many times as a child ... the attitude was far from complimentary. On the contrary, its effect was to set me apart from all that was normal, to identify me, once and for all, as a stranger, and to usher in an overwhelming feeling of being alone.
>
> I tried to hide the more obvious symptoms of my strangeness. But my biggest discovery was adaptation. ... It took me a long time to find out what I lost on the road between "sensitive" and "adaptable."
>
> I found out I was not the one. In fact, there were many of us, all lying low because of the same ignorant, suspicious voices, and all keeping inside the remarkable perceptive and creative powers with which we were born.
>
> —**Francis Martineau,** *The Sensitive Vein*

This is the first of two chapters focusing on relationships. After discussing the research on the relationships of sensitive persons generally and the assets they bring to relationships, this chapter focuses on the difficulty some have with meeting people and then committing to a longer relationship.

This chapter and the next benefit from the long-standing involvement of myself and my husband in the study of close relationships (e.g., Aron, Mashek, & Aron, 2004). Although these chapters do refer frequently to marriage, it is only because marriage is the context in which so much research occurs. This material can be applied to every type of relationship—friendships, family relationships, work relationships, and of course long-term romantic partners.

RESEARCH COMPARING SENSITIVE AND NONSENSITIVE PERSONS IN RELATIONSHIPS

By far the greatest influence on patients' relationships is prior relationship experience, as seen by the ubiquitous effects of attachment style on adult relationships (Cassidy & Shaver, 1999). According to our unpublished data, sensitive persons are no more likely than others to report insecure attachment styles. Still, highly sensitive patients who are insecure may be more affected by their insecurity, given that other aspects of their childhood affect them more.

In search of some direct role of temperament in relationships, I have been able to add the HSP Scale to a number of relationship studies using a variety of standard relationship quality measures, resulting in data from about 600 college students and a community sample of 200 married adults. There has been no direct, unmodified correlation with sensitivity on the standard variables—relationship success, satisfaction, closeness, and intimacy—once we had partialed out neuroticism (Aron, 2004a). In other words, there was nothing in these studies about high sensitivity per se that affected the ability to develop and maintain a close, satisfying relationship.

However, the role of sensitivity could be to effect the style of closeness or preferences in ways to be close, which in turn would matter in different ways depending on one's partner as well as one's own ability to negotiate conflicts arising from differences in temperament. One could imagine sensitive persons in close relationships either being especially capable or especially handicapped by their trait. This highlights once again the importance of the interaction (Aron et al., 2005) between sensitivity and childhood relationship experience.

In another type of study, however, reported in *The Highly Sensitive Person in Love* (Aron, 2001), sensitive respondents as a group did appear to be less satisfied than the nonsensitive, but most of the respondents in this case were women. This study was designed for another purpose, to compare the sexuality of the two groups, and it used a mailed anonymous survey that went to 1,200 and provided data from 443 respondents (a typical response rate for mailed questionnaires). These were 600 subscribers to a newsletter for sensitive people, plus a comparison group made up of one friend selected by each respondent as being similar in demographics but nonsensitive (and who were provided envelopes of their own with which to mail in their questionnaires separately).

These self-selected sensitive respondents were slightly less likely to be satisfied in their relationships than the group made up of nonsensitive friends. The highly sensitive respondents in a relationship with a nonsensitive person were also less satisfied, and since 50% of the respondents fell into this category, it may be the main reason for the reduced overall satisfaction. There are also likely to be substantial differences between the student and community samples we had measured previously and this one, of sensitive persons, mostly women, who subscribe to a newsletter and bothered to answer a questionnaire about their sensitivity. For example, they may have been more affected by knowledge of their own trait and that of their partner, so that they were more likely to think of it as a major problem when there were problems at all.

Bottom Line: Sensitivity alone does not appear to predict relationship satisfaction in the general population, although being paired with a nonsensitive person may. Further, given the strong negative effect of insecure attachment and negative affect (neuroticism) on relationships, sensitivity is able to have a dramatic effect on relationships through its intensification of negative affect in patients with negative histories.

THE ASSETS SENSITIVE PERSONS BRING TO RELATIONSHIPS

As already described, and more thoroughly explored in the Appendix C, the interaction of sensitivity and early environment points not only to vulnerability, but also to a greater susceptibility to the benefits of a good environment. If therapy can be such an environment, assets will surface that can be utilized and strengthened. For example, sensitive persons in general and sensitive patients at certain times can grasp the subtle meanings of a communication and see its many implications. Thus they can better detect and gain more than others from your supportive attention and sincere caring, which they will learn to watch for and expect more of from others, while their own generosity increases through your modeling. A relatively undistorted awareness of subtle social cues, along with other assets that come with the trait, may not be available to certain patients, at least at first. But watch for them and praise them when they are present. This is the sort of support sensitive patients especially need while engaged in the hard work of changing what they are not doing so well. Three such assets to point out and praise are discussed below.

Empathy

Especially when not overaroused, sensitive persons can be wonderfully sensitive to another's feelings and communications, both verbal and nonverbal. Of course, patients often misuse their sensitivity to know best how to cater especially well to others' needs and disregard their own. Also, as with anyone, their own issues can distort what they hear and the result is no real empathy at all. Often, however, you can comment on a sensitive patient's unusual degree of kindness and empathy for you and others as an asset he or she brings to relationships.

Depth of Conversation

Sensitive persons, even extroverts, usually prefer one-on-one interactions on deep subjects, which can make them increasingly fascinating as conversations expand and relationships develop. They also reflect deeply on what has transpired and are usually the first to notice when a conversation is off course and needs refocusing. Again, you can comment on this as you experience it, relating it to the patient's general sensitivity so that you do not imply that this only occurs between the two of you. If patients report feeling left out of conversations, it is often because they were thinking so deeply about what was being said that by the time they have formulated their thoughts into words, others have changed the subject. You may want to help them resolve to continue in a conversation until a deeper level is achieved and help them find ways to do this.

Loyalty

Sensitive persons are generally loyal, in that they do not like to betray others or leave a relationship that still has potential. The drawback of this, of course, is that they may stay too long in hopelessly flawed relationships, or the other may not reciprocate this level of caring or even exploit it. Loyalty in a relationship remains, however, a valuable quality and deserves praise even if you also must point out the drawbacks of it at times.

Sensitive patients are going to be very loyal to the therapeutic relationship, too, and they may need help to know it is all right to leave it when they are ready. Indeed, you can teach a new kind of loyalty, in which they are loyal in their fond thoughts of your special relationship but do not have to remain loyal in the sense of always being present.

Bottom Line: All sensitive patients bring assets to their relationships (e.g., empathy, depth, loyalty), including to the therapeutic relationship. Do not take these assets for granted, but rather highlight them when appropriate.

DIFFICULTIES MEETING PEOPLE

One of the most frequent complaints of sensitive persons is their difficulty meeting people with whom they would like to form a relationship. If they are introverts, like 70% of highly sensitive persons are, some of this difficulty will be due to their not being out among others enough. Or they may be shy due to past rejections. In addition, sensitive persons can be rather choosy about who they want to get to know. They are easily bored by superficial conversation, irritated by behaviors others would not notice, and quick to sense values and attitudes with which they disagree. These three difficulties typical of highly sensitive persons—avoiding overstimulation, shyness, and finding no one suitable—require quite different approaches. Sensitive patients, like all patients, will have their own issues due to their personal experiences, which will intertwine with their sensitivity and create additional problems, such as fear of loss or betrayal. Still, some general points and advice can be made about each of these difficulties.

Dealing With Overstimulation

As for the first problem—the overstimulating nature of getting to know people, especially in a "busy" environment—sensitive patients can best deal with this by being more selective about where and when they meet. It may help to meet new people during an activity involving something else, such as taking a course or joining a book discussion group. The process of getting to know another is not confronted head on, but gradually.

Rather than frequenting happy hours, for example, suggest the patient allow friends to introduce him or her to new people, one at a time. A quiet dinner of three or four provides the time to relax and get to know another person. The right friend will naturally screen out those who would not be a good fit, bring out the sensitive person's strengths, help with the initial conversation, and generally reduce the overarousal because of being familiar and supportive. The next step would be a one-on-one chat, again, at some quiet place. Your sensitive patient could have a few ideas of what to talk about—preferably questions about the other person that would open up to more topics. If they do meet someone in a highly stimulating place, they can at least appreciate the effect of it on them, expect less of themselves, and find ways to alter immediate aspects of the setting or compensate for it—for example, suggesting a walk outside or looking for a quiet spot inside.

Bottom Line: Avoiding overstimulation is a common reason for sensitive patients not to meet new potential friends, but once understood, there are many practical solutions.

Shyness

The second problem, shyness, is obviously more complex. First, I do not use the term unless the patient does, and I make certain that patients truly do have a chronic fear of social evaluation and are not calling themselves shy when actually referring to their sensitivity. Everyone fears or avoids social judgment, the essence of shyness. Maybe even Bill Clinton was shy when meeting Queen Elizabeth for the first time. People are called shy if they have this fear chronically, but this is a case where the diagnosis does more harm than good. Explore the specific situations in which they feel shy and the underlying feelings they are having, and also the situations in which they are not shy, experiences often forgotten.

Point out that overarousal can be mistaken for shyness. In a study I mentioned in Chapter 3 by Brodt and Zimbardo (1981), "dispositionally shy" women were assigned to two conditions—in both they were to converse with an attractive male confederate while they were exposed to high frequency noise. In one they were told the noise would create "side effects" of heart pounding and rapid pulse, common correlates of arousal and shyness. The others were told the side effects of the noise would be dry mouth and tremors, uncommon correlates of arousal and shyness. The misinformed women remained very shy, but those able to attribute their arousal to the noise were not shy at all. They talked easily, enjoyed the interaction, and readily agreed to converse with a stranger again if needed for another experiment. Further, the male confederate, not knowing what the women were told or about their dispositions, usually had no idea that these women were shy. I mention this study to shy patients because even when they are certain they were not just overaroused, it does make clear that even chronic or "dispositional" shyness is governed by our view of a situation.

Often some simple cognitive-behavioral methods can help enormously. But be careful of asking them to think what they know is not true—for example, that no one is noticing them. They know people do judge others all the time, some negatively. The needed change is in accepting negative judgments to be inaccurate or only superficially true. Yes, they are not as talkative as others, but not because they are boring or "not cool." They have great depths. It simply takes time to get to know them. Of course everything already said about helping them with low self-esteem and handling criticism applies here.

There are many books, Web sites, and clinics that offer help with shyness, and a few now take into account temperament. Some of the advice will be helpful, but again, patients should be forewarned that some will be too aggressive, like boot camp. Some will have goals they do not share—perhaps learning to "work a room" and be popular—or try to motivate clients with dire predictions of how bad life will be if they never conquer their problem. Basic social skills are often what is taught, which can be boring or insulting to a sensitive person, who usually has the skills. They will profit most, probably, from simply having a supportive place in which to become more at ease when meeting new people. The chapter on "The Slide Into Shy" in *The Highly Sensitive Person* (Aron, 1996) could also be helpful.

Being highly conscientious, they may do well with gradual desensitization through graded homework tasks. One sensitive adolescent, a thousand miles away at a 2-week program for college-bound high school students, called me to say he felt hopelessly lonely and wanted to come home immediately. Feeling desperate, I risked asking him to agree to a contract with me that he could leave in 3 days with my blessing if on each of those days he had a conversation with someone new. I knew he might not be able to follow through, but he also had come to trust me, so as it happened he did the assignment and stayed.

In all of this you should be gentle, patient, choose goals that can be met, provide a thoughtful analysis of perceived failures, and perhaps offer your own experiences of feeling shy to normalize it and tell how you managed the feelings.

When shyness arises from patients' deep sense of worthlessness and many prior rejections, beginning with their own parents, shyness will begin to heal first in your relationship. Indeed, the ability to open up to potential closeness with you and then with others may be the best measure of progress for these patients, and I keep it foremost in their minds with the analogy that social contact is like food, a true necessity. Without it, anyone will begin to feel strange and weak. Usually one has a meal or two every day, and a feast once a week or so. When a whole meal is not available, you fill up on frequent snacks—smiling at someone passing by, being friendly with someone waiting on you, or chatting with others while you stand in line. If it "tastes good," you follow up with more nibbles. If you are not getting enough food, that is serious. Human contact, some of it intimate, is necessary for everyone, no matter how sensitive.

Bottom Line: Patients need to distinguish sensitivity from shyness and understand that even when shyness is chronic, it is a state of mind determined by the situation and not a permanent attribute. Use whatever available methods you prefer for reducing shyness, but adjust them for sensitivity.

Finding No One Suitable

The third problem, sensitive patients being particular about whom they want to meet, can be a true difficulty or a defensive stance. It often is hard for them to find people who both appreciate them and think as deeply as they do. Some sensitive people lean toward intellectual depth, some toward deeper feelings, but they always hunger for something that nonsensitive persons may or may not want. Even if the nonsensitive person is attracted to this depth, they may not be able to give back as much as the sensitive person wants.

Sensitive persons who are also high sensation seekers have an even harder time meeting people who are both sensitive enough and adventuresome enough. If they have found a career, such as journalism, that suits both aspects, they often find their friends and a partner in their field. But it is a serious problem throughout their lives.

The highly gifted have a similar problem finding peers, and many sensitive persons are also highly gifted. In both cases, they have to accept that no single relationship will meet all of their various needs at once.

A few sensitive persons are so busy with other interests and frustrated by the combination of rejection and boredom that they do not value time spent meeting new people. They may need reminding that even if they have a few good friends, friendships can end for various reasons, such as moves, so it works best to be constantly shopping just a little.

Sometimes the problem of finding no one interesting is solved by seeking out other sensitive persons. These are remarkably easy for any sensitive person to identify, once the patient realizes he or she thinks much like the other does. The introverted ones can be found at the edge of the party, watching. Both introverts and extroverts will be found, for example, at places of natural beauty, art workshops, spiritual retreats, concerts, lectures on complex subjects, seminars on psychology, meetings regarding social causes, in the vicinity of children and animals, or in places of healing. They will not often be found when these settings become noisy and crowded, but they will be somewhere in the background or otherwise involved. There are a few activities specifically for sensitive persons (listed on my Web site, hsperson.com). Of course two people being highly sensitive is no guarantee whatsoever that they will like each other.

Perhaps the most important way to help sensitive patients get over their reluctance to try to meet others is to emphasize that they do not have to approach the problem as the nonsensitive do. There is no need to force themselves to go through speed dating. Nor do they need to criticize themselves for caution in social situations or for starting out by observing. Sometimes I joke that "We don't make good first impressions, but we make terrific second impressions." In short, they need to find their own way of meeting others.

Of course these feelings of disdain for others and for ordinary social situations may be defensive—a platform over a dark hole of inferiority. In these cases there will be problems in their current relationships as well. The defense is working—no one is being allowed close enough to discover their supposed worthlessness—but the cost is too high. It can be tempting to break through this nonchalance or indifference with a firm confrontation, but these patients are still highly sensitive as well. One has to tread very gently, making note of his or her own admittance of the problem.

Example Dialogue

The following is a typical dialogue between a patient and therapist working on the issue of meeting people.

Patient: You think I'm shy. A social misfit.

Therapist: I don't recall ever using the word "misfit." I was only reflecting on what you said a minute ago, that you doubted if there had ever been a time when you were at ease with anyone.

Patient: Well, other people feel at ease, so I'm a misfit.

Therapist: To never have been at ease with anyone. ... As I said before, I think everyone feels ill at ease sometimes. If you feel it all the time, you must be feeling uncomfortable right now, with me.

Patient: Don't take it personally. I'm not at ease with anyone. But it's not shyness. Like you said, shyness is a kind of fear of other people. I don't fear people.

Therapist: So it's another type of feeling. Since you are feeling it right now, maybe we can figure out what it is.

Patient: I don't know. I never could figure it out.

Therapist: But you feel it now, so maybe we can figure it out together. Does it feel good or bad?

Patient: As I said, I'm used to it. But, well, bad I suppose—"ill" at ease doesn't sound too good, does it? Sick.

Therapist: Are you saying that you see this feeling as almost a kind of illness?

Patient: No, it's not. It's not a weakness. It's almost a kind of strength.

Therapist: I sense that having a weakness of any kind would be very hard for you.

Patient: Doesn't everybody feel that way?

Therapist: Not at those times when they want to improve themselves in some way. You don't want to feel ill at ease. So to do that, you have to start by knowing what needs to change. What is this illness that is not ease? You thought sensitivity was a weakness and now agree it is not.

Patient: Not always. Sometimes it is.

Therapist: In this case I think it could be a strength. Being sensitive means processing things deeply, so perhaps we can use that strength to notice what's behind this feeling you have right now.

Patient: That's what I'm paying you to do, to figure this out.

Therapist: But it's not easy for any sensitive person, even me, to listen to someone and immediately know why they feel bad. Why you feel bad right now about being with me. It means talking, as we are doing, about deep, long-standing issues. Weaknesses even. Without falling into feeling that you are utterly worthless. Some kind of misfit.

Patient: So the issue is not if I'm a jerk, but what causes this "not feeling at ease with anyone."

Therapist: Exactly.

Patient: And exactly how that feels, how bad that feels.

Therapist: "Exact" is the word, isn't it? Looking at it very closely and seeing it for whatever it is.

Patient: So yeah, it's fear. I suppose I'm afraid of what people are thinking about me. That they don't like what they see. That even you don't like me.
Therapist: Even me …

Bottom Line: The highly sensitive can have a genuine difficulty meeting people they would enjoy getting to know better, as well as a defensive lack of interest due to an especially heightened fear of rejection.

DIFFICULTY WITH THE DEEPENING STAGE OF RELATIONSHIPS

Patients whose relationships never proceed past a few meetings or that only last a few months are always a challenge, especially when they do not see the problem as residing in themselves. With sensitive patients, especially some sensitive men, it is always possible that the problem is not so much due to them as to prejudices against them. For many others, the problem is simply not knowing how to move forward, taking the necessary risks, and trusting their feelings.

Initial Difficulties Experienced by Almost All Sensitive Persons

Mutual self-disclosure is central to deepening any relationship, but it requires taking many risks—of doing it prematurely, revealing something the other dislikes, or becoming disillusioned with each other. The highly sensitive do not like high risks with such uncertain outcomes, so it can be helpful to teach them some techniques to reduce the risks. For example, self-disclosure ought to be enough to maintain the other's interest, but not too much to be overwhelming or seem odd. Above all, it should match the self-disclosing of the other person, and then advance further when it seems right. Their excellent intuition should help here. They can grasp the advantages of being bold and jumping ahead to discovering a mutual fondness that was not there before.

We all know the steps toward intimacy, but it helps to make them explicit to patients. There is the initial chatting about the weather and movies, then the mutual disclosures about careers or where they live or came from. If things proceed well, there can be a bit more intimacy—about mutual likes and dislikes, opinions, feelings. Then the feelings discussed become more personal and immediate, such as a recent loss or success. A huge step is expressing feelings about the other—exchanging sincere compliments or the sense of pleasure being in each other's company. Ultimately there are those moments of deepest honesty when we know we can say anything, even about something not working well in the relationship, or how well it is working, or how lucky we feel. Each feels received and valued by the other. If highly sensitive persons have experienced such intimacy, either in the past or in the therapeutic relationship, and they see what is required to re-create it elsewhere, they can be very skilled and motivated to plunge ahead and lead others toward these depths.

Bottom Line: Progressing toward a deeper relationship requires mutual self-disclosure, which highly sensitive patients may avoid due to the risks involved. Actually, they should be able to manage this especially well, once they sense the goal, which should appeal to them especially.

When There Are Stronger Fears of Closeness and Commitment

For many patients, of course, the process of growing closer may be blocked at any point by fears that are more complex than those of rejection. These are fears of success—of becoming close and eventually losing the other, for example. Some of these fears are natural to the highly sensitive; some arise as they interact with childhood experiences.

Case Illustration

Steve, 53, had lost his first wife when he was only 30, while they were still childless. He felt his loss was long resolved and desperately wanted to remarry. In fact, he had been in and out of numerous relationships. Early on I had provided him with a too-easy excuse, in that he was both a high sensation seeker and highly sensitive, so that it was naturally difficult to find someone similar on both counts. However, each relationship began and ended and it became clear to us both that he was avoiding a new relationship as much as he wanted one, by spoiling each with his unspoken criticism of the other, which would soon become outspoken. This hardly endeared him to the woman, but by then he would be convinced she was wrong for him anyway. But underneath this, he was afraid of losing another beloved, of not loving his next wife as much as his first, and at the same time fearing the other would not love him as much as his first wife had. Further, he was aware of his natural quickness to notice flaws and that this hardly made him a desirable partner.

The problem was further complicated by his early home environment. Steve had been the only child of parents who loved him well enough, but disliked each other. Early on he won the oedipal conflict, in that his mother clearly loved him more, making this sensitive boy her special confidant. However, she put him aside when his father came home at the end of the day, because the father was highly critical of Steve's mother and she was trying to avoid his anger. Seeing this, Steve lost respect for her even while he loved receiving her special attention when they were alone together. His father, seeing Steve as effeminate only because he lacked an interest in sports, did nothing to pull his son out of his childish romance with his mother but rather consigned him to it. Steve came to associate his father's lack of interest and being a "mama's boy" with his sensitivity.

As he reached adulthood, it was his mother rather than his father who told him he would not be a "real man" until he lived on his own. As it is for many sensitive patients, living alone was a frightening idea. He was so used to his parental home being a shelter from an overstimulating world that he did not really know how to cope with it. Still, he set out to be a man, with his father as the only available model, but determined to have a partner as soon as possible, one who would re-create his early maternal paradise without the danger of his father coming home.

He was amazed by his luck in the second endeavor, until the sudden death of his young wife. As much as he wanted a third paradise, the project seemed doomed. Besides all of his other fears, we saw that he felt he was not man enough, and even if he were, fate (or his father?) was not going to allow it. Of course, again, he was the one dooming each relationship. He feared he would either lose the woman early on or she would live long enough to discover his unmanliness.

As our relationship became more like that first paradise, he tried to destroy it as well, with all sorts of caustic criticisms. This was not paradise—either I had to be worthless or he was. But this time we both understood the fear he was covering up. Further, I accepted and admired his sensitivity and saw him as no less of a man for it. Nor did I die or seem likely to. This time he was able to stay with someone until some of the idealization wore off, without the relationship being destroyed either. Most important, he was the one who controlled the ending, and he did terminate when he found another good-enough woman with whom he could share a semiparadise for many years to come.

The lesson for me from this complicated case was that there can be multiple reasons for avoiding the closeness that sensitive persons often claim to want. Further, bringing them into consciousness can take a patient a long way toward overcoming those fears because of their often-unusual ability to appreciate and counter their own defenses.

Fears of Long-Term Closeness and Commitment

A whole crop of reasonable worries also sprout up around commitment to a closer relationship, especially because it is the essential nature of sensitive persons to consider long-term consequences. I discuss these fears at length in *The Highly Sensitive Person in Love* (Aron, 2001). Again, many patients will also go beyond these normal fears that are intensified by their trait, as did Steve, and bring up issues that have interfered with closeness throughout their lives. Steve had also been having trouble maintaining friendships and staying at one job, but of course sensitive patients can turn out to be absolutely justified in their hesitations about committing to someone and have this insight more frequently than most people. It is important to consider whether the caution is specific to this relationship or has been repeating.

There are at least eight apprehensions that can arise, and I will make brief suggestions about resolving each. First, there is the dread of exposure and rejection—the core self, or simply the sensitive part—seems shameful. This was certainly so in Steve's case. Sometimes it helps to remind them that everyone feels that their own particular flaws and sins are worse than anyone else's. Because they have lived so long with the sense that something is wrong with them, it will require extra effort to reduce this fear. Hopefully it can be addressed in part by the therapeutic relationship and in part by an increasing ability to notice acceptance when it is occurring.

The second fear is of separation and loss, especially the other's death. Very often this has been dissociated and at first can only be inferred from the history—in Steve's case, the loss of his wife—or else from the reaction when the therapist goes away. I emphasize to them what a deeply instinctual response this is. The fear can be very intense, but once it is more conscious it can become a focus of the work and eventually coped with.

Third is the fear of abandonment or betrayal—a separation deliberately caused by the other. Most often this fear arises because it has actually happened and thus is very resistant to extinction, especially in a sensitive person. Most likely only time with a new, more loving person will reestablish trust.

A fourth is the fear of conflict—that one must capitulate for the sake of peace or endure endless overarousing shouting matches. (In the next chapter I will discuss how to help sensitive persons deal with conflict and the fear of it.) Steve was typical of many in that he "could dish it out" to each woman he dated and then to me, but he was deeply hurt when criticized in return. Other patients will never express any criticism, much less anger, fearing counterattacks or feeling they are unworthy to judge anyone else.

Fifth, sensitive persons can worry about the gravity of the responsibility to the other and perhaps in addition the consequent loss of independence. Can I earn enough money to support two if necessary? Can I be a good parent? Will committing interfere with my creative goals? Will it just make me like everyone else? None of this should be taken lightly. Some sensitive people with troubled backgrounds really could be overwhelmed if too many responsibilities came with the particular type of committed relationships they are considering. In particular watch for them trying to rescue someone. It is also true that some gifted sensitive persons are not meant to be in a committed relationship because too much of their soul is being given to something else. But they do need to be reminded of the regret they may feel later, and the loneliness—the high cost of rebelling against the family context in which humans were designed to live.

Related to this fear of responsibility and lost freedom is the worry of being controlled, engulfed, or smothered—the self being obliterated. Sensitive children are especially damaged by narcissistic, intrusive, overinvolved parents, usually at the root of this sixth fear. Of course avoiding closeness with everyone, often people not at all narcissistic, by one is still being controlled by these troubling people from the past.

Seventh, some sensitive persons fear their own instinctual nature—their potential for ruthlessness in their sexuality or moments of hate or complete indifference toward those they are supposed to love. Both the fear and the instincts are often below the threshold of consciousness—but not quite far enough. Sensitive persons need to appreciate these as instincts found in everyone and controllable.

Finally, some fear their irritability or criticalness, often a justifiable worry. For example, sensitive persons are easily irritated by habits or noises that would not bother others. Usually these criticisms are not voiced, but in an intimate relationship they will have to come out and perhaps make the other justifiably angry at being held to a higher standard, as the other person probably has no problem with the sensitive person's minor idiosyncrasies. Patients need to learn to quell some of this to get along with anyone. Being close always leads to some irritations. It is natural for sensitive persons to notice these things more, but by focusing on what they like about the other, they can often let some of them slide.

For other sensitive persons the fear of their own irritability is highly exaggerated—they feel it but rarely express it. They fear rejection for even thinking the negative thoughts that naturally come or expressing a few of the complaints sensitive persons naturally have, such as "Could you speak more softly?" So rather than live with irritations, they live alone. They think that because of their misanthropy they are simply unsuited for relationships. Again, sometimes the therapeutic relationship is the first place that these fears can be faced, when they are able to utter their criticisms and find that the relationship and some of the idealization survives.

With all of these fears, the carrot works better than the stick—the carrot being the need we all have for closeness as opposed to the stick of trying to push patients past their fears and possibly helping them make a serious error. This is almost not a metaphor, in that in my experience with horses—animals that are extremely sensitive to danger—when they refuse to do something, it is usually due to fear. Yet because they stubbornly resist and "win," being bigger than their rider, it is tempting to hit them with a whip, harder and harder. But this only increases the horse's fear. On the other hand, one strategy that works is to offer a carrot or handful of grass. This will often calm a horse—it is hard to munch while in terror—and then the fear can be faced again and often overcome. For sensitive patients, repeated appropriate, honest compliments and reassurances can have the same effect.

Bottom Line: There are a number of natural fears about committing to greater closeness as well as real reasons for hesitation. Sensitive persons will feel these far more deeply and the therapist must work with their fear patiently.

Making the Big Decision

It should be emphasized again that even if all of these other fears have been thought through, many sensitive persons will hesitate, rightly, to make the deeper commitment that especially arises in the case of choosing to live with a person, marry, or have children. They *know* the responsibilities involved. They know their own emotional and physical limits, especially their need for time alone. If they are taking on financial responsibilities, they may not like doing what is required to earn more. Even in the case of becoming much closer in a friendship, they know the vast importance of the role they are considering. So they may simply let time pass, sometimes so long that the opportunity is lost.

They need to be reminded that the burdens will be shared and that no one expects someone to take on all the responsibility for another's life, financial or otherwise, or to be given unstinted time and attention. Even children need this type of care for only a decade or so.

Naturally they will also have doubts about whether they are choosing the right person, or whether they will conceive a child with some genetic problem that will be an impossible lifetime burden for the patient. Here they need to be reminded that certain important decisions in life are laced with uncertainty, yet we still have to decide. Deciding not to decide is also a form of deciding.

Bottom Line: There are good reasons to fear committing to a long-term relationship and these will be stronger in highly sensitive patients, but both you and your patient much remember the consequences of continuing in a state of indecision and letting a good opportunity pass.

SUMMARY AND CONCLUSION

Temperament has a powerful impact on relationships. Sensitive persons specifically bring assets to a pair such as their ability to notice subtle cues from the partner or signs that the relationship needs attention, plus a preference for intimacy and staying together. If a patient does exhibit these assets with the therapist, they deserve acknowledgment.

Often these patients are struggling to enter relationships because of their "shyness." Sometimes they are not even truly shy but only introverted and sensitive. In these cases the problem is solved by their better understanding their sensitivity, which leads to increased confidence and a reframing of their past social behaviors. Other patients' fear of judgment will have deeper roots and require more time to resolve.

Once in a relationship, their fears of making a stronger commitment are partly quite understandable. For example, they may fear losing their independence, committing with the wrong person, or being unable to meet all the responsibilities involved. It is admirable that they are reflecting on these long-term implications, but waiting and doing nothing becomes a decision as well. The therapist has to see that all their fears of commitment are openly discussed.

Throughout this chapter I have imagined the many extroverted, secure, highly sensitive people I know who would be appalled by any suggestion to therapists that high sensitivity necessarily leads to shyness or a paralyzing fear of commitment. Again, I am speaking of difficulties frequently encountered in sensitive *patients*. Generally their shyness comes from painful social experiences in childhood and overall poor parenting, which then leads to depression and anxiety, and then to shyness (Aron et al., 2006). Without that history, sensitive persons are no more shy than others.

The importance of this chapter lies in the obvious fact that we are social animals, with strong social emotions, including anger and despair due to loss; shame; fear of rejection; and, above all, loneliness. For those reasons, sensitive persons undoubtedly benefit from having secure, supportive, long-term relationships even more than the general population and suffer more from the lack of them. Hence working with sensitive patients to improve their ability to relate to others may be the most important task and goal for their therapy.

CHAPTER

7

Helping Long-Term Relationships

Working With Conflicts, Degree of Temperament Similarity, and Sensitive Sexuality

> An attentive observer might have discovered that the elder daughter was rather more the darling of her parents than the younger. Her parents' esteem was due to the special kind of sensitiveness which this daughter displayed ... just those things which, because of their contradictory and slightly unbalanced character, make a person specially charming.
>
> —**Carl Jung (*Collected Works,* Vol. 4, para. 384)**

This chapter continues to consider the relationships of the highly sensitive, with a focus on the issues arising in long-term friendships and with romantic life partners, such as negotiating conflicts and reluctance to leave bad relationships. There are suggestions for resolving problems encountered by a sensitive patient with a nonsensitive partner and also those of a pair of sensitive persons. The chapter concludes with the results of a survey comparing sexuality in sensitive and nonsensitive persons.

As Jung suggests, sensitive persons can be very appealing to others, especially in a long-term relationship, as in a family or marriage. Your goal as a therapist is to bring out those qualities in your sensitive patients that make them successful in their closest relationships.

IS DIVORCE GENETICALLY DETERMINED?

In a surprising study that drives home the clinical importance of temperament, McGue and Lykken (1996) found in a sample of twins (used to study the influence of heredity vs. environment) that 53% of the variance in divorce risk is attributable to the genetic contribution of one spouse (the twin in this study). In a follow-up twin study, Jockin, McGue, and Lykken (1996) used self-report personality tests to measure traits known to be somewhat heritable. (Heritable means there is some genetic influence on a variable, but does not mean there is a specific gene for it—there is no gene for wearing skirts but it is highly heritable because of its link to gender.) Positive emotionality and negative emotionality were associated with divorce rate, while constraint was negatively related. Overall, some heritable personality traits, measured in some way by these tests, contributed to 30% of the divorce risk in women and 42% of the risk in men.

What is heritable about divorce? The negative effects of positive emotionality are probably attributable to high sensation seeking, since both are related to dopamine levels (Canli, 2008). Persons high in sensation seeking are known to be more easily bored in a relationship and likely to have an affair (Seto, Lalumiere, & Quinsey, 1995). As for the role of negative emotionality, I would expect it to have had its impact by way of the interaction already described. Something innate, sensitivity, interacts with a difficult past, something not innate, leading to chronic negative emotionality, and chronic negative affect (also called neuroticism) is known to be the largest single predictor of low marital satisfaction (Karney & Bradbury, 1997). The trait associated with less divorce, constraint, would certainly be another way of describing sensitivity, and it is my experience that sensitive persons think long and hard before leaving a relationship. In short, in a variety of ways innate temperament contributes to relationship longevity.

However, these findings do not indicate that divorce itself is innate or that *any* gene *causes* divorce. Just as in medicine, certain innate conditions become dangerous if not recognized, but otherwise are easily treated, so these innate personality traits probably become threats to relationships only when partners do not understand the role of their own and the other's unchangeable aspects so that they can make appropriate compensations. Being able to suggest how this is done gives a therapist important leverage for improving patients' relationships.

Bottom Line: Almost half of the risk of divorce is probably determined by innate temperament, which manifests as personality traits that have developed through genetic tendencies in interaction with the environment. A risk of divorce can be reduced when couples understand how to compensate for their temperaments.

LONG-TERM RELATIONSHIPS: GENERAL ISSUES

First, of course, we all have to be very careful about "helping" a relationship by discussing it with only one of the partners. (As in the previous chapter, everything here applies to family and friends as well.) The other person *always* has a different, equally important story to tell, and both contribute in some way to every problem. Having said this, I still do much work with sensitive partners on their relationships. On the one hand, they often have unusual insight and influence in these relationships. On the other hand, they may be in unusual difficulties, such as being the "identified patient" (even more than they ought to be) because of their sensitivity or failing to assert themselves enough. In any case, very often their own changes and insights help their relationships dramatically.

Case Illustration

Bella, 32, had met Jerry in Europe, where both were touring after graduation—Bella, Phi Beta Kappa from an excellent university; Jerry, an art major with attitude, from an indifferent state college. But each found the other fascinating from the first meeting, and they fell in love. They came back to the United States and worked as interns for various organization for several years, then settled "on the land," growing their own organic food and marijuana. The use of the latter was a part of their relationship from the outset. They both smoked daily.

Bella spoke often of how much she loved Jerry—he was attentive, funny, and highly creative. His goal in life was to become a successful cartoonist, and meanwhile he made some money painting signs and selling some of their produce. To her, the only cloud was a bright one: They hated to be separated from each other. As she put it, "Jerry is *not* my problem."

The problem was her "whole life," and she thought it might be related to her sensitivity. She taught in the elementary grades and thought this work important, but hated the noise and confusion in the classroom plus the inevitable tensions with parents and administrators. I asked her what she might do if she could do anything and received a quick answer: "Get my doctorate in history, then teach at a small college and on the side write books for travelers about the history of medieval sites in the various regions of France." But she and Jerry needed a steady income, so she had earned a teaching certificate instead.

Bella grew up in a large, well-to-do family in which noise—especially in the form of loud, bitter fighting—was constant. Her father criticized everyone and her mother raged back at him, to little avail. Bella was proud that she and Jerry were not repeating that sort of relationship. I asked whether she hoped to have children herself, and she appeared confused. She did, very much, but worried that she might unwittingly raise children as unhappy as she had been. As for Jerry, during his early years his family was very poor. He was an only child who had actually witnessed his father's death when Jerry was 5 years old. Then he had to deal with a succession of three domineering stepfathers. He also had some hesitations about having children. I noted to myself that given her age, the decision would have to be made soon.

Assessing the Relationship

Sensitive persons, because of their emotional intensity, tend to express themselves at the extremes about their relationships—they may know they need it so much that they do not want it analyzed, so they see it as and say it is almost perfect; or they are feeling the pain of it so deeply that they sound like they could be describing hell. Asking about their love for the other may yield some nonverbal information. The verbal response can be far from the truth. Some think of love as a virtue; some as an emotion they may or may not feel at the moment; some as a need or desire to be near the other no matter what; and some as the sense of attachment after years of proximity, which one can feel even for someone awful. A better definition of love for the therapist and patient is more like the degree of responsiveness—wanting to know the other and to meet the other's needs as much as possible (while not ignoring one's own most central needs, at least without negotiating first as equals).

In Bella's case, I suspected she was more loving in the responsive sense to Jerry than vice versa, although that was a risky assumption to make without hearing his side of it. After all, given that she had never lived on her own (even her trip to Europe had been with a brother), I suspected her love was equally or more of a desperate attachment. So, as I usually do, I assessed her relationship in terms of behaviors and attitudes, about which sensitive patients will attempt to be conscientiously objective. How much time did they spend together? ("All their free time," although that did not fit with Jerry's drawing cartoons until late at night and sleeping in while she was having to arise early and go to work, not seeing him in the mornings on weekdays.) How much did they confide in each other? ("Everything," but they had not yet discussed at all her worries about her "biological clock" or her dream of a doctorate.) What about sex? (Jerry liked a lot of sex; she did not discuss with me her differing needs until specifically asked about it.) Does the patient feel fulfilled sexually? (Her orgasms usually "fizzled," something else Jerry did not know.)

John Gottman (1999; Gottman & Notarius, 2000), a specialist in research on couple interaction, advises couples to get to know each other's "love map," or depth of knowledge of the other. He also sees it as an excellent assessment tool. Some of the "geography questions" are: "I can name my partner's best friends" (1999, p. 50); stresses he or she is under; his or her life dreams, philosophy of life, favorite music, least liked relatives; and so forth. Often sensitive patients can give the answers about their partner, but know their partner could not do the same. As one might guess, that was the case with Bella, but she was not interested in working on this with Jerry. Filling in the details of the love map is a way to increase closeness, and resistance suggests how poorly the relationship is going.

Bottom Line: Expect highly sensitive patients to speak in extremes about their relationships, so assess as much as possible from actual behaviors (allowing for the fact you are hearing only one partner's perceptions). Sensitive patients will usually strive to be objective about behaviors.

Love and Power

Paradoxically, in a love relationship the power issues can be even more important than love—how the pair deals with scarce resources, such as attention, time, and money, or how they resolve conflicts about, for example, child-rearing philosophies. Sensitive patients are often the less powerful of a pair. They tend to feel inferior, and their partners may have come to assume this as well. Partners have often learned quite unconsciously to take advantage of the sensitive person's desire to avoid overarousal by escalating conflicts to the point where they know the sensitive partner will give in. Plus, sensitive persons are slower to think of counter-arguments in the heat of the moment. And they often have the philosophy that letting the other have his or her way is somehow more moral. Indeed, in a certain way they may come to enjoy submitting—at least they can feel kinder, more virtuous. More often, they are hoping some day to be paid back for their generosity, whereas usually this becomes less likely as the other settles in to enjoy the favored position.

Even in basically good relationships, most partners are using power maneuvers without identifying them as such and have too much to lose by not changing their ways once the less powerful partner points out the unfairness. Achieving greater equality is a worthwhile goal, since as Gottman (1999) points out, happy and unhappy couples have the same number of unresolved conflicts—they differ in how they deal with them. If each feels heard and the resolution seems fair, the conflict can be tolerated within a larger context of mutual caring. There is further reason to deal with power issues and conflicts in that, as I said regarding the heritability of divorce, many conflicts arise due to temperament differences that seem irresolvable because partners do not know what each could change and not change.

At Gottman points out, at one time we taught partners reflective listening skills, but now we know that it is equally important, especially for the less powerful partner, to learn to speak his or her needs and reasons for them clearly. It helps to think of a need or desire coming with an attached number from 1 to 10 rating of how important it is to the one having it, along with the costs to the other to meet it. A fair outcome can only be determined by hearing each other out enough to know these ratings. Further, the couple must assess the valences not by how loudly or persuasively the need is asserted, but by the actual feelings and results of each course of action.

For example, Dick, a strong-willed, outspoken lawyer and father wanted his newborn son to be baptized Catholic, but sensitive, soft-spoken Lela, my patient, felt passionately about their son being raised in her Jewish tradition, beginning with circumcision. Dick did not believe in the key tenets of the Christian faith and never went to mass. He knew his son would receive no religious teachings from him, but his mother had been opposed to the marriage and made him promise that her grandson would be raised Catholic. Originally Lela agreed to this without telling her parents, but when their son was born the decision had to be made about circumcision or baptism, and Lela went into a deep depression. Dick said it was postpartum depression. I listened to her feelings about disappointing her loving extended family, who celebrated all of the Jewish holidays together and looked forward to their first grandson's bar mitzvah in 13 years. So I referred them to a trusted couples therapist who was willing to see them immediately. I knew that in therapy each would have to hear the other's feelings and base their decision on needs and feelings, not the loudest voice or most well-argued case. The therapist used the 1 to 10 scale to weigh what each of them would feel if the decision was made one way or another. The scale weighs feelings about both gains and losses for each because they can be different. Dick's own feelings having a Catholic son was a 2, and his loss would be having to tell his mother, a 5. For Lela, the gain for having a Jewish son was 10, and the loss was equally high. Their son was raised in her tradition after all.

Sensitive patients often need help appreciating their rights to their needs and to setting boundaries about fulfilling others' needs. As stated before, they begin life with thinner boundaries because of their awareness of the needs of other, and many have given up even those boundaries long ago in order to see the other happy, to submit to someone threatening, or simply to avoid being left alone. Sometimes it takes years to prepare for taking a stand. One way therapists can help is by being a role model in exemplifying how their own needs have been met while being kind but firm about boundaries.

When sensitive patients are ready to stand up for themselves, they still need practice learning what to say. At this point, their partners have well-developed comebacks for everything. Sometimes I role play dialogues, letting the patient be his or her partner while I demonstrate ways to respond. I emphasize that the subject can always be brought up again with the partner if the patient feels he or she left out an important point.

Bottom Line: Sensitive patients usually need help seeing the power issues in their relationships and exerting their rights.

Bella Stands Up to Jerry

Bella eventually admitted that smoking marijuana was both endangering her livelihood as a public schoolteacher and an obstacle to doing more with her life, in that she felt it "deadened" her to her own long-term goals. As she experimented with smoking only on weekends, she found she was dreaming again, which was important to her because whenever she had dreams and we discussed them, she found it very helpful. She also had more and better orgasms without pot. Because marijuana does not completely leave the body in a week's time, she began using it even less.

Now Jerry was nervous. He felt they were going to drift apart without pot to bind them. And it was true that they were accustomed to getting high when she came home from work, then having a mellow dinner together before he returned to drawing cartoons and she cleaned up.

I tried to stay neutral as she went back and forth about their use—again, it is my experience that the conflict needs to stay inside the patient rather than be split between the patient and the therapist, with the therapist the enforcer of the more conservative option. We often made contact with the part of her that did not want to upset Jerry, a little girl who was afraid to live without him and loved his playful ways and especially the fun they had on marijuana. But that little girl had other needs, to feel truly valued and to resume her development, and Bella felt those needs were not being met.

One day she announced she was giving up marijuana entirely, and even more drastic, wanted Jerry to stop. She said that she thought they both knew his cartooning was not at a professional level—it was a literal "pipe dream" that kept him from thinking about his actual future. She believed he had considerable talent but needed to attend art school. Her vision now was for them to live close to a city where they could both go to graduate school, supported by student loans. After that they would need "real jobs" to pay off the loans and start a family. But she wanted to take charge of her life right now, with or without him.

Then the storm began. She repeatedly backed down as Jerry argued persuasively against city life, for public school teaching being more socially valuable then studying medieval history, for his cartooning being ruined by formal training, and on and on. Because Bella could not think of answers in the moment, she discussed with me how she would respond next time. They could live in the country again in the future. She found it too risky being a schoolteacher with marijuana growing on their land. Teaching history at the college level had social value. If he was serious about his talent, and it was real, then it could only benefit from further training. He would gain in his ability to distinguish between what was good and what was not. Above all, she asserted that feelings are simply feelings, like the weather. They are not good or bad and cannot be ignored. She wanted to hear about his, and she did not mind suggestions, but she would not tolerate arguments that were really aimed at discounting her feelings.

Finally came the inevitable, the attack on her personality—her bookishness, moodiness, and turning into a nag like her mother. Once again she agreed at first. So I had to point out that name calling, labeling, and diagnosing are not allowed in fair fights; each must stay with the issue. As for their families of origin, she could say that Jerry was now being like his stepfathers as well as like her own father, and she could be like his mother, a doormat, or like her own mother, who fought and lost. Or she could ask him to stick with the issue rather than making these generalities and see what happened.

Next he blamed me. He said I was a bad influence. I was ruining what had been a perfectly good marriage. Again she thought this might be true, but I was able to point out that stopping smoking and going back to school were entirely her ideas. Tensions were mounting, and Bella was facing the possibility that marijuana and the country life were more important to Jerry than she was. When she questioned him more on marrying and having children, her other goal, he kept asking why things could not just stay as they had been. When she pushed on this, he said children did not fit with an artistic life.

Hearing that response, she realized she had to act, so she applied to graduate schools. When she was accepted at her first choice, she made plans to go. To her surprise, he decided to accompany her. She was delighted at first. Eventually she actually saw that she wanted to go alone unless he also agreed to marriage and starting a family after she had finished her class work but before her dissertation. He would have to agree to support them until the baby was 2—after that it would be his turn to go to school—and stop smoking marijuana, beginning immediately. To her it did not fit into the life she wanted anymore. If Jerry could not agree, she told him that she understood. These were his feelings. Meanwhile, hers were deep grief and then fear of being alone for the first time.

We continued intermittent phone sessions after she moved. The transition was extremely stressful—she had to find a place to live and then live there, alone, in the city, while starting a very difficult graduate program and knowing no one. Jerry visited often and supported her heroically, helping her find an apartment and furnishing it for her. In a year he had joined her, marijuana free. Five years later Bella gave birth to Jerry's son.

Conflict Avoidance Due to Dread of Overarousal

Frequently sensitive patients avoid conflicts or lose power in relationships because even the threat of a fight sends them into a higher level of arousal than it does their partner. Gottman (1999) found this true of men in general, but this may be particularly true of sensitive men. When anyone is overaroused, thinking is clouded and a fight often escalates into something irrational and nasty. Further, sensitive persons often know they have allowed their resentments to build. They have not wanted to bring these up, but when the big guns come out, they have more than enough ammunition to return fire and see it have very damaging results. Then, having had a negative experience with conflict, they avoid it even more.

Gottman recommended that if during a conflict either person has a pulse rate over 100—and they should learn how to take it and do so—that they take a time-out of at least 20 minutes to let the arousal drop back to normal. Sensitive patients and their partners should discuss taking time-outs ahead of time so that the rules are settled; for example, both should agree on when they will come back together. Wanting to "sleep on it" is not wise when one of them will not sleep. I also recommend that they only face conflicts when rested and not overaroused by something else, and maybe do it out of doors. A river, lake, or ocean especially puts things in perspective.

Having other "rules of warfare" are also helpful to sensitive patients, such as no name calling ("You're such a cry baby") or diagnosing ("Now you're behaving just like your father"); sticking to the current conflict rather than branching out into other grievances; not using "you do it too" or other deflecting defenses; using "I statements" and avoiding global truths ("It bothered me a lot when you left such a small tip, since it was really from both of us," instead of "you never tip enough"); and using many positive metacommunications (seven per criticism is ideal; "I wouldn't bother to bring this up if this relationship were not so important to me," or "Most of the time you are so thoughtful that it surprised me when you ..."). Finally, sensitive patients can be especially helped by shifting the conflict into the office of a skilled couples therapist who can referee, maintain an optimal level of arousal, and generally carry the hope and confidence that both individuals and the relationship can survive these painful disruptions in intimacy. That therapist should have a good understanding about the role temperament and especially sensitivity play in relationships.

Above all, the highly sensitive need to appreciate the importance of communicating openly around conflicts. They need to experience how much a relationship improves, sometimes literally overnight, once the feelings are out in the open. Indeed there can be a rebound effect in that the two love each other much more for having bridged together this frightening abyss that was between them. If this rebound happens, it should be highlighted so that it is remembered next time they fear entering into conflict. Often conflict dealt with in the therapy relationship dramatizes this positive effect especially well.

Bottom Line: Watch for conflict avoidance and provide ways of dealing with arguments that feel less catastrophic or overarousing, such as the two together developing rules that promote fair fighting.

Misuse of "My Extraordinarily High Sensitivity"

Not all sensitive patients are one-down in their relationships. Most have developed at least a few ways to use their trait to gain power, again usually unconsciously. It often helps to define power as influence in order to lessen the harshness of their self-judgments once they recognize what you are talking about. The fact is, they may have learned the power of crying in front of their partner or of being "ill" or exhausted for days after doing something they did not wish to do. In short, this type of sensitive patient can be extremely unpleasant to be around unless others cater to their needs.

Sensitive patients need to become aware of their power, even when at first they honestly cannot see that they have any. They often have astounding influence simply because of their ability to suggest the better way to do something or the problems that will result if their needs are not met. None of this is necessarily wrong to do, but it is power in the sense that power is influence, so that the inequalities in the relationship may need to be assessed. Plus, all victims of past injustices can very easily become unwitting dominators whom others do not dare cross for fear of being accused of being dominators themselves.

Once aware of their power, sensitive patients need to learn how to negotiate fairly for what they need. They must face the real costs to the other of their needs and even of their good influence. For example, their partners might simply be tired of them usually being right. Whenever the highly sensitive do agree to an activity to please the other or because they hope to enjoy it, it is essential that they take responsibility for their choice rather than become a victim. In an affection-based relationship, no one can *make* the other do anything.

Bottom Line: Help sensitive patients recognize and use their power ("influence") over their partner in ways appropriate to their values, without undue concern about upsetting the other or seeming bossy because they happen to see better what needs to be done and say so.

Discussing Their Sensitivity for the First Time

When the highly sensitive learn about their trait for the first time (or have any other insight in therapy), they are often eager to talk about it with everyone important to them, and naturally they expect an enthusiastic response. Sometimes I warn them in advance that the more a person loves them, the less delighted they may be. Sometimes it is a problem in the moment—they are full of enthusiasm and the other is thrown by it. Or the other may rightly want to know the source of this seemingly wild new idea. "Who told you this was true of you?" And the bubble has burst for the sensitive patient.

Simply bringing up a difference between two intimates almost has to create distance at first. It amounts to saying "we are less alike," and implicitly, less close. It also may suggest changes on the horizon. The power is shifting if the other is seeing new needs and the right to have them met. For example, if sensitive patients say they now understand why they do not like rock concerts, shopping malls, football games, or loud parties, and their close other has enjoyed their sharing these activities, something is going to change. From the point of view of the person who enjoyed the two of them doing these, it is not a change for the better. An especially dominant partner will immediately sense that the sensitive person is on the verge of realizing he or she has rights to assert rather than a weakness to hide. In these cases especially it is best that there be a third party, an excellent couples therapist, to help shift the relationship from one based on power to one based on love.

In other types of close relationships, parents of a sensitive adult, for example, can be particularly defensive if they feel their child is saying their parenting was damaging because they did not allow for your patient's sensitivity, or worse, had no clue about it. Parents naturally feel they know everything important about their child, or should. Great tact will be needed, something with which some patients will need help.

The key is empathy, which they should be very capable of, once they put aside their own enthusiasm and make a concerted effort to imagine how the other will take the news of their sensitivity and attune to the other's first, second, and third reactions. To be able to do this, the patient should wait until some of the initial excitement has settled. I sometimes add the dampening perspective that, although this high sensitivity seems like the most meaningful information they have ever received, in a few months they will take it into account very naturally and rarely even talk about it.

Bottom Line: Prepare the sensitive patient for a less than enthusiastic first response from partners, friends, and relatives upon hearing about the patient's newfound sensitivity.

Reluctance to Leave Unsatisfactory Relationships

Sensitive patients—particularly those with the strongest attachment issues, low self-esteem, and tendency toward depression and anxiety—tend to think they would be devastated if they had to live without their partner, no matter how bad the other is. They may feel they will not survive alone and definitely would not find anyone else. Sometimes this is actually the case, so one has to be very careful about pushing for a separation, or at least one that precedes the development of adequate internal and external support.

As with any patient, even if a relationship seems hopeless, I am very reluctant to urge he or she leave a relationship, especially if I have never even met the other person. There are times I have, however, supported a plan to leave when sensitive patients have wanted me to help them do that, but were continually backing down for the wrong reasons.

Although I tried not to side with Bella in her struggles about life decisions, once she made them, or seemed to have, I have to admit that I did enthusiastically back Bella's leaving Jerry. Even though Bella's taking action may have been the key to Jerry's changes, so that all turned out well in the end, I still was wrong about him. He became a devoted husband and responsible father.

Now, with more experience, I would not have been so one-sided even when she made up her mind, as sensitive patients especially can unmakeup their minds just as easily. Bella could easily have returned to Jerry and to pot, sensing all too accurately the emotional pain breakups entail for anyone, but that it will be worse for them. As they mull all this over, if the therapist has spoken out for separating, the patient's reverting to staying will make allies of the patient and the partner and leave you looking like the marriage ruiner, as the partner had probably been saying all along. Unless there is reason to think the relationship is simply too damaging, it is better to reflect on both sides of sensitive patients' feelings as they change back and forth, even if it takes longer for patients to leave. (But state that this is your plan, so that the patient is assured that you do care about the outcome—you simply want it to be his or her own decision.) Another great advantage of not taking a stand on one side of the patient's inner conflict is that if patients in the end cannot carry out "the right decision," they do not have to worry so much about disappointing you. (Once or twice, however, when sensitive patients have backed out of their plan many times, even though the decision felt so final and obvious, I have asked if they would like to sign a pact with me about when and how they would leave. This has worked very well because sensitive patients tend to feel strongly about keeping promises.) What matters is that you continually revisit the status of a troubled relationship, as sensitive patients may avoid the topic because either staying or going is too distressing.

Bottom Line: Most sensitive patients have difficulty making a major life decision such as leaving a long-standing abusive relationship, often reversing their position many times. Therapists should keep them focused on the decision, but try to stay neutral as long as possible so that the patient can work through the issues.

Helping Patients Discuss With Partners the Need for Change

Initiating changes or knowing whether to leave requires patients to explore the issues further with their partner. No partner deserves to be spurned or left without even being told exactly why, yet many sensitive patients will not have said anything before talking about leaving, or at least not at a "volume" that would have had any affect. When suggesting that patients bring the conflicts out into the open, I coach them about timing, avoiding a defensive reaction as much as possible, and having the right comebacks to the predictable responses from their partner. I make it clear, however, that they know the situation better than I do. It is up to them to decide whether or how to try to have such a talk at all. Especially if I have spent time making suggestions, I emphasize that I will be fine with whatever happens. Whenever a patient wants to act and utterly cannot, I indicate that this is simply more information for us to consider.

Often patients return from such attempts with a sad story of being ignored or talked out of their position. Listen for whatever argument they could not counter—usually a label or diagnosis by the partner that left the patient feeling it was all too correct. Correct or not, they failed to notice how well their partner effectively evaded further negotiations. Again, it is particularly difficult for a sensitive person to respond quickly in an argument, and any hesitation may seem to indicate to both parties that the sensitive partner is defeated. Responses have to be deeply ingrained as valid and almost overlearned, which is so important for these patients anyway if they are to believe their own words.

Feeling better prepared after practicing within a therapy session, they usually want to try again. This back and forth from the therapist's office to home and back again may go on for a long time, concurrent with other work. Whatever the outcome, it has the powerful effect of teaching sensitive patients how to speak up; respond well to defensive, invalid counterattacks; and keep trying if they wrongly backed down the first time. (Rehearsal dialogues work well for other settings as well—for example, helping a sensitive patient speak up about a well-deserved promotion.)

Of course I usually encourage sensitive patients to try to bring their partner to couples therapy. Sometimes all of these attempts fail. Then we face the larger problem of separating, an enormously difficult task for sensitive patients, as they feel the attachment and its loss so keenly, however bad the partner. I do not reassure sensitive patients that they will find another, better partner, or that it will be easy to live alone, even though they naturally want this reassurance and I want to give it. I do try to help them envision an alternative life, without the other, because having an alternative is the best predictor of whether a partner leaves.

All of the above can also happen with long-term friendships that are causing patients undo suffering, usually because they are being used while their own needs are ignored. Often this will have been a pattern with many friendships, so there has to be a change in the attitudes and behaviors that send a message that it is all right to use them. Again, learning to speak up, even in a doomed friendship, is good practice for them and will help them avoid the problem in their next friendship.

Bottom Line: The correct and fair decision about whether to end a relationship can only be made if sensitive patients have spoken up about their grievances. Often they need help in how to do this, which is invaluable training whatever the outcome.

LONG-TERM RELATIONSHIPS: WHEN THE PATIENT'S PARTNER IS NOT AS SENSITIVE

Now we turn to two situations, when the other person in a long-term relationship is much less sensitive, and in the next section, to long-term relationships when the two are similarly sensitive. With the former pair, generally the greatest problem will be their conflicts; with the latter, their boredom. At least the marriage of opposites is never dull.

The Advantages

The numerous advantages to the sensitive–nonsensitive combination are much like those for a sensitive patient having a nonsensitive therapist. As a couple they enjoy a wide range of abilities—one takes the time to notice subtleties while the other can quickly take action when necessary. One takes them on inner adventures; the other on outer ones. One makes certain they consider all the options; the other makes certain they finally choose one. One tolerates well life's dark moments and weighty mysteries; the other tolerates well life's changes and sometimes high levels of stimulation.

Both can find the other amazing, fascinating. Both will learn more about their "shadow," their rejected parts, than would a pair of similars. For example, if two nonsensitive partners both make life all work and no play, neither will notice the lack of balance. If the sensitive person needs more downtime and also insists on both giving sufficient attention to their relationship, the nonsensitive person will have to consider why he or she is so driven. Ultimately, the two will move each other to the middle—dissimilars do become more similar over the years (Karney & Bradbury, 1997; they even look more similar with time, Zajonc, Adelmann, Murphy, & Niedenthal, 1987).

Sensitive persons in these relationships benefit personally in many ways. Hopefully they are enjoying the healing experience of being valued for their sensitivity. At the same time, they have someone who can do some of the things they find most unpleasant—someone who may even enjoy these tasks. My not-so-sensitive husband loves to plan vacations, busily consulting schedules and making reservations. I hate such tasks—too many options. Once there, while I am resting, he likes to get out and explore to find what he wants to show me. He would hate just resting as soon as we arrive. Neither of us feels any guilt about doing what we most like.

At the same time, the sensitive partner experiences more adventures. I would not choose to go out in the evenings as much as my husband likes to, but I would very much regret not having been to the concerts and plays he urged upon me. I have compromised so that we could do together things I would never, ever have considered on my own, such as living in Manhattan for 3 months a year. Ultimately I have come to like our sojourns there. Generally, being married to him has made me far more flexible.

Nonsensitive partners can benefit equally or more. For example, he often consults me about his own decisions, knowing I will see all sides. I point out to him what he would never notice otherwise; he is safer and healthier because of me; and his spirituality is more focused. I can help him interpret dreams that would otherwise mystify him—and he takes dreams very seriously because of me and has learned enormously from them.

Bottom Line: When two friends or partners are dissimilar on this trait, as a pair they enjoy a wide range of possible benefits and probably find each other especially interesting. Each enjoys the admiration of the other for his or her differences, especially important for sensitive patients, and can help each other in a variety of ways.

The Problems

The possibilities for conflicts are numerous, but a few stand out. Sensitive persons will want more downtime than their nonsensitive partner, who may feel rejected. In these cases I urge patients to spend their quiet time with their partner—partners may think they will be bored yet come to enjoy these mostly silent interludes. If sensitive partners do go off alone, they need to be clear when they will return.

A greater problem is that the sensitive person will want less stimulation in general than the nonsensitive partner would prefer. The former often wants to live in the country, have fewer children, or work less intensely even if it means having less money. Many nonsensitive persons find these options unacceptable.

In addition, the sensitive one may want to minimize financial risks and maximize security, while the nonsensitive one may be eternally frustrated by this or else take over and leave the sensitive partner in constant anxiety. The nonsensitive one of the pair also may find the sensitive one generally too fussy, irritable, and emotionally unstable—quiet and boring one hour, frighteningly intense the next. The sensitive partner may find the nonsensitive one too talkative, superficial, or bossy.

An especially delicate problem is the sensitive person's disappointment that the other cannot go to the same depths without coaching, and never spontaneously. The nonsensitive person may feel judged for this. Indeed, the sensitive one cannot help being quick to notice flaws and irritating habits. He or she has to choose between saying something and being authentic but also sounding judgmental, which in fact he or she is, or else be quiet and endure, distance, devalue, and resent with all of this simmering mostly out of sight. Almost always if either feels an attraction to someone else, it will be to someone with their own temperament.

Finally, communication problems always arise, because the sensitive one communicates with hints or tones of voice that the other misses, while the other's simplest statements may sound like orders or unshakeable opinions. During conflicts, as just described, the sensitive person becomes overaroused and shuts down or has an emotional "melt down," which a nonsensitive person may find intolerable to witness or suspect is purely dramatics. These differences in style frequently become the focus instead of the original conflict, and because they are so acutely aware of each other's "flaws" (those behaviors that do not suit them due to their own temperament), each can fall into diagnosing or labeling the other all too accurately, in a sense. But they are forgetting the advantages that come with the very flaw they are now reviling.

The basic obstacle to resolution is that they do not usually know which behaviors the other could change but is stubbornly refusing to do so, and which behavior would be impossible to change. In our current social climate, the assumption is that anyone can change anything—we ought to change and grow all the time. Partners may even hear that they have a right to insist on it—adapting to the other would be giving in. This attitude does not work with temperament differences.

Bottom Line: Pairs dissimilar in sensitivity experience considerable conflict about the amount of time to spend together, the level of stimulation they prefer, the level of risk that is acceptable in life, the dislike of each other's general style of thinking, and the different intensity with which they communicate with each other. Further, they have no idea that their partner might not be able to change.

Helping Resolve the Irresolvable

Whether working with the sensitive partner alone or with the couple, the therapist who understands temperament can help this type of couple enormously. First, you can help them answer this question of what can be changed, what cannot, and how much to compromise. Second, you can help the couple reestablish a workable balance of power when the inequities are due to one or both of the partners still seeing sensitivity itself as a weakness. In this case, the sensitive patient seems flawed for this reason alone and therefore worthy perhaps of more sympathy but less influence. Such patients may need individual therapy to bolster their sense of equal entitlement and then couples therapy as a safe place to exert that.

On the other hand, if the sensitive patient is dominating or demeaning the nonsensitive partner, even without realizing it, that can require even more time before the patient can digest this fact and understand why it is happening and how much it interferes with what he or she desires, which is mutual love.

If their admiration is mutual, except for their confused exasperation with each other's attributes due to temperament, then they need to grieve and then move on. They need to face what they lose by having a partner with a temperament different from their own. This should not be so difficult to understand—one cannot have everything you want in life or in one partner. That only happens in the movies, when men and woman are touchingly sensitive but also heroically unfazed by extreme levels of stress. It makes no sense in the real world that someone can be both. However, the grief is real and should be faced and felt.

Without this grieving, each will still be secretly hoping for some miraculous change if the other could only take the right attitude, seminar, medication, supplement, exercise method, biofeedback training, or whatever. They will be unconsciously engaged in many small but systematic battles along a creeping front that is meant to end in final victory over this enemy hidden in the other's DNA. The victory will not happen.

You can ease the grief by simultaneously reminding the couple of the benefits that accrue from each other's temperament and even from simply being dissimilar. In addition, the truth is that anyone's character will be strengthened by accepting what cannot be changed in both themselves and the other, whether this is short stature, crying easily, or starting to look old—and loving the other anyway.

However it is achieved, once their temperament differences (not other issues) are truly accepted as inalterable, most feel a renewed love for each other. With the new love comes a surge of creativity. They find countless ways to arrange their lives so that both are satisfied: take two cars to the party so one can go home early; live in the city part of the year or part of their lives and in the country the other part.

I like Gottman's (1999) thoughts on conflicts as often being due to unspoken dreams for the future being threatened unwittingly by the other's actions. When partners differ strongly in temperament, their dreams may be very different. When A accuses B of spending too much money, it may be because in A's mind that money was being saved to buy a cabin at the lake to enjoy after retirement. These dreams have to be brought into daylight. Two people who love each other will find a way to have both, or perhaps one's dream must be sacrificed for the other, at least temporarily. But in a mutual relationship the mutual love could increase from the giving and the receiving of such a gift.

Bottom Line: When one partner is sensitive and the other is not, there will be many conflicts, but these cannot be resolved until both appreciate that temperament cannot be changed, grieve the resulting losses, appreciate the advantages of each other's traits and of being dissimilar in itself, and then come to creative solutions to their different preferences and needs.

WHEN BOTH ARE HIGHLY SENSITIVE

Again, these sections apply to friends and relatives as well as long-term partners. That said, what follows tends to be or sounds like it mainly applies to couples. For example, while analyzing data from our temperament and sexuality survey (Aron, 2001), we found that many sensitive persons, women especially, thought their partners were not sensitive when in fact they were. The discovery happened by chance. The survey required they give the same anonymous questionnaire to a nonsensitive person with an envelope so he or she could mail it in separately. To verify that the person was nonsensitive, he or she answered a brief form of the HSP Scale. Many gave these questionnaires to partners, most often wives gave it to their husbands, and many of these men did not qualify as controls because they, too, scored high on the measure.

Given this discovery, therapists may want to assess the sensitivity of the sensitive person's partner or friend rather than assuming both are being accurate about their difference. If the patient overlooked the other's sensitivity, then you will want to consider what that means about the relationship and in what way having both know this might reduce their conflicts.

Advantages

As for the advantages of this pairing, as mentioned at the outset of this chapter, some of our research found that highly sensitive persons were slightly happier when paired with another sensitive person. The reasons seem obvious, given that the problems specifically caused by being a mixed pair are usually not understood and go unresolved, while the similar pairs do not have nearly as many conflicts. These pairs communicate at the same "volume," agree more on how much time to spend quietly and on what is too stimulating, and conflicts are less likely to escalate to the point of overarousal. They can exchange strategies on how to cope with the nonsensitive majority. If they are comfortable with their sensitivity, they are a society of two that can raise each other's self-esteem. They can converse deeply about feelings, both those that need healing and those that are current. Hence they could well achieve more intimacy than other couples.

Bottom Line: Two sensitive persons in a relationship will probably be slightly happier than a dissimilar couple. They certainly enjoy many advantages, such as sharing the same needs and preferences.

The Problems and How to Help

The greatest potential problem is that the sensitive pair experiences what I call "couple low self-esteem." They may feel flawed in all sorts of ways—that as a pair they earn less money (if they do), have fewer adventures and do fewer "fun" activities, worry too much, do not take enough financial risks, are indecisive, are too nice to each other and put off conflicts too long, lack the courage to confront nonsensitive persons who are making one of them uncomfortable, and so on. Some of these can be serious problems for two sensitive people, and again, most can arise with two friends as well, who may feel they each have settled for an inferior friend because they are not more popular with others.

When sensitive patients are dissatisfied with a sensitive partner, it is important to look for projections of their own dissatisfaction with their own sensitivity: "He's too cautious" from an anxious patient, or "She's too emotional" from an equally intense patient. In addition, sensitive women (and nonsensitive women as well) may be critical of sensitive male partners because of their cultural training or their own fathers' reactions to their partner, either of which can lead them to look down on their choice after it has been made. The media and everyone else portray a real man as decisive (could your patient also see that this could be called impulsive?), outspoken (opinionated?), confident (narcissistic?), unflappable (lacking feeling?), assertive (aggressive and self-centered?), with "masculine" interests such as professional team sports or race car driving (violence?), hunting or fishing (more violence), politics and investments (an obsession with power?), and sexual jokes or pornography (sexism?). Of course many sensitive men have some of these interests, but the overall portrait of the ideal male is not typical of sensitive men. When sensitive women reflect on all of this, they are often very satisfied with their choice.

Perhaps the root of the cultural prejudice in women is a sense that sensitive men are not real "warriors" so are less likely to be good protectors. This can be worth exploring with women in these relationships, since they will usually admit that their highly sensitive partner has thought about how to deal with almost any emergency and would automatically take care of those they love ahead of themselves. (One patient even prepared for me and his family members "a terrorist attack preparedness kit," with touches of humor, such a chocolate bars, but also a face mask and iodine pills to protect my thyroid from atomic radiation.) If this kind of concern and forethought is not "manly," what are we actually saying about "real men"? Even though in an emergency sensitive people can become overaroused, their conscientiousness and forethought would probably make them better companions in even the worst emergencies.

While these homogenous dyads have fewer conflicts based on temperament than dissimilar pairs, they can have more problems with boredom. I will address that next.

Bottom Line: Sensitive pairs may compare themselves negatively to nonsensitive and mixed pairs; in particular a sensitive woman may think less of her sensitive male partner. Another potential problem is boredom.

Keeping Their Love Alive

Boredom is rarely identified as a problem in relationships, but my husband, myself, and our collaborators (Aron, Aron, & Norman, 2001;

Aron, Norman, Aron, McKenna, & Heyman, 2000; Reissman, Aron, & Bergen, 1993) think that it can play a large role. We have found that couples who do self-expanding ("novel, exciting") activities together, at home or in a laboratory experiment, report more love for their partner and more satisfaction with the relationship and, even more, positive communication patterns in laboratory tasks rated by blind coders. We believe this is because all of us are motivated to "expand the self," to become more competent, more complete persons. While sensitive people may not like to be overstimulated, they do like to expand themselves in ways they find appealing and interesting.

From birth, most of us are particularly fond of expanding ourselves through becoming close enough to someone to "include the other in the self." Through a long research program (for a review, see Aron et al., 2004), we have found that in fact the closer two people are, the more they will include the other in the sense of describing their relationship as two selves represented by closely overlapping circles; the more they will make cognitive confusions of self and other; be more generous to the other even when the other will not know; and have brain activation when thinking about a close other that is more like the activation when thinking of themselves. (All studies described in this section are summarized in Aron et al. [2004].) This is a nice solution to the question of whether love is based on altruism or self-centeredness: It is neither, or both, depending on how you view it.

When we fall in love, according to this theory, we experience a huge increase in self-expansion. A longitudinal study (Aron, Paris, & Aron, 1995) of those falling in love over a year's time found that they described themselves more complexly than they had before falling in love. So part of the ecstasy of falling in love is sharing ourselves with another and including the other in our self while the other includes us; in fact in one definition of the very essence of love each desires to include the other to the point of union.

As this sense of self-expansion through the other tapers off, the intensity of feeling declines. Love feelings can taper off to a flat plateau or even decline. But we have found that relationships will still be perceived as self-expanding if, again, the couple engages in self-expanding activities together. (Self-expansion not associated with the relationship does not have this effect [Aron et al., 2001].) These activities can be anything from competing in sports together to going to the opera for the first time—the pair decides what is self-expanding. Clearly it is a remarkably easy way to improve relationships and especially important for those who are similar. For them, in certain senses there has to be less of a sense of ongoing expansion, as many parts of the other were already present in the self almost at the outset.

Unless one of them happens to be a high sensation seeker as well, a sensitive pair may fail to do enough exciting, novel activities because they are using their relationship more as a refuge from an overstimulating world. They will stay at home together, or as friends will do the same activity each time, because it is more restful and easier than deciding on something new. But again, every relationship needs to provide some sense of self-expansion or it becomes dull. If you think about the people you consider boring, the problem is that you "don't get anything" from being with them. Getting to know them does not expand you.

Of course a sensitive pair can expand inwardly, by processing experiences together to greater and greater depth. But they still must take the time to do this, not simply adopt a sensible pattern of going to bed early, each reading a book, and then turning off the light. Further, some of their self-expansion should be outward, not inward. For the highly sensitive, especially those who are introverts, outward self-expansion is especially mysterious, exciting, and even pleasantly dangerous in the right amount.

The fact is that members of any dyad will be expanding out in the world somewhere, away from the twosome—perhaps at work or in other relationships. To stay close, they need some of these expanding experiences to happen together as well. You can point this out, and if your patient finds this difficult, you might choose to make suggestions about what the two would find exciting yet not too much so.

Bottom Line: Sensitive pairs need to engage in activities together that are *pleasantly* exciting and novel in order to provide the sense that their relationship is still contributing to their self-expansion.

DEPRESSION, MEDICATIONS, AND RELATIONSHIPS

Many sensitive patients will be depressed when they come for treatment or during the treatment, but often the only ones to notice are those closest to the depressed patient because the highly sensitive are so conscientious about carrying on at work. Not only do their partners notice, but of course they suffer, sometimes as much as the patient. Besides losing their companion to depression, feeling somehow to blame, and perhaps being blamed, they may be receiving increased criticism. Depressed sensitive patients may be more judgmental of their partners at such times. It is my observation that people feeling worthless and hopeless can also feel that way about their closest relationships, having included the other into their depressed self. This comes out harshly, especially when people are prone to being critical anyway. At the same time, sensitive patients probably benefit more from having social support during a depression, so it is important that the therapist monitor the sensitive patient's various relationships during these times to see that they do not completely founder.

Further, when sensitive patients want to put off trying medications, as they frequently do, I will mention their obligation to those who love them to at least experiment with a low dose. I sincerely mean it when I suggest it is to some degree a moral decision—they owe it to those they love. I might even point out what they may be too depressed to notice—that these people are wearing down and gaining very little from a relationship with them right now. One has to be careful not to overstate such matters to a depressed sensitive patient, especially since medications may not work for them. Usually just their being willing to try medication gives those around them the feeling that the sensitive person is willing to attempt to alter this mutually miserable situation.

SENSITIVE SEXUALITY

An innate temperament trait such as sensitivity, affecting one's "style" in every area of life, would naturally impact sexuality as well. To find out about that impact, we conducted a survey in 1998, as described in Chapter 6, with materials enclosed in an issue of a quarterly newsletter mailed to about 600 sensitive persons. They were asked to complete the survey themselves, anonymously, and return it in the envelope provided. Also, in order to obtain a control group as similar as possible, we asked them to give the same questionnaire to someone else, to be returned separately (not by the person giving it to them). Besides the questionnaire, we included a 15-item form of the sensitivity scale and a 6-item measure of sensation seeking. Finally, we invited them to say more about their sexual life, their sensitivity, or the questionnaire itself.

We received responses from 308 women and 135 men, 120 of whom were the friend controls. The average age was 46 for women, 48 for men. The response rate was high, 45% from the newsletter list, but the survey was open to numerous other sources of bias besides nonresponse. Perhaps most important, those not responding may have been less willing to reveal this type of personal information even in a purportedly anonymous situation. The much lower response from the nonsensitive persons asked to complete the survey (if respondents did indeed follow our instructions to help us gather a control group) suggests many sources of bias, both because of the subject and perhaps a lack of interest, not being highly sensitive, or feelings about the person giving it to them. Still the information can at least be generalized to sensitive persons who would respond to a survey such as this.

How They Did Not Differ

There were no significant differences between sensitive and nonsensitive persons on the number of sexual partners lived with, duration of their most recent sexual event, sex being viewed as one of the most potentially satisfying parts of life, liking to be the one who is active and deciding what the two will do, having fantasies of having power over another person, liking to talk during sex, and frequency of having an orgasm or of masturbating. In other words, they seem to be as sexually involved as others.

There were also no significant differences on physical or emotional problems or medications interfering with sex; having been sexually abused, and if abused, having these experiences affect their life; reporting a sexual dysfunction (such as lack of interest, not finding sex pleasurable, impotence, premature ejaculation); or feelings of satisfaction, worry, excitement, or guilt during sex. In short, they do not seem to have more problems with sexuality. However, all analyses controlled for depression and anxiety, making it a nonfactor. Since sensitive patients usually have more negative affect for a given level of trauma, these results may not apply to most of the sensitive patients you see.

General Differences

The responses of the highly sensitive were significantly different from the controls in that, not surprisingly, sex has a sense of mystery or power about it and that it is difficult for them to return abruptly to ordinary activities after sex. Given this reported intensity, it is also not surprising that they preferred to have things be the same each time and did not particularly enjoy variety in sexual activities. This difference in needing variety was even greater between sensitive and nonsensitive men, but for both genders being a high sensation seeker made the difference between sensitive persons and controls statistically nonsignificant. That is, even sensitive sensation seekers preferred variety.

It is not surprising that compared to controls, highly sensitive persons reported not being turned on by strong, explicit sexual cues; having areas of their genitals that can be touched in a way that is painful or too intense, even when aroused (this was true for sensitive men as well as women, although more true for women); needing to stop during sex because of being overwhelmed or overstimulated; having their sexual arousal terminated by being distracted or interrupted; and being easily disturbed by slight sounds, smells, or visual objects in the environment or connected with the other person.

Gender Differences

There were some differences that were only present when considering the gender of the sensitive person and their controls. Sensitive women were less likely than nonsensitive women to have trouble having an orgasm or lubricating and less likely to feel sad, scared, or afraid and more likely to feel loved. (They also liked having sex less, which may have been the result of a few extreme scores, or that sensitive persons are often stressed by already dealing with too many highly stimulating activities and sex is only one more.) I had to wonder if their general sexual pleasure might have been related to the following other differences: having fewer sexual partners over their lifetime and during that year, sex less often in the past year, having their first intercourse later in life, giving more consideration to the impact a sexual relationship would have on the other person, and being more concerned before entering a sexual relationship about sexually transmitted diseases or pregnancy. Perhaps caution pays off.

Compared to nonsensitive women, sensitive women also needed much more to love their partner in order to enjoy sex; enjoyed it less with someone they did not love; had less desire for a variety of sexual partners, even if not in a committed relationship; and were "less able to take sex lightly." The fusion of sexuality and love, desired by most people, seems even more important for sensitive women and is perhaps another reason for their general satisfaction and lack of negative sexual experiences.

Sensitive women were also less likely to have sexual fantasies while having sex with a partner, either romantic sexual fantasies or fantasies of another person having power over them.

Because of the smaller number of men responding to the survey, there were fewer significant differences between sensitive and nonsensitive men than are likely to actually exist. But some differences did surface. The sensitive men were more likely to be currently in a relationship. Sensitive men had a significantly greater dislike of music while having sex than did nonsensitive men, which perhaps suggests their general experience with stimulation, that less is more. Interestingly, unlike the women, they were more likely than nonsensitive men to have a sexual fantasy while having sex with a partner or while masturbating. Finally, compared to nonsensitive men, alcohol was more likely to adversely affect their sexual performance—not surprising given that alcohol has that affect on all men to some degree and the generally greater reaction of sensitive persons to alcohol, caffeine, and medications.

Bottom Line: Highly sensitive persons in general do not report more sexual dysfunction or experience with or harm from sexual abuse, and no less sexual involvement or satisfying sexuality, but they do see sexuality as more mysterious and powerful, desire less variety in their experiences or overt sexual stimuli (pornography), and can be easily distracted or overstimulated. Sensitive women, the majority of respondents, also had had fewer unpleasant sexual experiences, probably reflecting their preference to consider carefully before acting.

DISCUSSING WITH PATIENTS THESE RESULTS, AND SEXUALITY IN GENERAL

Clearly the survey asked questions I already suspected would be true of sensitive persons. I have found the results to be a great comfort to them. They see that they are not so unusual, but probably similar to the sexual behaviors and attitudes of 20% of the population. This gives them more permission to be themselves sexually, including being overwhelmed, overstimulated, distracted, or suddenly turned off in ways that might seem odd to nonsensitive sexual partners. Indeed, it often enables them to express their sexual likes and dislikes a little more freely. For example, if they like things to be the same each time and have felt uncomfortable doing the "strange" sexual activities their partner wants, they might ask for less of this variety or to at least be warned ahead of time. That partner might find that settling for less variety actually improves their sexual life. The sensitive person is not feeling anxious about perhaps having to do something uncomfortable or simply wondering what will happen next. Now each is adapting to the other rather than the sensitive one doing all the adapting. Very often sensitive patients feel much more sexual desire once they have discussed with their partner those aspects of sexuality that have not given them pleasure or that they have even come to dread.

In most good relationships the partner will come to accept that the sensitive person's preferences are part of the package deal. Everyone has preferences about sexuality. After all, they probably like their sensitive partner's intense emotional responses to sex, the sense that it is special when they make love, and that this person is less likely to seek variety through another sexual partner. So who needs constant change when familiar sexuality is already mysterious and powerful? What matters is that their partner be eagerly anticipating making love with them.

Knowing sensitive persons generally are easily hurt during intercourse is particularly important given that some patients will find it especially difficult to complain about pain, fearing this will interfere with their partner's pleasure. But pain is pain, and sensitive persons do have a lower pain threshold. Painful experiences are certain to lower desire for future intercourse.

Since the survey found that sensitive women tend to have fewer sexual fantasies with a partner (there was no difference about fantasies while masturbating), if they are having trouble having orgasms I might inquire about their fantasies. Many believe it is wrong to have a sexual fantasy while having sex with their partner, an idea I try to correct. Sexual fantasies are actually highly associated with marital satisfaction as long as these are not fantasies of someone with whom one is actually planning to have an affair (Griffin, 1990).

Although not a subject of the survey, I have also found it useful with some sensitive patients to discuss ordinary genital sensations that they can be so unusually aware of and often guilty about, since they often occur when it seems inappropriate or irrelevant. I point out that everyone's genitals can come alive when we are feeling good or like someone. They can "smile when happy." A genital "smile" implies a true sexual intent no more than a smile on the lips implies a desire to kiss.

I also bring up masturbation, especially as a way to "practice" and learn what does and does not work for them. However, therapists need to be especially attentive to a sensitive person's religious or cultural view of masturbation.

Of course sensitive patients are often especially inhibited about discussing sexuality at all. Frequently they do not mind discussing their own so much as their not knowing whether the topic itself is appropriate. I encourage them by pointing out that it is a very influential aspect of every person's mind and body, so that leaving it out of our discussions would be a failure on my part. Ours is a benign, appropriate clinical interest.

For therapists who would consider it to be relevant, sexual feelings arising in the transference of course need to be explored *sensitively*, in ways that are appropriate to the individual case. It is important to realize that even more than with nonsensitive patients, these feelings may be present and not discussed. They may be having these feelings with unusual vividness and at the same time be unusually ashamed of them. Once they are told that this, too, is a very acceptable feeling as well as valuable material for the therapeutic work, and that it will not be acted upon by either of them, they may become very conscientious about reporting it and thus be able to free up some of their natural impulses, so often too controlled.

Frequently both partners have viewed sensitivity as a flaw or weakness at the root of all the patient's difficulties. The research data regarding the positive impact of their sensitivity on their sexuality can be a revelation to both and help sensitive patients regain equal influence, leading to improvements in other areas of their relationship.

Bottom Line: The therapist needs to take an active role in discussing sexuality with sensitive patients. When they are a part of a sexually active dyad, very often these discussions not only lead to their experiencing greater sexual satisfaction, but also to greater equality and happiness in all areas of their relationship.

SUMMARY AND CONCLUSION

What sounds like the discovery of a "divorce gene" is actually the discovery of the importance of innate temperament, a good reminder that therapists can greatly improve their patients' lives by considering innate differences couples may be dealing with. In the case of sensitivity, it very often leads to inequality. Sensitive partners also need help to stop avoiding conflict due to fears of the consequences or of becoming overaroused. Both fears are usually solved by the therapist helping the couple use time-outs and other agreements about "fight behavior" that have the same effect of reducing arousal. Sensitive patients often need coaching as well on how to respond to a partner's quick comebacks when they would normally think through an answer slowly.

Couples in which one is sensitive and one is not have many conflicts to resolve, but they do not have to fear boredom. Each will be constantly challenging the other in new areas. Couples in which both are sensitive have to actively seek shared experiences that will challenge and excite them.

Discussing the sensitive patient's sexual style can free him or her to set up conditions that will encourage greater satisfaction in this area as well as enable the patient to speak more freely about it with a partner and stand up more generally for his or her needs and preferences.

All in all, understanding the effects of temperament on relationships, specifically sensitivity, may be the most ignored yet fertile way to improve the treatment of couples' difficulties and provide them with greater mutual satisfaction.

CHAPTER

8

The Sensitive Person in the Workplace

> I'll never forget temping as a typist in an insurance company when I was an undergraduate. I heard a fellow typist say she'd been at this same job for over 20 years, typing names and addresses on insurance forms. But it got more interesting, she said, when she worked on another form, where the information was *reversed*. You can imagine what I thought and felt at that moment. It doesn't matter what jazzes other people about their jobs, it's what jazzes you. Trust me, you can't tolerate "just a job." Even if you pigeonhole it into a neat tidy corner in you life. Of course, there are some HSPs who must do this, because of family or other intense responsibilities. But our souls will suffer a loss of some kind.
>
> **—Barrie Jaeger,** *Making Work Work for the Highly Sensitive Person,* **p. 29**

This chapter begins by examining the typical difficulties most sensitive persons encounter when trying to find a suitable career. The second topic is the workplace itself—how to help sensitive patients choose a good work environment and adapt to aspects that cannot be changed, having been designed to suit the nonsensitive majority. The third topic is how therapists might help more disturbed sensitive patients remain gainfully and comfortably employed.

Pearl S. Buck's quote at the start of Chapter 5 and this one by Barrie Jaeger both capture the reason I turned down offers to write a book on sensitive people in the workplace. There can be an almost tragic gap between their need for meaningful, creative work and the actual jobs they must take in order to earn a reasonable living. This is often a wider gap for sensitive patients. Jaeger's book emphasizes the need for the highly sensitive to find their calling, but more practical advice is harder to provide.

Nevertheless, there are myriad ways that being highly sensitive is an advantage in the workplace—these workers have abundant creativity, conscientiousness, loyalty, and empathy for customers and coworkers. Hence, as I describe their "typical problems," please remember that many highly sensitive persons have not experienced any of them. They have found work they love, are good at it, stay rested, and enjoy their colleagues and workplace. Still, some specific issues often arise.

CAREER PREPARATION AND CHOICE

Career choice deserves emphasis with sensitive patients because those with stressful histories will often have had an especially difficult time deciding or already have made a poor job choice. They may have had to change careers several times or have stayed with a career that was not working because they were afraid of making a second bad choice. Often they were not encouraged in their youth even to think about their future, as if written off. I urge young patients who are unsure of their plans to gain a liberal arts education plus internships in the summers to expose themselves to as many areas of specialization as possible. I also encourage career counseling, using vocational testing and the Myers–Briggs (most will be classified as either Introverts or Intuitive, and often both). Above all, in any of their chosen fields, they should gain the highest degree or training possible, in order to give themselves credibility and confidence, so that they can make the sort of contribution they want to make. However, for them higher education often requires taking time off for several periods and not taking too many courses in a term. Not all will have the desire or ability for so much education. For them career counseling is even more important.

When sensitive patients have difficulties with vocational choice, while hearing them out for how their personal difficulties are contributing to their problem, be certain they understand that their trait needs to be taken into consideration. Equally important, find out what kinds of pressures they are under from others. Patients rarely come for counseling with only career issues.

A CASE ILLUSTRATION

Les, a very young 29 when I first saw him, came from a long line of entrepreneurs and investors, mostly on his father's side—he got his sensitivity from his mother. It was assumed that he would follow the family tradition and attend a prominent business school. That part was easy and interesting, but his first job was not. For some reason he had thought finance and accounting, his specialty, would not involve high levels of competition among coworkers, but there was more of that than he cared for. Further, he had not minded studying long hours by himself, but did mind working long hours in a building. His father saw his struggles and suggested his son join him in the family firm, probably his father's plan all along.

Working in this company, Les was welcomed, made comfortable, and treated with more deference than he felt he deserved. Meanwhile, he was becoming sensitized to social issues he had been exposed to as an undergraduate and that had not come up at his business school. Although his father did not know it, in college he had taken some courses that had given him what his father would call a "liberal bias" and after that spent most of his time with friends who were politically active. While he had expected the corporate world to be less interested in social issues, he was distressed by the utter hostility toward these issues in his father's firm. He was feeling increasingly guilty about having so much while others had so little. He wanted to do something about this, but feared he would disappoint his father. Consulting now with his old college friends, he decided that he wanted to go back to school in the field of education and eventually become a principal in an inner-city school. First, however, he would have to do what he feared—disappoint his father.

I tried to stay neutral about his career dilemma, feeling that how he made this decision was more important than what it was. Evidently his father was a charismatic, driven man who had carefully managed the upbringing of his promising and compliant son. Distressed by the early signs of his son's sensitivity, he had taken the approach of overriding his son's hesitations with motivational lectures. Les had learned to override himself in the same way, but he drew the line on treating the disadvantaged that way.

Like Bella in the previous chapter, it required a year of increasing Les's volume before his father really heard him. This resulted in Les's father disowning him—no trust fund, no inheritance. Les was shocked. He did not wish to stay in therapy to discuss it. Therapy now seemed like another frill for the rich, a group to which he no longer belonged. He set out immediately on his new career path.

I was glad to hear from him 5 years later, but not surprised that his issue now was how to avoid burnout. He was finally ready to talk more about his sensitivity and his two career choices thus far. The first had lacked personal meaning and the second was too overstimulating. As we continued to meet, he decided he would now like to follow in my footsteps and become a therapist, but specialize in troubled, disadvantaged young adults.

Again we did not meet for several years. By this time he had obtained his license, married, and had two children. Now he found he could not support them on the fees he could charge his patients or the beginning salaries in the nonprofit agencies he admired. He was deeply upset with himself. In one session I found myself imaging a large foot trying to fit into a small shoe, which I shared with him. It seemed to me that he was squashing himself into a job that did not make use of the full range of his talents. This brought us back to him and his father and how much both of them had lost faith in Les the young man along the way. He was seen and saw himself as someone who had stepped down in the world to join the ranks of those who serve others with their hearts, not being tough enough in mind or body for a more competitive job. The next thing I heard, he had begun as a side line to help other therapists with their accounting and taxes, and then do the same for other friends with other types of small businesses. Most of the work was boring, but in the process of helping a friend with a start-up company he noticed an unusual business opportunity that had been overlooked by all but a few. For months I heard about his fears of investing in the idea. This time I was especially careful to stay neutral but energized—so much to gain, so much to lose.

At this point we were not meeting, but he told me later that At first he simply dabbled, but once he understood the parameters, it seemed that he could not stop making money. He hired several assistants to do the more tedious aspects of the job, mainly research, so that he was working only 2 hours a day. This freed him to teach seminars on how to do well in this area, but he found this teaching boring as well as stressful for an introvert, so he returned to working 2 hours a day in his firm and wondering what to do next. His family was comfortable, his marriage good—why was he dissatisfied?

I mostly listened as he recalled teaching someplace else, the impoverished high school he had fled from due to burnout. That was now 20 years in the past. He went back now to visit and then to volunteer and felt happier now.

Again I did not see him for several years. Then he came by for one session to tell me that he had decided to blend his talent with his deepest desire, by founding a nonprofit, self-sustaining program that tutored the brightest, most vulnerable male students in his city, helping them apply to college and for financial aid when they were ready. But each had to agree to contribute time mentoring the next wave of students. Les told me that his "six tries to get it right" gave him some cache with the youths he saw, most of whom had dropped out of high school and drifted from one bad job to another before entering his program.

THE TYPICAL CAREER PATTERN OF SENSITIVE PERSONS

Les's career struggles are typical of those faced even by some of the most emotionally stable, gifted, and affluent sensitive persons. Like Les, they often follow the urgings of their parents and teachers, who recognize both their talent and sensitivity, but worry a great deal about the latter. These well-meaning persons either wish to ignore the sensitivity by pushing the person into a high-powered career "as if nothing was wrong" or want to see him or her safely ensconced in a lucrative, high-status profession: medicine, law, dentistry, academia, engineering.

Others have considerable gifts that have led them in the wrong direction because they did not take their sensitivity into account. For example, they have the intelligence to pass the bar but often do not enjoy practicing law—not in a corporate setting, not in the discouraging offices of public defenders or district attorneys, and in not a private practice in which they must promote themselves. Susan from Chapter 1 is another example. Sensitive persons can rise fast in the corporate world, but near the top find themselves miserable for one reason or another. Sometimes, too, colleagues can be less fastidious about subtle issues of ethics, which can deeply trouble sensitive persons, who either must conform or be seen as sitting in judgment. I should add that I know highly sensitive persons in law and business who are thriving, but the point is that talent can lead some into highly stimulating environments that they cannot find a way to manage. We all know stories of great talents who collapsed under the pressure of too much success, and some were certainly highly sensitive.

Like Les, when these people find themselves backed into a corner, they often turn to one of the more creative fringes of their careers, such as practicing their profession in low fee settings; using cutting-edge, alternative methods; or working for a nonprofit. Very often they choose careers focused on righting some wrong, for example, whether by teaching in an inner-city school, as Les did, or entering medicine and then joining Doctors Without Borders. Alas, they do not belong on the "front lines." They are far more useful in other roles—consulting, strategizing, supporting, or training those who thrive on what they would find too stimulating and distressing. This does not contradict my assertion that sensitive persons are outstanding in emergencies or crises. They are not suited, however, to entire careers that place them in almost hopeless situations—confrontations with truly cruel persons or working with victims so distressed that they simply cannot be helped very much, be they starving children or harpooned whales (all of which can serve to goad the nonsensitive into an optimal level of arousal for heroic action).

Many sensitive persons turn naturally to the arts, or work close to the arts by running bookstores, galleries, small presses, or organizing concerts and teaching music. Still others feel they have to work outdoors, doing anything from organic farming or mountaineering to carpentry or running refuges for animals. Some turn to the sciences or liberal arts within an academic setting, where they can pursue their ideas with a little more freedom than is found in most business settings, although sometimes they have considerable difficulty teaching undergraduates or handling academic politics. Many choose to engage in body work or one of the many alternative healing professions.

Sometimes they decide they will have to choose between making money or making meaning, and a therapist might hold out the hope that they can find a way to make their passion profitable. There is no greater joy than loving a job that also supports you well, and that happens when you work at the point where your own greatest "bliss" intercepts with the world's greatest need. It can also make sense to do as Les did—focus on making money efficiently and spending free time "following one's bliss." This seems to be an especially likely course for those in the arts, where it has been shown that there are seven persons hoping to earn their living for every one adequately paying job (Eikleberry, 1999).

When highly sensitive persons are good at almost everything, as Les was, they need help establishing priorities and accepting that the cerebral cortex can dream up far more schemes than they can ever put into action. Further, some of these schemes are simply not suitable to their sensitive bodies.

Unlike Les, however, many sensitive patients stay too long in careers that are unsatisfying or too stressful simply because they are being loyal to those who have become used to counting on them. Jaeger (2004) distinguished between drudgery, craft, and calling. Drudgery jobs are those in which we count the hours until we can leave the workplace. Craft denotes the pleasure in one's work that comes from knowing you are usually competent at what you do. But once a craft is mastered, the work can become drudgery. When working at anything but their calling, sensitive people are usually miserable—tired as well as unsatisfied.

Bottom Line: Career choice is more difficult for the highly sensitive, and they may change directions several times before finding their niche, as they need work to be meaningful yet not overstimulating, have the talent to do many things well, and often feel pressured by others.

THE LARGER PROBLEM

A larger perspective helps me understand what sensitive people are struggling with and how much I may be able to contribute in certain cases. Although what follows is speculative, it seems that, traditionally, highly sensitive persons have filled more of the roles in society that required thought and education—greater depth of processing. I have the impression that in the past many more doctors, lawyers, teachers, nurses, clergy, scientists, historians, artists, and consultants to leaders were highly sensitive. I am not certain why this has changed, except perhaps that until recently the majority of nonsensitive persons could find employment in other ways, in jobs that were equally lucrative but emphasized strength and endurance or that required tolerating monotony or constant high levels of stimulation (e.g., factory work, farming, the military). Supporting the family, enjoying the work camaraderie, and looking forward to vacations or retirement were sufficient for many of these less sensitive persons. As the tough, boring jobs have been mechanized, perhaps the nonsensitive have turned to careers that had previously been mostly done by sensitive persons. Also, there has been a huge growth in numbers of those who want the services of doctors, lawyers, scientists, and teachers, so that they seem to be practiced now in an atmosphere of time pressure, limited resources, or the pursuit of very large profits. This atmosphere would seem to favor those who can do these jobs more quickly or are willing to work longer hours, with less thought about various outcomes and less regret about imperfections.

In some cases, it seems that the jobs sensitive persons once gravitated to simply require greater toughness now, as in the case of forest and park rangers. In the past we used to say, half jokingly, that these careers came up on vocational tests in order to provide something for introverts. Now rangers must learn crowd control and some carry guns. The clergy is another example. Seminarians have told me that sensitivity in the clergy is now discouraged, as they must work long hours, have competitive fund-raising skills, and handle large, contentious congregations. A passion for prayer, solitude, scholarship, and reflection is simply not quite as important.

Often it seems that if more of the highly sensitive were still in careers such as teaching and medicine, they would simply do the work differently and the quality of service might actually improve in some cases. But the working conditions are very trying. I could form a large support group of the many highly sensitive nurses I know who are struggling to remain sensitive to patients in the modern hospital environment. Further, in the arts, self-promotion and networking can be as important as ability. Hence, we may be losing a certain point of view by the inadvertent exclusion of many sensitive persons from these, their traditional fields.

Whatever the reasons, once the standards are set by the nonsensitive majority, it seems difficult for the highly sensitive to work alongside them. I do not mean any of the above as an excuse (and certainly not an accusation) so much as a topic for therapists to consider and perhaps explore with sensitive patients looking for the right field of work. I also like to think of the above ruminations as something of a challenge to the highly sensitive—to find a way to work in their traditional careers, doing it their way. More and more medical students, for example, are looking for humane training conditions, forcing a slow change in that field, and perhaps more sensitive doctors will result. If we consider Abraham Lincoln as highly sensitive, which seems likely, politics could certainly benefit from more like him.

The highly sensitive can do almost any job, if they can do it their own way. I know a sensitive realtor who specializes in grasping the real needs of clients and matching them to the right home. Another sells fine wines. I find them in roles one would never expect—motivational speaking, law enforcement, and fire fighting. The policeperson was a special investigator. The motivational speaker succeeded by having unusually interesting messages. In a community telephone survey in our unpublished data (Aron & Aron, 1997), the only trend we found for occupations was that slightly more persons who are highly sensitive stayed home to care for children.

In general, the highly sensitive are best at reminding others of the "big picture" and the possible long-term advantages or dangers that could arise from a particular decision. They are usually very attentive to ethics and quality control. They do well in roles that involve creativity, strategizing, training, consulting, and problem solving. We need them back in some of their old roles and for them to reinvent these professions.

Bottom Line: Keep in mind the larger picture, that times have changed and many of the traditional roles of the highly sensitive are now more difficult for them to pursue. When possible, encourage them to return to those roles, but in their own way.

TYPICAL INTERPERSONAL PROBLEMS IN THE WORKPLACE

Turning to problems in the workplace, I find that most of these are interpersonal. The others, involving overstimulating environments, are addressed below. What was said in the previous chapter about sensitive persons' assets and problems in personal relationships applies here as well. They are good listeners, thoughtful coworkers, fair managers, and generally good morale builders, so they can often develop a loyal following, especially if they are extroverts.

As for the problems, many of the suggestions from the previous chapter will apply here, but not all of them. Coworkers and supervisors are not as obligated as friends and partners to adapt to the sensitive person. Rather, the sensitive person must state his or her needs as supporting the organization's needs—"I will perform better if ..." or "Since you value my creativity, it might be better fostered by ..." Unlike in a relationship, they cannot ask for a timeout during a confrontation at work. When possible, have them role play in therapy a confrontation they are anticipating and find ways to make it less threatening—for example, having a coworker present who also understands the issue.

It is especially important at work to turn up the "volume" of speech in the sense of being as brash or straightforward as the nonsensitive people around them are and not expecting others to hear hints or suggestions that are meant to be more than that. On the other hand, the highly sensitive can be so alert to flaws that others find them too critical, so they also need to learn to choose their battles and let some things go. When delivering criticism, they need to remember the rule of seven positives to every negative. Seven can be fit into a normal conversation far easier than they may think: "I value you so much as a coworker. I know I can count on you when I need help. You always come through.

I especially value your sense of humor. I just thoroughly enjoy working with you. Since I do value our relationship so much, I guess I feel I have to discuss what happens for me when you do. ... We've always been able to talk things over, and I sure hope you do not take this as some blanket criticism of your work, which overall I so much appreciate."

If sensitive persons are also introverted, they may be initially misperceived in new workplace social settings as less intelligent or mentally unhealthy (Paulhus & Morgan, 1997) unless he or she makes a concerted effort to engage socially and in meetings. Then, as time passes and they do the job quietly but very well, they are usually underappreciated. This is especially true if they persist in believing that hard work is always rewarded and it is wrong to brag about accomplishments. They need to learn to promote themselves and at a volume that will be noticed.

Sometimes a less sensitive person can do this for them: One sensitive person waited 10 years for friends in his graduating class, who knew his unusual abilities, to obtain high positions and be able to hire him, which they did. Or they can use their sensitivity to observe how others promote themselves, note what works and what does not, and develop their own ways, in accord with their own personality. Give them permission by discussing the fact that not providing the full, factual information about one's value raises ethical questions of its own, since the organization needs to know the talents of its employees in order to utilize them fully and not lose them to another organization.

A major workplace dilemma can arise for the highly sensitive working on team projects or in meetings. Frequently they can see the right solution to a problem before others do, or be the only one to see the long-term negative consequences of a course of action. But speaking up has high costs. Having a better idea ought to please others, but in fact it may threaten them or the suggestions may seem too outlandish. Pointing out problems with a plan can affront those promoting it or earn the sensitive person the label of naysayer and pessimist. But not speaking up also has costs. Holding back leads to feeling increasingly alienated from the group, and others will usually sense it and perhaps attribute it to something else.

In these situations, the sensitive again need to be encouraged to use their intuition to perceive the defenses, worries, allegiances, capacity to understand, and all the rest of the qualities of the others in the room, and then to work around these. Just as teachers must teach at the level the students can understand, sensitive persons can teach the nonsensitive their point of view if they do not accept defeat before they begin. But this requires confidence in one's capacity to persuade others, which often means getting over their own low opinion of themselves. Also remind them that a solution that is almost as good as theirs but that increases group cohesion may be the best one after all.

Another issue is power. Most workers are over someone and under someone else. Sensitive persons often rise in status and power with time, yet can view these as almost intrinsically unethical—they do not wish to control others or make them feel they have a lesser status. Remind them that another definition of power is influence, which can be used for good or ill, and that if someone responsible does not assume power, someone else will. Joseph Badaracco's *Leading Quietly: An Unorthodox Guide to Doing the Right Thing* (2002) can be helpful. Badaracco described his quiet leaders as people who "don't fit the stereotype of the bold and gutsy leader ... what they want is to do the 'right thing' ... but inconspicuously and without casualties" (dust jacket). The book provides role models of ethical leaders at all levels of organizations who are not naive or submissive, but rather use their power effectively by being exceedingly perceptive, realistic, and strategic in upholding the values sensitive persons tend to have.

A few other suggestions can be made. First, just as when preparing for a career, sensitive persons should obtain all the additional training they can in order to give their opinions more credence and to feel more self-confident. Second, some interpersonal environments are far more distressing that others, so when a manager or coworker seems almost pathologically problematic, they should consider whether anyone else is troubled by the person. If the problem is being denied, it is not going to get better. It is better to move on rather than tough it out, hoping somehow things will improve.

Finally, highly sensitive workers are often promoted to management positions and need to be warned of or helped with certain potential difficulties. They will have to turn up their volume even more and be ready to act quickly in response to problems of discipline. They may have to be alert to illegitimate power moves by those under them. They will almost certainly have to work longer hours and have more trouble leaving their work behind when they go home to rest or fulfill other responsibilities. I suggest they at least take courses in management, even if their organization does not offer them, or consider edging sidewise into more of a consulting-to-management role.

Bottom Line: The highly sensitive need to turn up their volume at work, especially if they manage others, so that their needs are met, their viewpoints heard, and they are not perceived as weak or less intelligent. They should continue to seek training in order to gain more influence and move on if they are in hopeless interpersonal situations.

TYPICAL WORK-ENVIRONMENT PROBLEMS

Almost all sensitive persons who are not self-employed face work environments that are designed for those less distressed by noise, bad lighting, lack of windows, cubicles without floor-to-ceiling walls, open floor plans where talk and traffic are constant, "sick" buildings, and so much else. If the organization values a sensitive employee, he or she has some negotiating room and should use it. For example, a sensitive scientist working in a laboratory complained to me that she could not concentrate because her coworkers played the radio. Because she was the only one bothered, they refused to wear earphones. I asked her if her work was valued, and she said that when the others had problems they could not solve, they brought them to her. I suggested she explain that she simply could not take on these extra acts of concentration unless the radio was off or they wore earphones. With my support, she was able to make this demand and it worked.

When sensitive employees are in a less powerful negotiating position, or correctly intuit that they are better off giving no indication of this side of their sensitivity, then they must reduce stimulation in whatever way they can. They can go outdoors on breaks, shorten their commute time in some way, and do the work that requires the most concentration when others are not around, perhaps by working staggered hours. Some sensitive nurses choose the swing shift, for example, when there is no traffic getting to work and it is after business hours.

There is a problem, however, with withdrawing too much, in that they may become socially isolated and misperceived as loners or even troublemakers. Worse, they risk becoming blind to the many aspects of office "politics" that can only be discerned and directed through casual talk among coworkers. Hence, the stimuli to be reduced should not be primarily interpersonal.

Finally, sensitive persons tend to be conscientious and perfectionists, and so may feel they need to work longer hours to do things right or else suffer anxiety that they will be reproached for an imperfect job. Help them keep a balance between work and the rest of their lives. The highly sensitive have to be creative and figure out how they can "do less to accomplish more." For them, the basis of good work is being rested. When rested, their sensitivity will help them find ways to be more effective.

When appropriate, bring up self-employment. The self-employed are disproportionately more likely to be highly sensitive (Jaeger, 2004). To many sensitive persons the mere thought of starting a business will seem overwhelming—too risky and more work than a regular job. Others will find self-employment easier, in that the politics are largely gone, one sets one's own hours, and conscientiousness works entirely in one's own favor. Nor need it be overwhelming or risky provided they enter self-employment gradually, for a while keeping steady income from elsewhere. Making a large initial investment of funds is less important if one plans to rely on slow growth based on quality rather than starting out with a large permanent site and extensive promotional advertising.

Bottom Line: The highly sensitive will be bothered by working conditions that do not disturb nonsensitive employees. If these organizations value them, they can ask for changes. Otherwise, they will have to adapt on their own without withdrawing too much from others. They can also consider self-employment.

THE WORK PROBLEMS OF SENSITIVE PATIENTS WITH DEEPER PSYCHOLOGICAL PROBLEMS

Therapists are familiar with all the problems their more disturbed patients face in their efforts to stay gainfully employed—for example, their constant anxiety about their performance. Depression may keep them from work or impair their performance. Interpersonal difficulties leave them feeling left out or victimized. They may have boundary problems if they use work relationships to fulfill unmet early needs or cannot draw a line when meeting the needs of others. Their general low self-esteem can hamper them at every turn, either when applying, trying to get along with others, or asking for a raise. Sensitive patients, however, might show a few specific differences in their work problems that are worth noting.

A CASE ILLUSTRATION

Richard, 31, was a highly gifted man with two master's degrees who was unemployed and living on a dwindling inheritance when he came to see me about his high sensitivity, which was causing him "some interpersonal problems." As he saw the depth of his problems, due to the interaction of his sensitivity with the effects of being raised by two narcissistic parents, he wanted to begin seeing me several times a week. First, however, I had to discuss my concern that he would run out of funds before we had completed the work that seemed needed. I also knew that if a large percentage of his remaining resources was spent on therapy that may have to end prematurely due to lack of funds, he might well blame the therapy for leaving him penniless and no better.

I suggested he might find part-time work to stretch his money further or to create a reserve earmarked for therapy. He exploded. Part-time work was beneath him. My suggestion was a repeat of his mother's nagging. The very discussion of it indicated that I was flawed in my approach. Surely, he said, his finances were his business. In a sense, of course, that was true, and I certainly prefer to leave patients in charge of such things without any advice from me. I backed down and privately decided to have less ambitious goals—to help him develop some interpersonal skills and insight.

Even before the payment issue was resolved, I came to know Richard's physical ailments—the headaches, nausea, muscle pains, and sudden bouts of fatigue, which we agreed were probably psychosomatic, since his parents had given him a bit more nurturing when he was ill and no one expects much of a sick person. So these symptoms were an additional reason for not working—he feared he could not handle the physical stress. Of course I suspected a deeper general fear of failure.

His dreams came to our rescue—a figure appeared in a wheelchair, a veteran named Sam whom he knew in childhood. In real life, Richard had heard that, regardless of the wheelchair, Sam's actual illness was "shell shock" from battle and a fear of going back to work and revealing his inner damage. Richard thought now that Sam had been highly sensitive and never belonged in a war zone. The dream helped Richard see and accept his wounded mind and its relationship to his health.

We got to know Richard's inner Sam, and Richard began to see that he, too, feared someone he might work with seeing his inner damage, which was far worse than others because of being "too" sensitive and not a real man. The more menial a job, the more shaming it would be to fail at, and failure at any work seemed inevitable to him.

Eventually, in order to continue our work together, he had to risk applying for a part-time job, and chose a specialty bookstore. To his amazement he was hired, in spite of the owner seeing him as "dangerously overqualified." Richard suffered acute anxiety before the first day on the job, but we discussed ways he could prepare himself. In particular, he had a relative train him ahead of time on the type of cash register the bookstore used. Once he was through the initial training, he found the work easy and the staff interesting. He even took pride in how quickly he had learned the store's procedures and intuited the basic principles of sales, which he also began reading about on his own. In turn, they were delighted to have such an erudite person helping customers.

Within a few weeks, however, the morning nausea and muscle spasms had returned and he was missing work. We explored what had happened on the day he first noticed his symptoms. After much delay, he admitted he had been rebuked for reading on the job. In response, he became furious with the owner and stomped out of the store. They later talked it over to the owner's satisfaction, but Richard was deeply ashamed, even too ashamed to tell me until now.

The first task was reducing this shame. We agreed that his sin was hardly the same as stealing. No harm had been done. The store was empty. He was simply bored, and with a mind like his, of course he would read. Indeed, having skimmed some of the featured books might cause him to recommend them more enthusiastically. Then, feeling less shame, he was able to accept the owner's point of view and admit to the trouble caused by his highly defensive response. Later that day he went to work with fresh energy and renewed pride.

With every reoccurrence of his symptoms, we were eventually able to locate the cause—some incident that rekindled his desperate fear that others would discover his core worthlessness. When the fear was resolved, the symptoms backed off. But we faced another problem. With every year of his life, his peers were advancing in what seemed to him to be highly successful careers, while he, once seen as the most promising of all, was working in a bookstore.

It took a while for him to accept that it might be a few years before he could pursue a true full-time career, but that, as for many sensitive persons, a slow start was normal. For him it was because he first needed to see his therapy through. The work he was doing with me and at the bookstore was for him the necessary foundation for his other goals.

Richard knew it was a true sign of progress when he could answer people's polite inquiries about his career with "Actually, I am still studying." If asked what, he would smile and say, "Myself. You know the saying, 'Know Thyself'?" If his part-time work was the subject, he would say that it was pleasant to be around books while pursuing, without distraction, his vision of his life's work, which, no, he did not care to divulge at this point. That he could explain himself honestly, even interestingly, without shame, was a great boon to his social life, since he had been avoiding meeting others partly because of his simple inability to answer the question "What do you do?" When one person reminded him that Einstein had worked in a patent office while developing the theory of relativity, he was gratified and at the same time able to admit that he doubted his life's work would be quite that impressive.

SPECIAL CONSIDERATIONS WHEN TREATING THE WORK ISSUES OF SENSITIVE PATIENTS

Many of Richard's problems are also particularly true of the highly sensitive. For example, their sense of specialness, real or defensive, can make their work difficulties even more shameful. Work often exacerbates their swings between feeling unusually gifted and unusually impaired socially and emotionally. As for Richard's physical complaints, having physically sensitive bodies anyway, these patients often develop more intense symptoms under stress. Some also have environmental sensitivities that may be augmented by tension. Finally, there is no doubt that since work is something every adult must do, if one feels unable, an adequate excuse is physical infirmity. I have never seen a case of malingering—a true choice to feign illness—in highly sensitive patients. I have no doubt, however, that the body can cooperate when this is the only solution to a terrible problem.

Highly sensitive patients are especially prone to feel victimized. Some will silently submit far too much, until you both have to admit that the situation has become abusive and they must quit. Others will blame, complain, or be passively aggressive until they lose their jobs.

Fortunately, sensitive patients are often the first to raise the necessary question about what their role is in a string of job failures. But be careful not to take advantage too quickly of this opening. Again, inadvertently shaming them is not helpful. They must learn to accept their basic goodness as well as their real, deep problems, and they are likely to be placing more emphasis on the latter, even if you do not hear about it. I try to help them stay aware of this task of simultaneous self-love and self-criticism. I might bring up only one issue at work and focus on that, or let a few more repetitions of something like being late occur before questioning what might be going on. The task is to help them, gently; to allow us to see more clearly their role in the process.

The best cues about what the patient is doing with others will often come from your own experience of the person: How does the patient allow me to victimize him or her in subtle ways, such as thinking "This is my easy patient—no need to focus my attention there." Or does the patient more often make me feel victimized or blamed? Is this what is repeating in the work situation?

When sensitive patients justifiably do leave a job, have them look closely at the next one before they take it, rather than feel so grateful for being hired that they do not consider that they, too, are making a selection. Return to the criterion of "goodness of fit"—the compatibility between the temperament of the individual and the demands and expectations of the environment. For example, since all sensitive workers thrive on a diet of praise and positive feedback, but the distressed ones even more so, I might suggest that patients bring up that they respond especially well to positive reinforcement and see how the interviewer reacts.

In a sense, the most important factor for the patient's success will be the interpersonal skills of those around him or her. That is something hard to assess through the patient's filter, but a sensitive patient might be able to judge something about a company's culture—a focus on teamwork or competition—if told to focus on that during interviewing. I speak to them about those who "connect" and those who do not, urging them to be around the former as much as possible, and to try to connect themselves—be as present, honest, and interested as possible—with anyone they interact with. When they cannot, they should try to note why, which usually you can describe as their being in their "complex" of feeling inferior, unfairly treated, or ashamed. This keeps them understandably overpreoccupied with themselves.

I have not discussed career choice in the context of more troubled patients. They may have begun with glorious plans meant to provide a permanent solution to feeling flawed, such as becoming a doctor or a great author. When these plans fail, they are in a deep crisis. Even as other issues are improving through therapy, the passing time only adds to the pressure to "become somebody." Their self-esteem may seem to be moving one step forward and two backward as they see peers enjoying the fruits of successful careers.

As with Richard, I may try to help them accept that for now their inner work is their true career. Or I may risk encouraging that they resume their career or professional training, hoping their determination in combination with their new insights and our working together through each crisis will triumph. This, however, entails the risk of another failure. Preparing them for failure can actually help them succeed by reducing the pressure, at least from me: "We both realize this may not work out, but if it doesn't, that will be information for us too—nothing to be ashamed about, just more information." Again, it helps to speak respectfully of the *work* they are doing in therapy and their integrity in pursuing it.

With others who are too impaired to pursue careers that match their talents, the choice might be to encourage accepting a lesser career, but one with equal or more real meaning for them than one meant to impress others or heal a sense of unworthiness. Instead of becoming a doctor, doing massage therapy. Then in their free time they can pursue their calling, without having to endure the pressure of medical school. For example, a would-be doctor might volunteer to assist at a clinic for the homeless.

Bottom Line: Highly sensitive patients may blame others, feel victimized, or develop debilitating psychosomatic symptoms to avoid feeling ashamed of their work performance, especially if they cling to the idea of being someone special and without personal problems. They can also look at their role in repeated job failures. Often they need help making better choices. You might want to reduce their shame about falling behind their peers by validating the importance right now of their "inner work."

OPPORTUNITIES TO REDUCE SHAME

While work creates problems, it also offers important opportunities with sensitive patients. If they are succeeding in this area, their productivity can be a point to bring up when they are feeling ashamed. Work also provides opportunities to discuss boundaries, idealizing, feeling victimized, and other issues that are impeding their life in all areas—and sensitive patients are often quick to appreciate the parallels, for example, between their reaction to the work group and to their dysfunctional families. Coworkers rekindle sibling rivalry. Reactions to superiors mirror parental issues, such as idealizing superiors, seeking their love, being disappointed, and then angry to cover the deeper shame of rejection.

Sensitive patients can also gain insight from their work behaviors and reduce their shame by noticing how they handle their sensitivity. Do they hide it, overly compensate for it, use it to guess the needs of others and to please them at all costs, or do they fail to notice its assets and how it can help them succeed?

Finally, work issues may be the avenue by which you both see the depth of your patient's problems. You may eventually learn that a particular sensitive patient simply cannot work right now, and may not ever be able to. The interaction of their trait and their sensitivity has simply done too much damage. Hopefully, someone else can support them—their family or government programs. Sometimes when they can stop trying to earn a wage they may even begin to contribute in other meaningful ways to society, be it through poetry, music, writing, or volunteering. Indeed, many great cultural contributors could not support themselves, some for emotional reasons, and required patronage. That may, however, place too much pressure on them again. Perhaps it is simply all right that some people live modestly on some external source of money, earned by others who are less damaged, and contribute nothing tangible except their sensitivity itself. In that case, however, sensitive patients will suffer more shame than others might, and it will be your task to help them accept their situation and that they are not to blame for the traumas they have endured.

Bottom Line: Events in the workplace provide opportunities to reduce sensitive patients' shame by discussing their work successes, gain insights from how their work behaviors have replayed family dynamics, or see in what ways they fail to make use of their sensitivity. If they are not suited to gainful employment, or not yet suited, they will experience greater shame than others would and it will be your task to reduce their shame.

SUMMARY AND CONCLUSION

Too frequently the highly sensitive have chosen or been forced into careers that did not take into account their sensitivity, especially their need for work that is meaningful. Once they do find the right career and settle into their life's true work, they can still have difficulty feeling comfortable with social and physical aspects of their work environment that others find tolerable. Helping them with these issues is especially meaningful, in that as you see them improve you sense that something especially valuable is now free to express itself. Someone is flowering, ripening, and without therapy it would not have happened.

We need highly sensitive people in every workplace, in every field, but especially in those that were once their traditional roles. Those with the confidence that comes from successful inner work with you will be far more influential as they call into question unwise plans and offer instead fresh, well-considered ideas with a careful eye as to how they can explain these to the unconvinced. One could even imagine that if some of them were in places of power, the world situation could improve. That is the type of positive outcome therapists like to think they can contribute, and in this case they very well might.

CHAPTER

9

Personality Variation in Highly Sensitive Persons

[Extraverted sensitive persons find social events] draining because of the seemingly endless social chit chat, niceties, and surface exchanges about a myriad of unimportant topics. ... I think this comes from our natural tendency to want "to know and be known" and to connect in an authentic way with others. ... [But] if we are not very careful and conscious of our intentions, when we are "out" in the world we can be found wearing our emotions on our sleeves, making ourselves unusually vulnerable.

—**Jacquelyn Strickland,** *"An Insider View of the Extravert High Sensation Seeking HSP," HSP Highlights and Insights, Winter/Spring 2007, www.lifeworkshelp.com*

As a conclusion, this chapter reminds therapists of the broad variety of sensitive patients they may see, who are still highly sensitive in spite of these other traits and interests. Cases from earlier in the book and imagined combinations are used as examples.

You now have, hopefully, a cohesive portrait of highly sensitive persons and patients, from DOES, presented in Chapter 1, through the chapters on the various clinical and life issues they face. In particular, you learned in Chapter 2 how to assess for sensitivity, but the subject needs to be revisited now that you know so much more. You have developed a template to place over each patient in search of a match indicating whether he or she is highly sensitive. However, the possible variations in sensitive persons are infinite. Each is unique. Now we need to consider further how other traits, innate or not, would then fit over that original template like transparencies, each contributing something to the final image. With enough such overlapping pages, the original template for sensitivity might almost be obscured, yet it is still there and exerting its influence.

VARIATIONS ALREADY DISCUSSED

I have already discussed the role of gender, age, ethnicity, and the interaction of personal history with the trait. Important also are the clinical symptoms of being emotionally over- or undercontrolled and being overexposed to stimulation and perhaps chronically overaroused, versus living a life that is too protected and unstimulating. These create major variations that you will have to consider for every patient.

You already know about the broad variations of introvert versus extrovert and being high or low in sensation seeking, differences worth mentioning again because, introverted sensation seeker that I am, I tend to come from that perspective.

Extroversion

The author of the epigraph for this chapter, Jacquelyn Strickland, views herself as an extrovert. She has described some of their attributes in the article cited. For example, she wrote that this type "can make new friends easily, but only in the right environment ... alone while riding the bus, alone while eating in a restaurant, or alone while on the beach." They are "definitely not comfortable in malls, at national conventions, or at board meetings." Overall, extroverted sensitive types report feeling quite different from other extroverts—more sensitive.

Strickland sees many of this type working as "social justice activists," but they "would never think about running for public office, though sometimes our passionate convictions make us seem as though we would be a likely candidate." Like other sensitive persons, extroverts enjoy the creative process, but immediately want to share the results with others. They also enjoy any collaborative process, such as committees.

In short, you will find many sensitive patients who are quite outgoing, talkative, and have many friends or at least are at the center of a large social network. They still have the characteristics of needing time to themselves, strong emotional reactions, a preference for deeper conversational topics, concern for others, easily hurt feelings, and sometimes a high level of creativity or intuition, love of nature, and strong spiritual interests.

High Sensation Seeking

Finally, do not forget the astounding differences in sensitive persons due to being high or low sensation seekers. As I explained in Chapter 2, I consider this to be an innate difference that, when high, often leads to extroversion, but not necessarily. Introverts can be high sensation seekers in ways that do not involve increasing their level of social interaction with nonfamiliars. This trait affects careers, choice of friends and partners, recreation, and overall involvement in activities. Sensitive persons who are also sensation seekers show their sensitive side in their conscientiousness, concern for others, and dislike of risk or impulsive behaviors. They may use their sensation seeking to travel or to serve a cause, for example, by fund raising.

DEMOGRAPHIC DIFFERENCES

Sensitive persons who grow up in a highly urban environment versus those who live in the country will differ in that the former will be habituated to far more stimulation, although still trying to avoid some of it. They find the social density itself familiar and even reassuring in that sense. They feel more secure with busy sidewalks and stores, conversations with strangers, friendly neighborhoods, and even using subways rather than cars. They will especially enjoy cultural activities. They make frequent forays to the country, but say they would not be happy living there. These city dwellers often seem more confident, outgoing, loud spoken, and humorous. In some patients, identifying with the urban scene will meet narcissistic needs at the expense of their sensitivity.

Those in the country are usually there because, born there or not, they prefer it. They like the quiet and visual calm. They live close to the earth and animals and often raise their own food. They are not content, however, with conversations limited to the best chain saws or composting methods. They will stay in contact with some aspect of life that affords them deeper intellectual or artistic meaning—perhaps by being authors, artists, or amateur scientists. The Internet makes this aspect of life much easier for them. Of course, some sensitive patients use the country as a way to withdraw, too.

Socioeconomic differences also have strong effects. Wealthy sensitive persons tend to use their money for others and to purchase quiet and privacy. Sensitive persons I have met who were poor or without higher education were remarkable in their unusual interests and were well read in at least one area, such as opera, meteorology, history, or psychology. If their income was low, they managed their money well (although some patients have had particular issues with money, often learned from parents, that kept them poor). As for variations in intelligence, I have not seen the combination of low intelligence and high sensitivity, and perhaps their thorough processing would not make that possible.

PERSONALITY DIFFERENCES

Whether these are innate, learned, or a product of dysfunctional families, the highly sensitive will vary widely in other personality traits. A place to begin is with those found to be noticeable as early as 3 months old and are perhaps innate traits. Thomas and Chess (1977) provided the first list of these traits based on observational research. Besides low sensory threshold, they identified eight others: degree of flexibility (changing course when asked to by others), biological rhythmicity (sleep, hunger, etc.), approaching versus withdrawing behaviors, distractability, persistence (separate from distractability because an individual can be distracted but if persistent will return to his or her focus of interest), activity level, intensity of emotional expression, and positive versus negative mood (this last trait is now in doubt as to it being innate). Evans and Rothbart (2007) developed an Adult Temperament Questionnaire based on the work of Thomas and Chess that lists four traits: negative affect, extroversion, orienting sensitivity, and effortful control.

Below is a partial list of other individual differences, whether innate or the result of experience, that are probably at least partially independent of being highly sensitive.

- Curiosity, open mindedness, and eagerness to learn versus disinterest or even suspicion.
- Anger proneness. I have found no relation between this and sensitivity, although its expression may be over- or undercontrolled.
- Messy versus neat. While sensitive persons might seem to be universally neat, tidy in dress, and punctual, those who are engaged in very creative lives may forget about these details. They may try to protect you from their disorder, but you will see it in other ways, such as losing things.
- Degree of physical coordination and involvement in sports.
- Noticeable independence, dependence, or interdependence. Related to this is the degree of personal power felt in various relationships. This varies from high levels of leadership to intense feelings of inferiority.
- Variations in appearance and attractiveness, although perhaps not a personality trait, are certainly noticeable and affect personality.
- Particular talents.
- Particular values and attitudes toward politics, religion, race relations, and myriad other topics.
- Health.
- Attachment style.
- Effects of trauma and stress in personal history.

IMAGINING SENSITIVE PERSONALITIES

The variations just described naturally appeared throughout the book in the case illustrations: Susan, Anna, Ida, Bella, James, Kevin, Tom, Josh, Julian, Les, Richard, and others. Their histories and demographics ranged from wealth to poverty and from confidence to severe personality disorders, and their traits went from introvert and artistic to extroverted and business oriented.

In closing, I suggest that you use the following exercises to solidify your ability to recognize and treat sensitive patients.

Filling Out the Case Illustrations

Think about the cases I have just listed. Imagine other qualities you do not know about your patients and how that might change how you would understand or treat them. For example, suppose you had learned that Susan was an extrovert, Josh was shy, or Richard intensely conservative politically.

Imagining Entire Personalities

I will suggest some types; see if you can imagine them. Then I will suggest alterations in the portrait, and you will see if you can imagine how that factor changes the overall person without changing the fact of his or her high sensitivity. Go back to DOES if necessary—imagine two or three of the four being mentioned in early sessions and how that would affect your sense of this person.

To begin, imagine a sensitive man who has not finished high school, poor, living in the country, single, and not interested in marriage. He is also confident and highly creative. What would he be like? How might he be supporting himself? Why would he come for therapy? What might his problems be? There is no single right image of a person that should come to mind, but what matters after all of this is, how might you recognize his sensitivity and how might these other attributes change how it might manifest?

Now change the man to a woman with all of the above characteristics except that she is married and lacks self-esteem and self-confidence.

Now put her in the city—still sensitive, poor, without much education, married, not confident, but creative. How would she seem and how would you uncover the fact of her sensitivity?

Now imagine her wealthy and single, but still creative, uneducated, and lacking confidence.

Imagine her now with average income and high in sensation seeking.

Imagine a woman with a PhD, wealthy, single, and sensitive. Her mother had been severely depressed and finally committed suicide when this patient was 10, but she was adopted into a wealthy family who raised her with skill and patience. She is also politically conservative, very introverted, African American, and a devout Muslim.

Imagine this same woman as European American, extroverted, and without the wealth or a PhD.

Imagine a sensitive man with average education and money, married with children, Hispanic, and low in confidence.

Imagine him South Asian and a Buddhist.

Continue imagining these variations—I am sure you have the idea. Do it now while the book is fresh in your mind.

Assessing Well-Known People

Unless I know the person and have their permission, I try to stay with a policy of not declaring whether he or she is highly sensitive. I cannot really know, and it seems like an invasion of privacy. After Michael Jackson's death, however, an article appeared on a blog suggesting he had been highly sensitive. Of course I began imagining how I would have decided if he was. If I had had him in therapy for an hour, what would I have asked him? What behaviors would I have watched for? What would I have wanted to find out if I could interview his family, friends, and associates?

If you could spend an hour with the following people, how would you assess whether they were highly sensitive (keeping in mind the possibility that they were or are extroverted or high sensation seekers): former president Jimmy Carter, Marilyn Monroe, "Unabomber" Theodore Kaczynski, Abraham Lincoln, Martin Luther King Jr., Coretta Scott King, Al Gore, or National Public Radio interviewer Terry Gross. Apply the above questions to a few famous people you know well from reading their biographies.

Assessing Those You Know

Coming closer to home, you might want to think about friends and family if you have not already. Of course, be careful how you handle your insight, but especially if you know of a sensitive child, you might be very helpful to the child and the parents if you bring up that possibility.

And What About You?

If you are highly sensitive, consider how the rest of your personality characteristics interact with the trait. What types of sensitive patients might you miss because they are unlike you in these other ways? This holds true if you are not highly sensitive as well. How would characteristics you might hold in common with a sensitive patient cause you to miss his or her high sensitivity? For example, suppose you love the arts, are conscientious, and like time to yourself?

By the way, if you are highly sensitive, congratulations on the choice to become a psychotherapist. I find all too few in our profession, even though high sensitivity might seem a prerequisite and is certainly one of those roles we belong in. However, we encounter problems because, for example, we do not like risks, and being a therapist does involve risk. It might help to know that data collected between 1995 and 2001 about licensed psychologists found that only about 2% of licensees have complaints filed with licensing boards in a given year (Van Horne, 2004). Fewer than 20% of those will result in any action, and only 13 of 10,000 will face any formal disciplinary action. If you follow practice standards, know your limits, document, and consult, the risk of adverse action is "negligible" (p. 177).

Aside from not liking risks, we do not like being overstimulated, and at those times when your case load has become too high or even one patient is in crisis, you will be overaroused. We do not like being aware of the potential adverse consequences of our actions beyond ethical and legal considerations. We fear doing harm. We are emotionally reactive, so our patients affect us more, especially the angry, critical ones. Obviously all of the usual methods of self-care should be used, but you need more self-care than others do. That will limit your income and perhaps hurt your professional pride, but that is simply how it is.

Screen your patients more carefully than others might, as you will be very effective with some patients, but much less with those who are stressful for you. We all know therapists who love such cases. For them, the more challenging, the better. Refer to them and put your energies where you can do the most good. Frequently that will include sensitive patients, but not all of them even. They can be very demanding if deeply disturbed, and remember it requires less in childhood to make them that way.

If you are not highly sensitive, congratulations on becoming so knowledgeable about this trait. You will be a far better therapist, I promise. You will enjoy your sensitive patients more and see them light up when they understand better who they are.

SUMMARY AND CONCLUSION

In spite of their basic similarity, there will be wide variations in the sensitive persons you will meet and patients you will see—differences resulting from demographic variables; other traits, whether innate or developed; interests; and attitudes. You have imagined some of these different possible presentations. You also may want to reconsider some of your patients whom you thought were not highly sensitive.

We have come to the end of both chapter and book. You now have a thorough sense of what high sensitivity looks like, how to assess for it, how to adapt to sensitive patients as a therapist, what their typical problems are, how the trait affects their relationships and work, and how broadly they can vary while still being highly sensitive. Your current and future sensitive patients will be grateful.

APPENDIX

The HSP Scale

Are You Highly Sensitive?: A Self-Test

Instructions: Answer each question according to the way you feel. Answer true if it is at least moderately true for you. Answer false if it is not very true or not at all true for you.

T F I am easily overwhelmed by strong sensory input.
T F I seem to be aware of subtleties in my environment.
T F Other people's moods affect me.
T F I tend to be very sensitive to pain.
T F I find myself needing to withdraw during busy days, into bed or into a darkened room or any place where I can have some privacy and relief from stimulation.
T F I am particularly sensitive to the effects of caffeine.
T F I am easily overwhelmed by things like bright lights, strong smells, coarse fabrics, or sirens close by.
T F I have a rich, complex inner life.
T F I am made uncomfortable by loud noises.
T F I am deeply moved by the arts or music.
T F My nervous system sometimes feels so frazzled that I just have to get away by myself.
T F I am conscientious.
T F I startle easily.
T F I get rattled when I have a lot to do in a short amount of time.

T F When people are uncomfortable in a physical environment I tend to know what needs to be done to make it more comfortable (like changing the lighting or the seating).
T F I am annoyed when people try to get me to do too many things at once.
T F I try hard to avoid making mistakes or forgetting things.
T F I make it a point to avoid violent movies and television shows.
T F I become unpleasantly aroused when a lot is going on around me.
T F Being very hungry creates a strong reaction in me, disrupting my concentration or mood.
T F Changes in my life shake me up.
T F I notice and enjoy delicate or fine scents, tastes, sounds, and works of art.
T F I find it unpleasant to have a lot going on at once.
T F I make it a high priority to arrange my life to avoid upsetting or overwhelming situations.
T F I am bothered by intense stimuli, like loud noises or chaotic scenes.
T F When I must compete or be observed while performing a task, I become so nervous or shaky that I do much worse than I would otherwise.
T F When I was a child, my parents or teachers seemed to see me as sensitive or shy.

Instructions for Scoring the Self-Test for High Sensitivity (These are the instructions for the general public, but therapists should follow them as well.)

If you answered more than 14 of the questions as true of yourself, you are probably highly sensitive. But frankly, no psychological test is so accurate that an individual should base his or her life on it. We psychologists try to develop good questions, then decide on the cutoff based on the average response. If fewer questions are true of you, but *extremely* true, that might also justify calling yourself highly sensitive, especially if you are male.

Reprinted from *The Highly Sensitive Person* with the permission of Kensington Books. For a research version of this test, email aron@ic.sunysb.edu.

THE HSP SCALE AND GENDER

As mentioned in Chapter 1, there is no evidence that at birth there are more sensitive girls than boys. However, throughout our studies women have scored somewhat higher on the HSP Scale than men, in spite of our efforts to write a scale that was without gender bias. For example, crying easily correlated highly with the rest of the scale, but far fewer men agreed to it than women did, so we left it out. In contrast, there was little gender difference on items such as sensitivity to hours of available daylight, which were biological and neutral. Still, in the end, there was a gender difference in overall scores, which surely reflects a Western cultural ideal for men to be nonsensitive. It seems likely that any set of items, no matter how flattering or gender neutral, would bring to mind for men certain cultural stereotypes of sensitive people that would make it difficult for them to agree to as many items as women could without evoking negative feelings about themselves.

APPENDIX

B

Distinguishing Sensitivity From DSM *Disorders*

The distinction is made between high sensitivity and disorders generally, and then between it and the specific DSM-*defined disorders likely to be confused with it, such as posttraumatic stress disorder (PTSD). In the same discussion of each such disorder, there are also suggestions about how it might differ in the highly sensitive patient who does meet the criteria. At the end there are suggestions for working with these patients when they have disorders that could not be confused with sensitivity, such as substance abuse.*

IS SENSITIVITY ITSELF A DISORDER?

The American Psychiatric Association's *Diagnostic and Statistical Manual of Mental Disorders* (*DSM*) definition of a disorder is "a clinically significant behavioral or psychological syndrome or pattern … associated with present distress (e.g., a painful symptom) or disability (i.e., impairment in one or more important areas of functioning) or with a significantly increased risk of suffering death, pain, disability, or an important loss of freedom. In addition, this syndrome or pattern must not be merely an expectable and culturally sanctioned response to a particular event, for example the death of a loved one. Whatever its original cause, it must currently be considered a manifestation of a … dysfunction" (APA, 1994, p. xxi).

Clearly this definition is informed by the problem that *dysfunction is to some degree in the eyes of the beholder.* In the case of sensitivity, a nonsensitive clinician in particular might look at a sensitive patient and reason: "Is there distress? Clearly. This person admits being distressed merely by spending a few hours in a crowd or watching the evening news. Impaired? She has refused promotions because she found managing people is too difficult for her. Increased risk? According to the research, she has an increased risk of being disabled by depression and anxiety, and she already experiences an important loss of freedom to engage in a wide range of activities—she can't even enjoy a normal party. Are her reactions to events expectable or culturally sanctioned? No. She can't eat at a restaurant that's a little noisy when a hundred other people are obviously having a good time. I have to consider her to have a disorder." And the patient might even reluctantly agree.

On the other hand, as these or similar reactions become understood as quite expectable in 20% of the population, as bestowing as many benefits and abilities as it does vulnerabilities (e.g. Belsky et al., 2009), and as the highly sensitive themselves no longer see themselves as impaired but having a subculturally sanctioned response, then the above position will become increasingly untenable and even ridiculous. (For a discussion of distinguishing temperament generally from disorders, especially in children, see Kristal [2005].)

It is important to be aware that when diagnoses are usually made, in the first few weeks of psychotherapy, sensitive persons will not be exhibiting their normal behavior, but rather extremes. These distortions may occur because of their initial overstimulation, fear of criticism, culturally induced shame about their trait, or overconscientiousness about reporting symptoms and flaws. These initial reactions lead to arousal, and anyone outside of the optimal level for arousal will perform poorly at any task. The poor functioning could be mistaken for low intelligence, chronic anxiety, or any number of problems. A state of overarousal can also lead to an anxious unrelatedness that could wrongly be interpreted as extreme shyness, a disorganized attachment style, or an avoidant or schizoid personality disorder. These of course could be present, but my point is that they might not, yet they could *seem* to be there.

A final note is that increasingly patients use the Internet and *DSM* to diagnose themselves, correctly or not. Because the highly sensitive reflect more than others about themselves and also must in some way account for being different from others, they are especially likely to come to the first session with well-developed ideas about what is wrong with them. It only makes sense to listen well to their reasoning. They have known themselves much longer and have listened to many others comment about them. While listening, the clinician can consider whether the patient is correct, and if not, whether this false positive is due to misinformation or defensiveness, leading to the least self-damaging diagnosis, sensitivity, or whether theirs is a false negative and they have mistaken the normal characteristics of their trait for a disorder.

DISORDERS FOR WHICH HIGH SENSITIVITY COULD BE MISTAKEN OR ALTER THE PRESENTATION

Disorders Usually First Diagnosed in Infancy, Childhood, or Adolescence

Mental Retardation

It is rather strange to begin here, but this is the first relevant disorder listed in *DSM*. A few sensitive patients whom I have seen were briefly misdiagnosed as mentally retarded in childhood because they performed so poorly on intelligence tests due to overarousal (or in one case, refused to perform) and were not adapting well in two of the criterion areas, such as communication and social or interpersonal skills. However, all three of these were misdiagnoses given later performance in school. In fact, the highly sensitive are more often at the other end of the continuum (Silverman, 1994).

Autism Disorder and Asperger's Disorder

Innate sensitivity, especially when mixed with shyness, is sometimes viewed as the mildest form of autism (Ratey & Johnson, 1997). However, distress from sensory stimulation is not listed in the *DSM* criteria for these disorders. It appears only in the description as "odd responses to sensory stimuli" (APA, 1994, pp. 67–68), including a high threshold to pain, not a low one. Inconsistency seems to be the main feature of these odd responses—a focus on certain stimuli while ignoring others. Still, sensory distress is a feature popularly associated with autism disorder (e.g., Mark Haddon's *The Curious Incident of the Dog in the Night-Time*, 2003). Otherwise, not one of the criteria for autism or Asperger's would be met by a highly sensitive adult or child as defined here, mainly because *the highly sensitive are unusually responsive to social cues* and skilled at social interaction, at least when they are in a familiar social environment. Also, sensitive persons have *intense imaginations and varied interests* rather than narrow preoccupations.

The mistake is usually made with sensitive men (since these disorders do appear more often in men), who are especially prone to withdraw emotionally due to not fitting the masculine stereotypes in our culture. They still need to prove themselves in some way, have social contacts, and support themselves, so they often enter into nonsocial professions, such as certain types of engineering and technology innovation, where they can meet these needs while usually avoiding overarousing emotional encounters. When a man or his family members seek a nonblaming explanation for why he always retreated to his room as a boy and still has not married, they may find it in a biological explanation involving the "low end of the autism spectrum."

On the other hand, men with undiagnosed Asperger's disorder might well come to therapy thinking or having been told that they are highly sensitive as an explanation for why they feel they do not fit in. You can do the differential diagnosis by closely observing patients' actual social empathy with you (after a few sessions to become comfortable) and by how they describe their relationships with others. In their history, the question is whether their low sociability is the result of trouble with social-emotional cues, commented on by themselves or others, or is it due to fear of rejection. One study found that even shy children usually know well how to behave in a social situation (watching a video they can identify or suggest good social behavior), but perform poorly due to low self-confidence (Cartwright-Hatton, Hodges, & Porter, 2003).

Attention Deficit/Hyperactivity Disorder (ADHD)

ADHD and ADD are confused surprisingly often with high sensitivity, mainly because this is such a frequent diagnosis for any child who has any difficulties in school or any adult who feels overwhelmed or has problems adjusting to life. But *when not overstimulated, the highly sensitive lack all of the outstanding* DSM *characteristics of ADHD*. That is, the characteristics for ADHD with be noticeably lacking: inattention to details and a lack of sustained attention during activities, not seeming to listen when spoken to, not following instructions or finishing tasks, not being able to organize work, avoiding sustained mental effort, losing things necessary to a task, and being generally forgetful. Sensitive persons even more definitely lack the hyperactive or impulsive symptoms. Further, ADD and ADHD are almost surely related to excess dopamine, which is associated with impulsivity and high risk taking rather than the opposite strategy of "do it once and do it right" associated with high sensitivity (and probably serotonin levels). Highly sensitive persons can also be high sensation seekers, but this is balanced with their inherent caution.

True, a sensitive child who is overwhelmed by stimulation in the classroom might have trouble paying attention or following directions and thus appear to have the distracted form of ADHD. In the safety of home an overwhelmed sensitive child may have tantrums or be oppositional, much as would a child with ADHD. But these behaviors would not usually occur at school or when in others' homes, and once the overstimulation has passed, the sensitive child is generally considerate, calm, attentive, and very conscientious.

Sensitive persons, like anyone else, will avoid or fail at tasks requiring focus or following directions if they have failed at these in the past. The original cause, however, would not have been a general inability to focus. Rather, sensitive persons sometimes do not realize how much they must practice and prepare in order to overcome the debilitating levels of arousal that accompany tests, performances, and other evaluated tasks. So the original cause of their failure was overarousal, and after a failure they will be even more overaroused and expecting failure the next time. It is no wonder they consciously or unconsciously avoid such tasks or cannot focus when they try.

Outside of the problem of fear of failure, the adult with ADD (Hallowell & Ratey, 1995; adult ADD is not in *DSM-IV*) and the adult who is highly sensitive, especially those who are also high sensation seekers, might both seem to be tackling too many projects at once. The sensitive person, however, is doing it because of seeing so many possibilities, not because of poor executive functioning. Generally, the sensitive person will eventually establish priorities and finish some projects, letting others go. In addition, both might complain of being scattered or overwhelmed, but upon inquiring about their "to do" list, the ADD person's will be much longer—if there even is a list! The sensitive person's will be a normal length or even shorter than normal. The source of a sensitive person's distress will be the desire to have everything done.

Other characteristics attributed to those with ADD (Hallowell & Ratey, 1995) but not in the *DSM* description of ADHD are probably the main reason for the confusion. These are underachievement, procrastination, being "creative, intelligent, and highly intuitive" (Hallowell & Ratey, 1995, p. 74), tending to worry, being insecure, and having chronic problems with self-esteem. All of these could be found in sensitive persons for reasons other than having ADD. If one stays with the *DSM* criteria, there is no chance of confusing sensitivity with ADD or ADHD.

It is not clear if these disorders and high sensitivity can co-occur. Chess and Thomas (1987) consider distractibility, up to some undefined limit, to be normal and could definitely be found along with the traits of low sensory threshold, low adaptability, and withdrawal (in their set of traits, these are probably the behavioral, observable equivalent of high sensitivity). I have met persons who thought they had both. If excess dopamine is the main differentiating factor, perhaps attention deficit disorders are much like high sensation seeking and could, like it, co-occur with sensitivity. The genes involved in all of these are still not fully identified and no doubt are more numerous and varied than simply those governing dopamine and serotonin.

Mood Disorders

Major Depressive Disorder and Dysthymia

Regarding a misdiagnosis, the highly sensitive are going to "ruminate" or process the negative events in their lives more deeply. *Their normal intense emotionality means one must be even more careful about a diagnosis of mood disorder.* The question is duration and impairment. Sensitive patients cry far more easily than others do, and so may cry in the first session, as would a depressed person. They can have a passing low mood or spate of pointless worry due to stress. Quite often their down mood has to do with something they have heard or seen. Simply listening to others' troubles or reading about the sorry state of the world may leave them depressed and anxious, which hardly amounts to a depressive episode or mood disorder. They also should not be diagnosed with mild chronic depression only because of a pessimistic view of the future of the world or of their own abilities (a pessimism that may well be accurate, as in the case of depressive realism [Alloy & Abramson, 1979]).

As for co-occurrence, again, highly sensitive persons are *more prone to depression if they have had a difficult childhood,* as already emphasized. Further, anxiety or sadness in the present, over something quite reasonable, such as a sick relative, or completely appropriate grief after a death will then lead to depression if it continues for too long, as it would in anyone. This progression may be quicker and more common in the highly sensitive, given their stronger emotional reactions.

Other less predictable triggers are possible as well. A sensitive friend contracted a strain of influenza that his primary care doctor had noticed was causing depression in some of his other patients. After 6 months on antidepressants, my friend was able to stop the medication and never had a recurrence.

As for making a diagnosis, depressed sensitive persons usually appear to be feeling better than they are because of their ability to manage their persona and their desire to carry on as usual, being very conscientious. Thus the more important criterion is "clinically significant distress" due to subjective states they hopefully are discussing with you, such as worthlessness, emptiness, or unending sadness, rather than "impairment in important areas of functioning" due to fatigue, loss of focus, or anhedonia. These might also be present but covered up. Often only those living with the patient who have previously seen this person during a depression will be able to recognize a current episode.

Paradoxically, sensitive patients may admit more often than others would to suicide ideation and planning because they are looking so far ahead at all the potential consequences of what they are feeling, want to be scrupulously honest, and are trying to express accurately the depth of their despair. At the same time, they are probably more likely to keep an agreement that they will not act on these, since they know how it would affect others or be a mistake in the long run. However, deciding on suicidal risk obviously requires careful clinical judgment in each individual case.

Mania, Hypomania, Bipolar, and Cyclothymic Disorders

Bipolar disorder is relatively rare in this population and probably has separate genetic causes, but its strong positive and negative reactions and the often intense creativity associated with it can lead to something resembling it, especially resembling cyclothymic disorder. Indeed, the criteria for a hypomanic episode seem vague enough that a sensitive person could easily fit at times, given that *DSM* indicates that it does not lead to impairment and could be met with the following three criteria (of the seven listed in *DSM*) if they lasted 4 days. One would be "uncritical self-confidence" (APA, 1994, p. 336) rather than the inflated self-esteem of a manic episode. A second would be an increase in "efficiency, accomplishments, or creativity" (APA, 1994, p. 336), such as writing a letter to an editor or clearing up paperwork, rather than the risky behavior of a manic episode. The third needed criterion would be, rather than a true flight of ideas, speech that is more rapid than usual or full of jokes and irrelevancies (what is irrelevant is, again, in the eyes of the beholder) or an increase in sociability. A sensitive person (or anyone perhaps) who reacts to high praise, such as an award or unusual opportunity, could well fit these.

A manic or hypomanic episode needs to begin suddenly, however, and involve a distinct change in personality that others can identify. Still, these others might easily mistake a sensitive person's greater emotional reactivity for cyclothymia.

It is going to be unclear, therefore, whether observing certain behaviors and calling these a hypomanic episode would be a misdiagnosis that confuses this disorder with high sensitivity, or a true co-occurrence.

What about a true manic episode? If not a case of misdiagnosis, a co-occurrence could present differently in these patients—for example, as being carried away by suddenly heightened intuitive or psychic abilities, "to the point of engaging in enjoyable activities with potential painful consequences" (p. 332). The enjoyable activity with painful consequences would be using these newfound activities to prophesy or misadvise others. It may well be that the *DSM* criteria need to be adjusted for sensitive patients to deemphasize inflated self-esteem and risky behaviors so that the disorder is more easily recognized in them.

Anxiety Disorders

Panic Attacks, Panic Disorder, and Agoraphobia

Most sensitive persons have had something like a panic attack—moments of feeling overwhelmed and all too aware that their bodies are on the edge of something they have never felt before. As with a hypomanic episode, this could lead to a misdiagnosis or be a co-occurrence. Again, every sensitive person will have at some time felt four or more of the required symptoms: pounding or palpitating heart, sweating, shaking, feeling unable to breathe, feeling of choking, chest pain, nausea, dizziness, faintness, chills or hot flashes, numbness, feeling unreal or detached, and a definite fear of losing control, dying, or going crazy.

Something like a panic episode probably has to happen to the highly sensitive sometime in life, almost by definition, given that they are easily overstimulated by their thorough processing of input. Until they realize how much they differ from others in this regard, their response will be frightening to them. In addition, they feel the sensations of overstimulation in themselves more strongly, adding to their panic. This decisive event usually occurs in sensitive youth, who, wanting to fit in, have tried to ignore how their bodies react to high levels of stimulation. A typical situation for a panic attack for them would be taking a recreational drug at a rock concert.

In most cases the anxiety about these sensations as they happen and the fear of their happening again disappear as soon as they understand about their being easily overaroused in general by strong stimulation. Thus, agoraphobia is usually stopped as well when they learn how this innate predisposition interacted with the situation they were in when the first attack occurred. With that information, they can develop plans to avoid being so overwhelmed in the future, or at least not to be so worried when it happens. Hence, the diagnosis might be deserved initially, but not usually for long, while there must be more than one spontaneous, unexpected, uncured "full" panic attack to meet the *DSM* criteria for the disorder.

As for their co-occurrence, if they do meet the full criteria, their panic disorder still may be more easily resolved than others'. At the other extreme would be cases in which the disorder is due to some deep conditioning to a threat, also a potential with the highly sensitive, and that has generalized to being in the world generally.

Social Phobia

The criteria for social phobia are perhaps some of the vaguest in *DSM*, in that almost everyone has had, at some point in life, bouts of "marked and persistent fear" of being scrutinized and humiliated that they knew to be excessive. The fear impaired them in that it prevented them from functioning as well and freely as they would like to have.

The issue for diagnosis is the persistence of the fear or its frequency. You must keep in mind that sensitive persons are even more aware of the fact that people do scrutinize one another and that these situations are overarousing, and overarousal impairs their response, causing them to feel even more scrutinized, and this cycle may well make their fear a reality. All of this becomes a disorder when they are utterly powerless to overcome their fear in almost all situations. Whether they have social phobia would depend how much the avoidance has become an impairment. Perhaps this diagnosis should be made based on whether receiving it will be useful for the patient in some way, which it usually is not.

Of course, you may also see persons with true social phobia who are not highly sensitive. Those who are sensitive would have other signs of their trait besides extreme shyness.

Obsessive-Compulsive Disorder

Misdiagnoses could easily occur, in that *most sensitive persons are aware of persistent or recurring thoughts or images that they find intrusive, wish were not happening, and try to ignore—the definition of an obsession.* These intensify under stress or during episodes of depression and anxiety, all of which probably occur more in the highly sensitive. For obsessive-compulsive disorder to be diagnosed, *DSM* requires that these thoughts "are not simply excessive worries about real-life problems" (APA, 1994, p. 422). You certainly see sensitive patients who admit to these kinds of worries. The question would be, again, what is "excessive"? *DSM* helps here in being very specific, in that these obsessions and compulsions must take up more than an hour a day and clearly interfere with one's functioning. Further, there would be no attempts to neutralize obsessions through compulsive, highly repetitive, or unrealistic measures. The highly sensitive usually can regulate their affect enough to avoid this type of solution.

On the other hand, a co-occurrence could be difficult to diagnose correctly, as their ability to adapt and their conscientiousness might cover up compulsions in particular. A person with obsessive-compulsive disorder who organizes support groups for them believes all of those with the disorder are highly sensitive and that most can recall the distressing event that first turned their sensitivity into obsessions and compulsions. I do not have enough experience with this disorder to corroborate that thought.

Posttraumatic Stress Disorder and Acute Stress Disorder

The criteria for PTSD require *trauma-related* nightmares, distressing recollections, and excessive stress responses, plus detachment from others, restricted range of affect, numbing, or fears for the future that were not present before the event. It can also manifest as insomnia, hypervigilance, or an exaggerated startle response (an item on the HSP Scale). The decisive issue is whether there has been a trauma that meets the specific criteria. If there has not been, a person with all of these symptoms technically would not have PTSD.

Still, in the moment, this diagnosis might come to mind if a sensitive patient mentions some of these symptoms—for example, autonomic signs such as a frequently racing pulse (the highly sensitive can show extreme sympathetic arousal from even one cup of coffee if they are not used to it) or bizarre, vivid, frightening recurring dreams. It would be easy to make the mistake of looking for the cause in some traumatic event, perhaps one with a delayed onset of symptoms. Indeed, highly sensitive patients unable to regulate their affect due to a combination of traumatic childhood events and an insecure attachment, for example, could easily develop what I would be happy to call chronic PTSD if it were a comforting explanation for a patient. You will see many cases in which sensitive patients meet most of the pure symptom criteria. However, again, for the PTSD diagnosis, *DSM* requires a specific type of event.

There are many co-occurrences, however, because sensitive patients, with their stronger emotional reactions, might develop PTSD after events that would not be traumatic for others. It might also involve a triggering of the sensitive person's strategy of avoiding future risks that are now more vivid.

Generalized Anxiety Disorder

As with social phobia, *the* DSM *criteria for this disorder are highly dependent on defining "excessive"* ("excessive anxiety and worry occurring more days than not for at least 6 months"; APA, 1994) so that the diagnosis could easily be given to anyone highly sensitive, depending on the level of distress and impairment judged to be present. Knowing where the fire exit is in a hotel or theater might seem like excessive worry until there is a fire. A sensitive person under some stress, or even just working a 40-hour week under an unpleasant boss, could easily meet the other criteria, which is 6 months of having, more days than not, three or more of these symptoms: feeling on edge, easily fatigued, trouble concentrating or mind going blank, irritability, muscle tension, and sleep disturbance. This might as easily be diagnosed as an adjustment disorder with anxiety or not diagnosed at all because it is normal for this population.

There are co-occurrences of course, and the history helps to determine if past events have rendered a patient more chronically anxious than others with the trait.

Somatoform Disorders

Sensitive persons are easily misdiagnosed as having somatoform disorders (somatization, conversion, pain disorder, hypochondriasis, and body dysmorphic disorder). First, sensitive persons are by nature more aware of their bodily processes, so that they will notice symptoms sooner and be more concerned and affected by them. Second, they have lower pain thresholds, more reactive immune systems (Boyce et al., 1995), and undoubtedly stronger reactions to consciousness-altering substances. Third, they have more side effects from medications, so they need lower doses and still may not be able to tolerate these effects (Jagiellowicz, Aron, & Aron, 2007). It is very easy to assume that most of these needs for extra medical attention are "all in their heads," but in fact it is all in their DNA.

For these reasons and others (e.g., having more questions about tests and treatments), sensitive persons probably account for about 45% of office visits to physicians (Kowal, 1998). Since most physicians are presumably not highly sensitive, their view of these time-consuming, complaining patients is understandable, and psychotherapists may accept the perspective of their fellow professionals. After all, "the essential feature of Somatization Disorder is a pattern of recurring, multiple, clinically significant complaints" (APA, 1994, p. 446). True, the pattern has to have begun before age 30, but it often does in sensitive young persons, who have not yet learned how to interpret and manage their stronger bodily reactions.

The other somatoform disorders require similar subjective judgments. Again, unfortunately these are generally made by physicians who are not as sensitive and observant about their own bodies. Conversion disorder "involves unexplained symptoms or deficits" (APA, 1994, p. 445) but attempts to find explanations may be fewer when the patient seems to be abnormally sensitive. Pain disorder is diagnosed when pain is the predominant focus and "psychological factors are judged to have an important role" (APA, 1994, p. 445). Again, if a patient is unusually sensitive a doctor may judge this to be a psychological factor, not a genetic one.

Hypochondriasis is "the preoccupation with the fear of having ... a serious disease based on the person's misinterpretation of bodily symptoms" (APA, 1994 p. 445) that "persists despite appropriate medical evaluation and reassurance" (APA, 1994, p. 465). I suspect that every sensitive person (and perhaps everyone period) has had such a preoccupation. Sensitive persons could easily misinterpret their bodily symptoms or fear that others have incorrectly diagnosed them as normal. Knowing that doctors do make errors, the highly sensitive might worry even after having been assured otherwise. Being conscientious and disliking risk, they may want more tests than their doctor might recommend. Occasionally patients have been right and their doctors wrong, at which point the diagnosis of hypochondriasis is removed. You will have to consider all of this when making a diagnosis.

Finally, body dysmorphic disorder is the "preoccupation with an imagined or exaggerated defect" (APA, 1994, p. 445). This does occur in the highly sensitive. Whether it is within the normal range for them is, again, a difficult question to answer.

In sum, for sensitive patients the criteria are too easily met because these disorders require judgments from others who are quite unlike them, about whether a symptom "cannot be fully explained by a known general medical condition," and is "in excess of what would be expected" (APA, 1994, p. 450).

Co-occurrences are also seen, of course. If sensitive patients have for many years lacked ways to handle their more intense emotional reactions, the body's heightened and prolonged stress response will definitely create symptoms or lead to chronic illnesses for which there are no definitive tests, so that the symptoms and illnesses are or seem to be primarily psychological in nature.

In addition, if sensitive patients lacked adequate soothing and emotional containment early in their development, as with anyone else with that history, they will understandably seek, unconsciously, to have these needs met by the only caregivers available to most adults, medical professionals. A difference between the sensitive and nonsensitive with these disorders, however, is that the sensitive patient's symptoms may abate more readily when psychotherapy contains and addresses those needs for attentive understanding, thanks to their probable ability to utilize the therapy environment better.

Another difference is that, compared to nonsensitive somaticizers, even if these patients feel more discomfort they may *complain less to their doctors,* and certainly less aggressively and accusingly. This is because they will be more aware than others that their doctors have doubts about their having a real illness. (Because of this overcompensation, one sensitive patient suffered a burst appendix because she was too ashamed of her somaticizing.)

Sensitive persons generally make more use of alternative medicine than does the general population, and sensitive somaticizers will, too—the practitioners pay more attention to the sensitive person's subtler experiences of symptoms and treatment. The sensitive nonsomaticizer will be more alert to scams, however, while the nonsensitive somaticizer may stay more with standard medicine.

Personality Disorders

First, *the general definition of a personality disorder is very close to that of a distinctive temperament type such as high sensitivity*: "An enduring pattern of inner experience and behavior that deviates markedly from the expectations of the individual's culture, is pervasive and inflexible, has an onset in adolescence or early adulthood [or presumably even earlier, although it cannot be diagnosed earlier], is stable over time, and leads to distress or impairment" (APA, 1994, p. 629). There are certainly some judgments required in interpreting the meaning of "deviates," "pervasive," "inflexible," and "leads to distress or impairment." But again, these judgments can too easily be made about an unusual temperament, especially when the judgment is made by a member of the majority not possessing that temperament. Any temperament is certainly a deviation that is pervasively inflexible and can certainly seem like a source of distress and impairment happens, especially when a talkative mental health professional rates the mental health of someone quiet (Gough & Thorne, 1986).

In sum, even the least impaired highly sensitive persons are statistically abnormal and have been throughout their lives, and these differences can seem to them and others to create impairments that will not change substantially with any kind of treatment, even medication—they are very "inflexible." Genes are that way.

Of course co-occurrences are very real, too. These are mostly what I treat. The personality disorders most easily confused with high sensitivity are, not surprisingly, those that sensitive persons are also mostly likely to develop: schizoid, borderline, avoidant, dependent, and obsessive-compulsive. Interestingly, these disorders cut across the three *DSM* clusters of odd-eccentric, dramatic-emotional, and anxious-fearful, perhaps because the various kinds of developmental traumas and defenses against them that lead to these three categories can impact anyone, sensitive or not, or else the type of personality disorder is the result of an interaction of trauma with other personality traits these patients may have. In addition, regarding the other personality disorders, the highly sensitive can *seem* paranoid when they describe subtle motivations in others that most do not notice; schizotypal due to their unusual perceptions or spiritual proclivities; narcissistic because of their greater "self-absorption" or, if they speak of it, their giftedness; and histrionic in their intense emotional reactions. But these disorders are easier to separate from temperament variations. Now we turn to the five disorders most easily confused with sensitivity.

Schizoid

There is really very little resemblance between a normal sensitive person and a schizoid patient, yet I sometimes hear them equated. The source of confusion seems to be that the highly sensitive also have an easily observed tendency to "prefer spending time by themselves rather than being with other people" (APA, 1994, p. 638). Every sensitive person needs more downtime to process the day's sensory input. This is especially true if their careers require a great deal of stimulation or mental effort, whether it is computer programming or wedding planning.

Similarly, both those with the sensitive trait and those with schizoid personality disorder are often drawn to fields such as engineering, mathematics, or computer programming, and both may even like these fields for their lack of social stimulation (for social animals like humans, social interactions are the most common source of stimulation). But more often the sensitive are in these fields because their creativity and intuition help them excel at solving abstract or spatial problems. Further, these are areas where sensitive men can be accepted and admired, and sensitive women are not expected to be constantly social. (Sometimes sensitivity is viewed as mainly a warm, fuzzy trait, especially by sensitive women who are Myers–Briggs "feeling types." But my data [Aron & Aron, 1997] on the Myers–Briggs found there were no differences in "thinking types" as opposed to "feeling types" among the highly sensitive.)

As for the co-occurrences, it is true that sensitive persons who are too withdrawn, even by the trait's standard, are more likely than other patients to be schizoid.

Borderline Personality Disorder (BPD)

Although the impulsivity and rages expected to accompany this disorder are far from the behavior of most sensitive persons, even *this diagnosis can be misapplied because of the intense emotions of the highly sensitive.* After all, one criterion for the disorder is "affective instability due to a marked reactivity of mood" (APA, 1994, p. 654). Here is another case where a nonsensitive therapist especially might see something wrong in what is normal for a sensitive person.

Mostly, however, it would be difficult to confuse, in person, a typical sensitive person with someone who struggles with BPD. The confusion seems to occur only "on paper," when the idea of sensitivity arises. For example, Stone (1988, 1991) and Grotstein (1996) have used the term "hyperirritability" to describe a symptom of borderline disorder that can be innate as well as traumatically induced. Using an analogy to physical systems, they argue that this sensitivity leads to a lowered threshold, exaggerated response, and chaotic oscillations.

It seems equally reasonable that an innate lowered threshold in a living system accompanied by more thorough processing leads to more accurate, orderly responses rather than to chaos. Chaos would be the result in humans only when affect regulation is lacking. In fact most sensitive persons do learn to regulate their affect. So if the harmful overreactivity being described by these clinicians is inherited, it does not seem likely to be the same innate trait as is being described here. Sensitivity involves a preference for reflection or action that has persisted throughout the long course of evolution.

True, as van der Kolk (1996) observed, "Exquisitely sensitive children may interpret normative growth experiences as terrifying. However, our study suggested that shyness and biological vulnerability are not the predominant factors leading people to develop BPD; the superimposition of childhood terror upon adult situations is most likely to be the key" (p. 189).

Sensitive patients can have what could be better seen as extreme attachment insecurity and meet very well some but not at all of the DSM *criteria for BPD.* For example, they may seem to make "frantic efforts to avoid real or imagined abandonment" (APA, 1994, p. 654). But the effort is more directed at trying to contain, perhaps ineffectually, their fear of or actual loss during separations rather than attempting to coerce another person into remaining with them.

While a sensitive patient, like those with BPD, might defensively idealize or devalue others, they would rarely do both to the same person at different times. The self-esteem of sensitive persons does fluctuate more than others according to events, but they do not usually show a "markedly and persistently unstable self image" (APA, 1994, p. 654), and especially not in the grandiose direction. Furthermore, as said before, affective instability is somewhat in the eyes of the beholder. Dissociation and "chronic feelings of emptiness" (APA, 1994, p. 654) may also be felt and described more by sensitive patients coming for treatment or during it, but the bottom line for diagnosing any disorder (although it is mentioned less for personality disorders) is always impairment.

At the same time, *there are many co-occurrences*. Indeed, there is a strong relationship between BPD symptoms and sensitivity, no doubt in interaction with a damaged early development or abuse. One study

(Meyer, Ajchenbrenner, & Bowles, 2005) found a .43 correlation between the HSP Scale and self-reported borderline *features* in a non-clinical population. Another provocative study (Park, Imboden, Park, & Hulse, 1992) compared outpatients with BPD to a control group with other personality disorders. A substantial 74% of the BPD subjects were rated as both gifted and psychologically abused, compared with only 13% of the controls, suggesting to the authors that some of the symptoms represent exceptionally high perceptual skills—perhaps due to high sensitivity—recruited into defense mechanisms due to trauma.

Behaviors atypical of sensitive persons, such as raging and impulsive behaviors, do occur in sensitive patients with BPD, but will feel less like an aggressive attack and more like the evacuating of overwhelming negative feelings, which sensitive persons reliving early trauma might indeed need to do. More often, sensitive patients with BPD assiduously avoid behaving in a way that would disturb others, even if they inadvertently do so. When they realize it, they usually become depressed immediately afterward, concerned about the harm they may be doing to a relationship that they understand they need. They are also more able to reflect later on the reasons for their responses (even if it does not prevent them), as one would expect of those who specialize in processing before or after acting.

In Kleinian (Klein, 1935/1984) terms, you could say that their innate sensitivity and conscientiousness make it a little easier for them to move from the paranoid-schizoid position, so typical of this disorder, to the depressive position, which takes into account the actual feelings of others.

As I discussed in Chapter 2 (the case of Anna), patients with this disorder or something like it can appear in initial sessions to be functioning surprisingly well because their sensitivity allows them to observe and re-create appropriate behavior. The best key to a correct diagnosis, in my experience, is a childhood history of severe trauma or abuse. It seems that no sensitive person escapes that without some type of personality disorder. Even if the good presentation only represents a regrouping behind the persona, any form of adapting that helps a patient maintain some stable, supportive relationships and a job or other resources that pay for treatment will have a better outcome. In Grotstein's (1995) terms, patients with personality disorders have two selves—one that functions well and one that does not. To work with them at all, therapists need them to be able to employ that better functioning self when they are not in a therapy session, and in my experience sensitive patients are often able to do this. In sum, the co-occurrence of sensitivity and BPD may mean that the disorder will be easier to treat, although perhaps not faster.

Avoidant Personality Disorder (APD)

A paranoid sensitive person might say that the sensitive minority have been wrongly targeted by the *DSM* criteria for APD. Of course the actual disorder does exist and cripples many sensitive persons. But *it is essential that clinicians be able to distinguish between APD and a quiet, introverted, or shy highly sensitive person who is simply being cautious, perhaps rightfully, about being misjudged in social situations.* Overall APD involves "Social inhibition, feelings of inadequacy, and hypersensitivity to negative evaluation" (APA, 1994, p. 662). *The specific criteria, requiring only four to qualify, can be seen as a tidy list of ways that the highly sensitive merely use their trait to detect potentially distressing situations that probably rarely bother others.* The seven criteria are "avoids ... activities ... because of fears of criticism, disapproval, or rejection; is unwilling to get involved ... unless certain of being liked; shows restraint within intimate relationships because of the fear of being shamed; is preoccupied with being criticized or rejected ... ; inhibited in new interpersonal situations ... ; views self as socially inept, personally unappealing, or inferior to others [in this case, because of feeling different due to their lifelong sensitivity]; and is unusually reluctant to take personal risks or to engage in any new activities because they may prove embarrassing" (APA, 1994, p. 665). Almost every introverted sensitive person, even if not shy, would display at least four of these in an unfamiliar or threatening social situation. (Maybe anyone would.)

The main distinction is that those with APD are *always* hindered by their fear of negative evaluation. Normally sensitive persons are secure and confident enough to trust that at least those who get to know them well will like them and do not fear negative evaluations from familiars. They are simply more hesitant about meeting strangers or being in large groups (remember, about 70% are introverts) out of fear of being misjudged. Sensitive persons do have close friends and are highly motivated to have intimate contact with them. Whether you make this diagnosis depends on how unrealistic the patient's fears are and how many potentially valuable, not-too-stimulating social encounters he or she is avoiding.

As for co-occurrences, they definitely occur. Two studies by Meyer and colleagues (Meyer & Carver, 2000; Meyer et al., 2005) of nonclinical student populations looked at sensory-processing sensitivity and self-reported behaviors from the *DSM* list of criteria for APD. In both studies, the combined features of the disorder correlated about .43 with sensory-processing sensitivity.

As for how APD might appear differently in sensitive persons, I have found that the way many avoid social life is by substituting for it an inner life, a spiritual path, or perhaps the appreciation of animals, nature, or the arts. Many sensitive and nonsensitive persons might pursue these, but the sensitive ones in particular will do so for avoidant reasons and reveal deep pain around the lack of close relationships if you probe for it. Sometimes the sensitive person with APD will successfully substitute an entire career for close relationships, if they can find one that does not require social interaction (I recall one who was completely content with a job repairing parking meters). Of course, they are extremely cautious about any transference relationship, although they can seem more attached than they are out of the desire not to hurt the therapist's feelings, while nonsensitive patients with APD might to be less concerned.

Dependent Personality Disorder (DPD)

Sensitivity and dependency, even to the point of a disorder, are easily confused because highly sensitive persons are often in a close relationship in which the nonsensitive member of the dyad supplies skills that are not as available to sensitive persons. Usually they are conscious of this division of labor. (If not, it should be brought up.) The nonsensitive one of the pair may handle everything potentially overstimulating, even to the point of making most phone calls that involve talking with strangers. This person may manage their shared funds if the two want to spend more freely, while the sensitive one of the pair is recruited when the two need to budget. Over and over the nonsensitive member of the pair will seem more effective, if you do not look at the contributions they also make—creativity, empathy, loyalty, careful observations, thorough processing of information, and so forth.

Still, when the sensitive one is struggling with a decision, the nonsensitive person may help by arriving at a final decision and appear to have made it. The nonsensitive one may be earning more money and share this with the sensitive person who earns less or stays home. This division of labor makes the pair stronger than other pairs, and sensitive persons in such relationships might confess that it would be very difficult to live outside of it. Still, they do not have the disorder if in some areas of their lives—career or other relationships—they can make independent decisions.

Even if they did see themselves as dependent, both therapist and patient should look closely, because, again, usually the nonsensitive person is gaining a great deal as well. Indeed, it seems likely that the trait could not have evolved in humans without a dependency developing *between* the sensitive and nonsensitive, so that even if sensitive persons would have had difficulty in some settings managing alone, the nonsensitive would compensate in other settings. Together in groups, the trait would remain because groups that have sensitive members would survive better in competitions with groups without them (Sober & Wilson, 1998). For example, the nonsensitive might depend on the sensitive to supply superior insights about the physical or social world (the weather, the strategies of enemies) or spiritual support (the highly sensitive were no doubt the early shamans and priests). If in a pair both turn out to be dependent on each other, this could be called interdependence, which is not a personality disorder.

Co-occurrences could still occur, in that sensitive patients may seem simply far too strong on the criteria for DPD. In that case, they *still will differ from nonsensitive patients with DPD in that their lack of life skills and sense of needing others will be related to their sensitivity, such as avoiding overstimulation*, as well as such issues as traumas that shake their confidence, an insecure attachment style, or an upbringing in a patriarchal family. Also, there may not be much true interdependence because, for example, the sensitive patient with DPD has a debilitating sense of shame and places no value on his or her insight, which may be too distorted anyway. That is, shame and self-expression may be the core problems rather than a lack of the skills necessary for an independent life. Such sensitive patients may be caught in a cycle of their low self-esteem, being kept from using their offsetting talents, and the inability to express those talents, which causes them to go unappreciated. As a result, their dependency becomes even more shameful and necessary, so that self-esteem is lowered still further and self-expression even more constricted.

Obsessive-Compulsive Personality Disorder (OCPD)

Sensitive persons usually give considerable attention to "doing things right." *Most would not do all of the behaviors identified as criteria for OCPD, but all would do some of them.* For example, they might seem "overly scrupulous" about recycling; keeping their living space, workplace, collections, or personal papers orderly; checking their work to avoid mistakes; checking schedules several times to be sure they read or remembered correctly; or controlling their emotions through methods such as meditation or through spiritual teachings about equanimity. The question would be whether these are "pervasive" and arising from a "preoccupation" that leads to the point that the true reason for the activity has been lost.

Here the *DSM* criteria are very helpful. Unlike the person with OCPD, *the normal sensitive person would not allow these preparations or activities to interfere with life or lose their purpose*—for example, they would not recycle in a way that obviously costs more to the environment (e.g., driving a long distance) than would be saved in the long run by the recycling effort. They definitely would prefer to complete projects on time rather than see that all the details are perfect. They would not live an unbalanced life, emphasizing productivity over relationships, or tolerate clutter rather than throw things out.

On other points, it is less clear. What "overconscientious" means is a matter of opinion. Most people these days consider it normal to copy what is copyrighted, turn a personal dinner into a tax deductible one by having a few moments of chat about work, or not reporting a colleague's unethical behavior. But some sensitive people would not do these, ever, and take pride in it. Are they overly conscientious?

As for being reluctant to delegate to others "unless they submit to exactly his or her way of doing things" (APA, 1994, p. 673), this would certainly depend on the situation. You would not see it as an impairment in a brain surgeon or even an auto mechanic. The judgment of how much money to "hoard for future catastrophes" (APA, 1994, p. 673) will certainly differ between the sensitive and nonsensitive person, but can be a legitimate cause for debate, even among economists. General "rigidity and stubbornness" (APA, 1994, p. 673) can also be viewed in the eyes of the nonsensitive beholder.

As for the co-occurrence of sensitivity and OCPD, these patients would probably be less visible than the nonsensitive equivalent, as they might not impose their behavior so much on others. They also might have more plausible rationalizations for their extreme behaviors, such as their need to reduce overstimulation. In Chapter 2 I described a patient who boarded up her house to keep out the sounds of school children. Her unusual behaviors extended so broadly that it clearly fit the criteria. For example, her house was full of tidy collections that took up all of her time to the point that she had no friends or contact with family.

DISORDERS THAT MIGHT DIFFER IN APPEARANCE OR CAUSE IN THE HIGHLY SENSITIVE

Substance-Related Disorders

The reasons humans overindulge in their favorite mind-altering substances are clearly vast, from genetics to social class. But some research has found a significant role for temperament traits, especially high sensation seeking (Andrew & Cronin, 1997), impulsive sensation seeking (Robbins & Bryan, 2004), and either high novelty seeking or low harm avoidance or, more often, both (Galen, Henderson, & Whitman, 1997). In the same studies low levels of these traits are associated with responsible use or abstention. While a sensitive person can be a high sensation seeker, generally they are not impulsive and do avoid harm, so they would avoid unhealthy, irresponsible, or risky behaviors.

The exceptions usually reach the stage of dependence or abuse because they are seeking relief from overstimulation or unconsciously wishing to avoid the responsibilities of adulthood, which they intuit all too well. The substance can be seen as a transitional object to which they have formed a comforting attachment (Denning, 2000/2004). In others, it is less obviously about sensitivity and more about biology, social environment, or trauma. Still, in these cases they are generally aware of the dangers to themselves and in greater conflict than would be seen in other patients with the same level of "acting out."

Sexual and Gender Identity Disorders

From the questionnaire survey reported in Chapter 7, it appears that there are no differences in the number or type of sexual disorders. Still, there could be some confusion because of sexual "style." Sensitive persons were more affected by unpleasant sounds and odors and less interested in pornography, which could be mistaken as a sign of sexual aversion disorder. They more often reported being so overwhelmed by sensation that it became painful and they needed to stop, which could be mistaken for dyspareunia. They had difficulty with distractions during sex and making transitions after, as well as being far more cautious about risks involving unfamiliar partners, sexually transmitted diseases, or pregnancy, behaviors that might be confused with hypoactive sexual desire without other criteria being met.

As for gender identity disorder, one would expect that the general cultural view of equating sensitivity with femininity may sometimes play a role in a sensitive man's confusion about gender identity.

Sleep Disorders

One of the items eliminated from the HSP Scale was on difficulty sleeping, as it did not distinguish highly sensitive persons. If a sensitive person does complain of insomnia, it is usually due to overstimulation (probably the reason for most insomnia).

Adjustment Disorders

As one would expect, the highly sensitive have more adjustment disorders because these patients have generally stronger responses to stressors and are more easily stressed by high levels of stimulation, more emotional in their reactions to events, and more concerned about long-term consequences than nonsensitive persons. The presentation might differ in that sensitive patients would appear to be used to strong emotions, perhaps habitually over- or undercontrolling them, which you would hear in their histories. A nonsensitive person with an adjustment disorder would be more likely to describe emotions that are stronger than they have ever had before. In addition, the life stressor for sensitive patients might be more subtle or future oriented—for example, fear of losing one's job rather than having actually lost it.

APPENDIX

C

Overview of Research on the Concept of High Sensitivity

This appendix reviews in more detail the research evidence regarding the concept of high sensitivity. It begins with the initial research in which the concept and the HSP Scale were developed, followed by other research by myself and others using the HSP Scale, including neuropsychological data, plus research by others on similar traits in humans and animals. Finally, you will find some theories about the genetic and evolutionary underpinnings of this trait and the answers to some questions you might still have. (Please note that when searching databases such as PsychInfo for studies done on high sensitivity, you will find most of them by using the term sensory-processing sensitivity or SPS.)

INITIAL RESEARCH

Preferring to develop a qualitative feeling for the concept before beginning a quantitative study, I first interviewed persons who identified with the term highly sensitive. I described this as either a high degree of introversion (still being convinced that I was studying an underemphasized aspect of introversion) or being easily overwhelmed by stimulation such as noise, emotionally evocative situations, or shocking entertainment (Aron & Aron, 1997, Study 1).

Interviews: Methods and Findings

Interviewees were recruited from psychology classes at the University of California at Santa Cruz, where I was teaching at the time, and, to gain a broader sample, through announcements in a campus staff newsletter and a local arts association newsletter, asking for "mature nonstudents."

About 10% of students in the psychology classes identified with the term and volunteered; response to the announcement in the newsletters was also strong. The interviews lasted for 3 to 4 hours each and were only with those whom I ascertained by telephone to have understood what was intended by the announcement and felt that it applied to them (about 85%). After recruiting the first 30 participants, I sought a more representative sample by giving some priority to certain ages and to men, artists (hence the art newsletter), and those who had careers deemed successful by conventional standards. In all, 39 people were interviewed, of whom 12 were students, 17 were men, and 30 were single (8 of these were single by divorce). One of each gender self-identified as homosexual. Ages ranged from 18 to 66, with at least four participants in each decade.

The interview protocol began with background data, then moved to general questions on what respondents had thought about the announcement's description of sensitivity and how they understood it for themselves. Questions then advanced from less personal (kinds of movies enjoyed, environmental preferences) to more personal (first memories, relations with parents, school life, friendships, dating and romance or marriage, creative activities, and philosophical and religious views). Afterward interviewees answered a brief attachment-style questionnaire (Hazan & Shaver, 1987) and the Myers–Briggs Type Indicator (MBTI; Myers, 1962).

About half of the interviewees had already thought considerably about being highly sensitive, even though they did not have an exact term for it. For others, the announcement brought their sensitivity into focus for the first time. (In three cases, during the interview it was mutually agreed that the interviewee was not highly sensitive as the researcher was defining it; the data from these interviewees were not included in the quantitative data analysis.)

Perhaps the most surprising result, again, was that of the 35 interviewees who completed the MBTI, 28 were introverted, but 7 were extroverted, despite the recruitment notice being explicitly biased toward introverts (because I thought introversion and sensitivity might be identical, given the research on introverts' greater physical sensitivity). One of the extroverts had been raised on a communal farm and found people, even strangers and large groups, to be calming rather than arousing. She was, however, sensitive to city noise. (Her attachment style, and that of one of the other extroverts, was secure.) Two others seemed to have adopted an extroverted persona as a defense or under pressure from family dynamics (and responded as avoidants on the attachment style questionnaire). Three seemed to have adopted an extroverted attitude out of a kind of energetic, restless giftedness. (They were undecided in their attachment style between secure and insecure styles.)

Another impression from the interviews, corroborated this time by the attachment-style questionnaire, was that about half of the respondents had had "good enough" childhoods but were clearly highly sensitive anyway—that is, their sensitivity was not simply a reaction to chronic family dysfunction or early trauma. These highly sensitive respondents with adequate childhoods were generally successful, either as students or in their careers, and saw many advantages to their sensitivity, although it had shaped their lives considerably. Their close-relationship histories were also far better than those with troubled childhoods. Among those with difficult childhoods, some had received considerable psychotherapy, and these accounted for almost all of the respondents who were undecided between secure and the two insecure options on the attachment questionnaire. The others with unhappy childhoods evidenced fairly severe adjustment or personality problems in adulthood, although these problems were not necessarily related in an obvious way to their sensitivity (e.g., two had eating disorders). However, there was a sense in which their sensitivity also seemed more problematic, affecting more their schooling experiences, career, and relationships. They were particularly likely to feel vulnerable, handicapped, or flawed because of their trait.

Another observation that held for over 70% was their sense of being different, especially in regard to their need to take more frequent breaks than others during busy days (and then feeling something was wrong with them for needing to go off alone). Other observations were their conscious arrangement of their lives to reduce stimulation and unwanted surprises; the importance of their spiritual and inner lives, including dreams; and a general conscientiousness both about details and a concern with "doing what is right."

There was a pervasive impression of at least mild low self-esteem, which could not always be explained by poor parenting or trauma. Some saw their difference as a weakness in itself. Others thought felt there had been many failures in their lives due to their sensitivity. They felt they had less control than others over their reactions to situations, such as being observed on the job, taking tests, speaking up in a group, or performing. They thought they were too concerned about being judged in regard to their general worthiness.

The HSP Scale

From the interviews a number of characteristics were identified that ought to be true of sensitive persons. These formed a 60-item questionnaire (Aron & Aron, 1997) that was given to 604 psychology students, from two samples—319 at the University of California, Santa Cruz, and 285 from statistics students in seven classes around the country. It was also given to 301 respondents in a community sample using random digit dialing and female student interviewers (there was a 37% respondent rate, quite good for these methods, and 8% of interviews were conducted in Spanish). From these data we reduced the 60 items (in a series of factor analyses and various-item evaluation methods) to the 27 on the final Highly Sensitive Person Scale (HSP Scale) used in this and subsequent research. In extensive testing, this questionnaire was highly internally consistent—that is, these seemingly diverse items were highly correlated: Cronbach alphas ranged from .64 to .75. (If you are unfamiliar with this statistic, Cronbach alphas range from 0 to 1, but extremes are unusual, so these alphas are relatively high, particularly for the very diverse set of items included in this scale.) Subsequent studies (reviewed below) have found similar alphas.

For each sample there was also a clear single-factor solution with a dramatic drop in eigenvalues (overall variance accounted for) from the first to second unrotated factor, with the remaining factors clearly showing a scree plot (low values tapering off without any sudden drop). Thus, based on the standard scree test approach, the measure appears to tap a single construct. (However, some subsequent studies have argued for subscales or multiple factors—an issue I will turn to shortly.) Given the wide range of behaviors and attitudes covered by the items, from startling easy and being affected by caffeine to having a rich inner life and appreciating the arts, a one-factor solution also fits with the theory that the construct describes something fundamental underlying most or all behaviors of those with the trait. (Most measures of a trait or behavior with alphas above .60 have nearly identical questions in order to have a scale that has an adequate Cronbach alpha and is unidimensional.) In this initial paper (Aron & Aron, 1997, Study 5) we also reported on the external validity of the HSP Scale, finding with a new sample of 119 students a substantial relationship between the HSP Scale and an already validated measure of a similar construct, Mehrabian's (1976) scale assessing low sensory screening.

Interestingly, the distributions of scores on the HSP Scale in all of our samples (N = 1,494) mirrored the experience of others with the temperament construct "inhibitedness" studied in young children (using formal taxometric methods; Woodward, Lenzenweger, Kagan, Snidman, & Arcus, 2000), that the trait is distributed more like an approximately dichotomous category variable rather than as a continuum with a normal distribution. That is, we found a break point somewhere in all of our sample distributions, and the "curve" was flattened, rather than most individuals falling in the middle. Again, between 10 and 35% fell into the highly sensitive category, depending on the sample—for example, psychology classes tended to attract more sensitive students than other classes. (For a discussion of typological conceptions of personality, see Robins, John, and Caspi [1998]; for a discussion of the related idea of global traits, see Funder [1991].)

The HSP Scale and Social Introversion

Systematic statistical comparisons were made of the sensitivity measure and several measures of social introversion (Aron & Aron 1997, Studies 2–4) used in the university and community studies. Using our own brief measure of social introversion, which varied from two to four questions (do you like meeting strangers, have a large circle of friends, avoid crowds, "recharge your batteries" alone or in the company of others), correlations ranged for the different samples from .25 to .52 (all significant), suggesting a clear relationship to social introversion, but also demonstrating that the variables are distinct.

We also used others' measures of social introversion. In one sample using the MBTI, the correlation with sensitivity was .14. In two samples, we measured introversion using Eysenck's (1981) *earlier* Eysenck Personality Inventory (in which items measuring both impulsivity and sociability were included) and the correlations were .27 and .29 (both significant). Using John, Donahue, and Kentle's (1992) Extraversion Scale, based on the Five Factor Model (McCrae & Costa, 2003), the correlation was .12 (not significant). John, Donahue, and Kentle's (1992) measure is shorter than other five-factor measures but has levels of reliability comparable to them (all five-factor measures of introversion emphasize sociability). Although most of these correlations were significant, as one would expect, they were not high.

Using another way to separate introversion from Sensory Processing Sensitivity (SPS), we compared the scale to items measuring sensitivity that were from the original 60 and not on the final scale for various reasons but still obviously about sensitivity, such as crying easily, falling in love intensely, sensitivity to alcohol, and sensitivity to daily and seasonal variations in sunlight. We used these items as a second "external" measure of sensitivity to do a series of partial correlation analyses.

After statistically partialing out introversion (having the effect, more or less, of testing sensitive people who are only average on introversion), the HSP Scale was still strongly correlated with this "external" sensitivity scale. When partialing out the HSP Scale from measures of introversion, the "external" sensitivity scale was not correlated with introversion. As an additional test of the specificity of the HSP Scale in relation to introversion, we also went at it the other way, making an "external scale" of introversion questions (e.g., "prefer to live in the country") that correlated with the measures we had used for introversion. When partialing out the standard measures of introversion, the HSP Scale did not correlate with the "external" introversion scale. However, when partialing out the HSP Scale, the standard introversion measure still correlated with the "external" introversion scale.

The HSP Scale and Neuroticism

We also carried out the same series of analyses in the same samples focusing on three measures of neuroticism (negative affectivity). The first was our own three questions, used in all studies: "Are you prone to fears?", "Are you a tense or worried person by depression?", and "Are you prone to depression?" Correlations of this three-item scale with the HSP Scale ranged from .47 to .62 (all significant). The correlation with five-factor measure of neuroticism in John et al. (1992) was .41 (also significant).

Although the correlations between neuroticism and SPS were always moderate to high, they were very far from perfect. Further, applying the same set of partial correlation analyses to "external" measures of neuroticism and sensitivity, we again found the two constructs to be clearly distinct. That is, statistically partialing out neuroticism, the correlation of the HSP Scale with "external" sensitivity items remained; partialing out the HSP Scale, the standard neuroticism measures still correlated with "external" neuroticism items.

Especially important, given that the SPS trait involves greater emotional reactivity, is our finding that this reactivity is both to negative and positive events and is present independent of neuroticism. For example, after partialing out neuroticism measures, the HSP Scale still correlated with general (not specifically negative) emotion questions—for example, in one sample (Aron & Aron, 1997, Study 6), with crying easily (.54 before partialing out neuroticism, .33 after), feeling love intensely (.31, .24), and "when you are happy, is the feeling sometimes very strong?" (.50, .30). These results support the idea that those high in SPS, neurotic or not, have stronger emotional reactions in general, including positive emotions. This was further corroborated by an experimental induction of positive and negative emotions (Aron et al., 2005, Study 4) described below and has since been demonstrated using neuroimaging (Bar-Haim et al., 2009).

Finally, the HSP Scale does not represent a simple combination of introversion and neuroticism, even though introversion and neuroticism were significantly correlated with each other (.16, .22, .16), as were the multiple correlations of the two with the HSP Scale (.56, .62, .47). In contrast, across all the various samples in our initial report (and in every study since that has conducted such analyses), nearly all of the correlations of the HSP Scale with sensitivity-related "external" items or variables remained strong and significant after partialing out both introversion and neuroticism.

In the initial series of studies (Aron & Aron, 1997), individuals who had a troubled past were not systematically separated out in these analyses. If they had been, it seems likely that the correlations with neuroticism would have been substantially reduced. Whatever remained would have been explained by items that neurotic and nonneurotic sensitive persons would both agree to, even though their reasons would differ somewhat—for example, being distressed by performing before others, sudden changes, deadlines, or having "a lot going on at once." For the nonneurotic sensitive person the main reasons would be related to disliking overstimulating situations. For the neurotic individual, there would be primarily fear of failure and humiliation or the consequences of depression and low self-esteem.

Sensitivity and the Five Factor Model

Neuroticism was the only one of the five factors (neuroticism, extroversion, conscientiouness, agreeableness, openness to experience) that correlated significantly or near significantly with the HSP Scale in our 1997 samples. However, the multiple correlation of all five scales with the HSP Scale was .54 ($p < .01$), a figure only slightly higher than just considering neuroticism and introversion without the other there. This small increase is probably because there are some questions in the other scales that do describe highly sensitive persons, but the scales themselves do not. Even given that a .54 association is clearly substantial, it means that 71% of the variance was not accounted for by the Five Factor Model at all, suggesting that SPS is not fully contained within these widely used constructs.

Smolewska, McCabe, and Woody (2006) also compared the HSP Scale to the Five Factor Model, using the NEO-Five Factor Inventory, and found a correlation (.45) with neuroticism, similar to what we had found, in addition to a .31 correlation with openness (which we had expected to find but did not in our sample). They also replicated the lack of a significant relationship with the Five Factor Model's other three scales, most notably introversion-extroversion. This is not surprising given that the Five Factor Model equates introversion with a lack of positive affect, while sensitivity is strongly associated with a positive answer to "When you are happy is the feeling sometimes very strong?"

Bottom Line: The initial research (Aron & Aron, 1997) on SPS began with interviews, from which 60 items were selected and administered to several large samples before the 27-item HSP Scale was finalized as a unidimensional, reliable, internally and externally valid measure of a trait thought to involve a strategy of preferring to process information before acting.

THE INTERACTION OF SENSITIVITY WITH TROUBLED CHILDHOOD PREDICTS NEGATIVE AFFECT AND SHYNESS

Again, although sensitivity was clearly distinct from neuroticism in our 1997 results, the two did correlate around .45. However, the interviews indicated that depression and anxiety were reported mostly by those with troubled childhoods. In these 1997 studies we did find a distinct subgroup of sensitive persons, about 30%, who evidenced substantially more introversion and negative emotions and whose negative affect seemed associated with a troubled childhood. But we had not looked for the interaction—that is, that chronic negative emotions or unusually positive outlook and behaviors are better predicted by considering sensitivity and childhood together rather than using either of these alone. (Specifically, the interaction pattern we expected from the interviews was that, although anyone would be affected by the quality of their childhood, the effect of childhood would be much stronger for the highly sensitive. Thus, those with a troubled childhood should show an especially high level of neuroticism, but those with a good childhood should if anything show *less* neuroticism than nonsensitive persons.)

Three Studies

The first study by Aron et al. (2005, Study 1) measured childhood environment, using a six-item scale of a few childhood experiences that could be answered relatively objectively (e.g., was there mental illness or alcoholism in the family, was a parent absent, were you especially close to your parents, etc.). We also used the three-item scale of negative affect or neuroticism we had used in the 1997 studies ("Are you tense or worried by nature?" "Are you prone to fears?" "Are you prone to depression?"). In all three studies, we also measured shyness, using Cheek's (1983) revised measure. We measured shyness because it is so often equated with sensitivity and because it is another variable we thought from the interviews would be predicted by the interaction of SPS and childhood environment (for a full discussion of the relation of sensitivity to shyness, see E. Aron [1999]). In addition, in all of these studies, we assessed introversion, but when introversion was partialed out, in every case the result was unchanged.

In this first study ($N = 96$) we found the predicted interaction, but more for shyness than neuroticism. For the highly sensitive, the worse the childhood, the greater the shyness, while there was a near-zero correlation between the childhood scale and shyness for the nonsensitive. The interaction was marginally significant ($p < .07$) for negative affect. The correlation of the childhood scale and negative affect for sensitive persons was .40 and .12 for the nonsensitive. The best "path analysis" found that sensitive persons with negative affect were likely to be shy—that is, negative affect was an important mediator. If high-SPS persons with troubled childhoods had managed to avoid chronic negative affect, they were not considered shy (Figure 1).

In the second study ($N = 213$) the same hypotheses were studied, but we also measured negative affect, using the Beck Anxiety Inventory (Beck, Epstein, Brown, & Steer, 1988) and the Beck Depression Inventory (Beck, 1978), and childhood environment, using the Parental Bonding Instrument (PBI; Parker, Tupling, & Brown, 1979). With this larger sample and these more standard measures,

(a) MODEL:

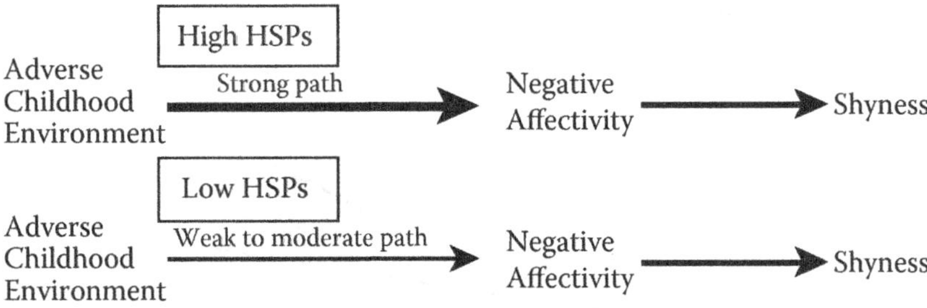

(b) RESULTS (AS PREDICTED BY MODEL):

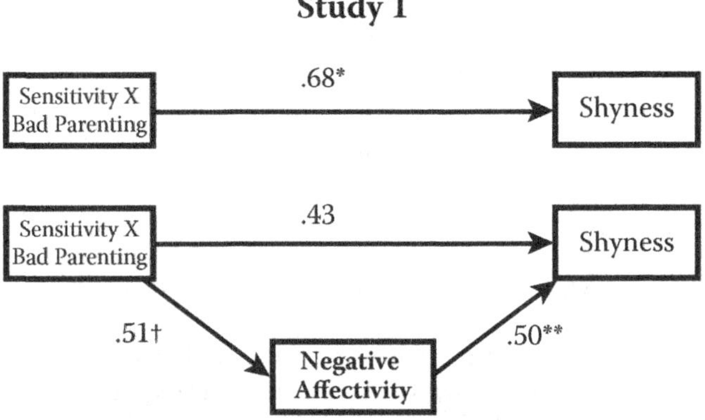

Figure 1

there was a clearly significant interaction such that SPS in combination with either poor parental environment or with negative affect was significantly related to shyness. Again, in our search for the best fitting path to shyness, negative affect was the mediator between bad parental environment and shyness. In Study 3 (N = 396) the same results were obtained using only ratings of the mother: a composite score of the mother version of the PBI and ratings of actual and desired closeness to the mother at ages 5, 9, 13, and 16 (Figure 2). Note that, although positive outcomes were not being measured for, those with positive scores on the PBI were less neurotic and shy than nonsensitive persons with similar positive scores on the PBI—that is, sensitive persons were doing especially well. Study 4 (which involved an experimental manipulation) is described later.

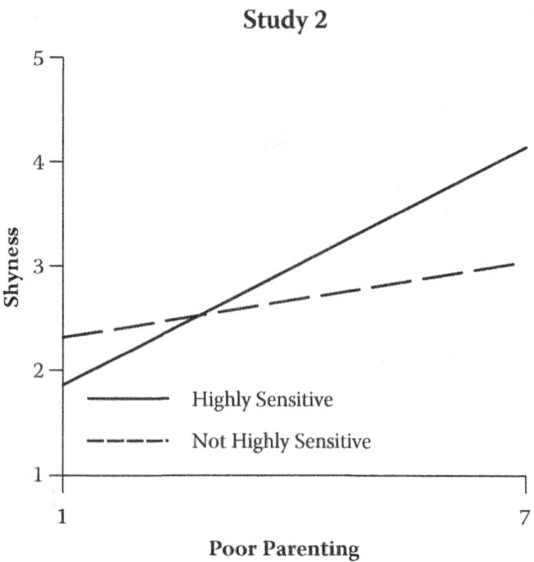

Figure 2

About the Use of Retrospective Self-Reports

Persons high on neuroticism are likely to describe a memory of an experience more negatively than they described the experience at the time it occurred (Barrett, 1997; Cutler, Larsen, & Bunce, 1996; Larsen, 1992), and the depressed tend to report most past events more negatively than the nondepressed (Feldman, 1995). Therefore, longitudinal data would have been preferable for studying these variables, but there are reasons to suppose such memory biases were not affecting our results.

There are no doubt problems with retrospective self-reports under conditions in which the obtained or predicted pattern of results corresponds to the likely direction of bias, as would be the case, for example, when correlating adult depression with retrospective reports of having had a bad childhood. But this type of correlation cannot explain why the association of negative childhood and negative affect should be higher for the highly sensitive. In fact, if high SPS were the same as having more negative affect or meant a more negative view of their life, including childhood, if when comparing a sensitive and nonsensitive person who each have the same current level of depression, if such a bias were operating, then the highly sensitive one would report a more negative childhood. The reports of depressed sensitive patients would be more biased than others' when depressed. However, the observed pattern of results is that with the same current degree of depression, high SPS subjects report a *less negative* childhood. (That is, the pattern of our results is that it takes a less negative childhood for them, compared to nonsensitive persons, to grow up depressed.)

To put it another way, if you made the mistake of equating being sensitive with being neurotic and having a negative bias, when a sensitive person who is upset by being jobless comes to you and describes a terrible childhood, you would think to yourself that this patient is certainly distressed, but his childhood was not as bad as he says—he is just a negative type of person.

In the next hour, a nonsensitive patient comes in equally upset by being jobless and has had a similar troubled childhood. This time you believe his childhood was as bad as he says because you think a nonsensitive patient does not exaggerate—he has had the terrible childhood he describes. Our results, however, show that for the sensitive patient to have the same degree of impairment—the same distress about being jobless—he would have had to describe a better childhood, not a worse one, than the second patient.

Given the results as described above, clearly we did not find this bias in our study, and this suggests that it is appropriate to conclude from the retrospective self-reports that the interaction of SPS and a troubled childhood leads to neuroticism (the negative affects of depression and anxiety) rather than SPS being the same as neuroticism. Rather, if this bias—that sensitive people all see their pasts more negatively—had been present, it would have worked against the obtained pattern of results. Thus, when longitudinal, observational research is eventually done, one might expect the same pattern that we observed to be even stronger.

Study 4: An Experiment

When we planned the next study (Aron et al., 2005, Study 4), we were only beginning to look actively for the interaction of sensitivity and a good childhood—that this combination leads to more positive outcomes than not being sensitive and having a similar good childhood. Our main goal was to begin to understand the process by which certain events might affect sensitive children and more. Assuming this process would have some similarity for those who are past childhood, we looked at the reactions of college students right after something occurred that should have been important to them. This time we tried to include a positive experience, but unfortunately, to measure emotional impact of the experience, we used a scale that measured degree of negative feelings. Still, participants could choose "not at all" anxious, sad, etc.

The experiment involved giving college students a test of "applied reasoning ability," for which (unknown to the participants) half were randomly assigned to receive a very difficult version and the other half a very easy version. Those doing the easy version saw people around them struggling (in fact, some problems had no right answer), and those doing the difficult version saw others finishing quickly. (We verified by a manipulation check that, regardless of whether they were highly

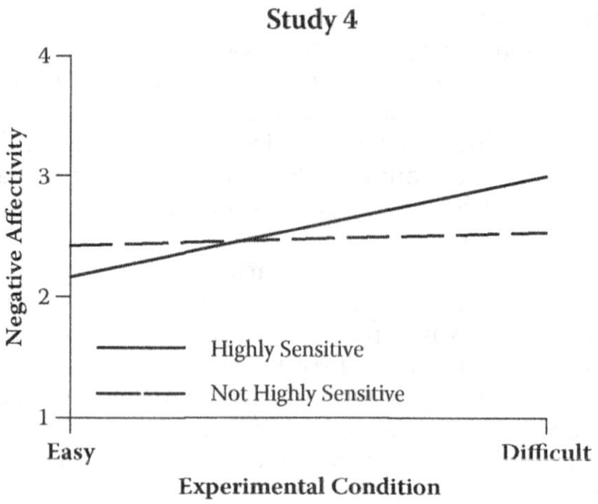

Figure 3

sensitive or not, those with the difficult version believed they had indeed done very poorly on a test of applied reasoning ability; those in the easy-version condition, that they had done very well.) Again we found an interaction, in that sensitive students who thought they had done badly felt worse than nonsensitive students who received the same feedback, whereas sensitive students who thought they did well had a stronger positive (less negative) emotional reaction than nonsensitive students who received the same news (Figure 3).

Indeed the nonsensitive students had almost no reaction to either type of test. Presumably the sensitive students were more affected by feeling they had done well or poorly on the test because they processed the subjective meaning of it more thoroughly. At any rate, it seemed that if sensitive adults responded more strongly to emotionally valenced events, the same might be true for children. Note that, as said earlier, the sensitive students were more sensitive to positive as well as negative feedback, replicating in another way the finding in the 1997 research that sensitive persons report stronger happy as well as unhappy reactions to situations. Research by others, described below, has found the same greater-than-typical positive effect of positive experiences on sensitive persons. One group (Boyce et al., 1995), studying school children in good and bad home and school environments, suggested that children with a heightened sensitivity to psychosocial processes "might also be better able to notice when social cues denote encouragement and acceptance" (p. 420).

Bottom Line: Following up on results in the initial research suggesting a differential effect of a troubled childhood on sensitive persons, we (Aron et al., 2005) looked for and found an interaction between a troubled childhood and sensitivity such that sensitive persons with troubled childhoods were more likely to have negative affect in adulthood and also to be shy, but it is the negative affect that mediates the outcome of shyness. In an experiment looking for how negative experiences might affect sensitive children more, sensitive college students were found to react more than others to a negative experience, but also to a positive one.

NEUROSCIENCE FINDINGS

The HSP Scale is a useful instrument for conducting research. However, ultimately the concept and the scale require the type of validation that indicates that this trait is based on a physiological difference between sensitive and nonsensitive people that affects behavior.

Highly Sensitive Individuals Show Less Cultural Bias in Perception

In a study (Hedden, Ketay, Aron, Markus, & Gabrieli, 2008) designed to test brain response to a known cultural difference in perception, 10 Americans of European descent and 10 East Asians recently in the United States were administered the HSP Scale and underwent functional magnetic resonance imaging (fMRI) while doing simple visiospatial tasks emphasizing judgments that were either context independent (typically easier for Americans) or context dependent (typically easier for Asians). Each group exhibited greater activation for the culturally nonpreferred task in frontal and parietal regions associated with greater effort in attention and working memory. However, in a subsequent analysis focused on the HSP Scale result (Aron et al., 2007), this overall effect was found to be dramatically and significantly moderated by individual differences in SPS.

Specifically, consistent with theory, highly sensitive individuals showed little difference as a function of culture; low sensitives showed strong culture differences. This interaction remained significant ($p < .05$) controlling for negative affectivity (neuroticism), social introversion, gender, and individual differences in strength of cultural identity. In other words, the sensitive persons needed to use less or no effort to overcome a culturally biased perception found in nonsensitive persons (Figure 4).

SPS Associated With Increased Activation in Perceptual Areas During Fine Perceptual Discriminating Tasks

In an fMRI study (Jagiellowicz et al., in press), students who varied in their scores on the HSP Scale carried out a series of tasks in the scanner, in which they rated each of a series of landscape scenes as to whether they were similar or different from the previous one. The presentations were in blocks, in which the variations (when there were variations)

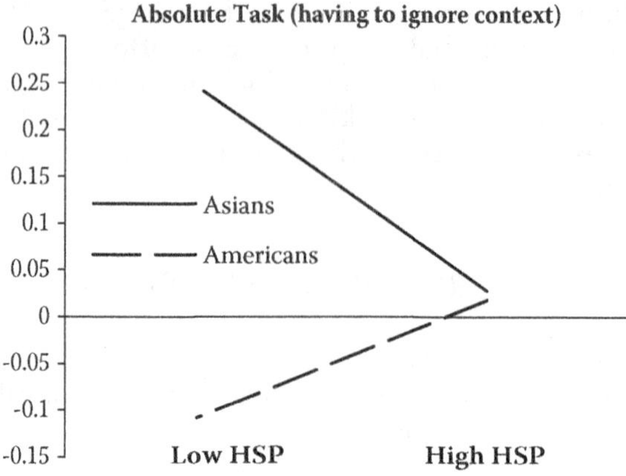

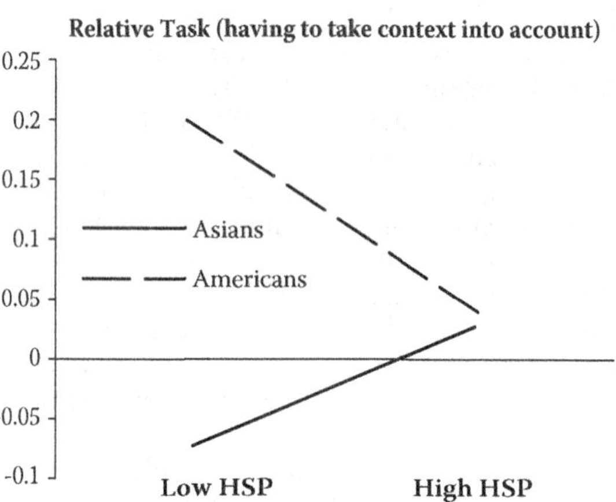

Figure 4

were either gross or subtle. There were 12 blocks of each type, presented in random order. Those scoring higher on the HSP Scale showed dramatically more activation in a variety of regions (especially visual processing) during subtle (vs. gross) tasks, suggesting that they were more actively working on the subtle tasks than nonsensitive subjects. These results suggest that even with such a small sample, sensitive persons can be found to respond quite differently from the nonsensitive on varying tasks.

Voxel-Based Morphology, Difference in Brain Structure Between SPS and Non-SPS

A study (Ersner-Hershfield et al., 2007) using a new method, voxel-based morphometry, which identifies differences in density of gray matter, looked at variations in SPS in two samples of U.S. college students and one sample of Asian college students recently in the United States. Across all three samples, this trait was strongly associated with complex but consistent differences in gray matter.

Bottom Line: Neuropsychological studies, even though using very small samples, have found that scores on the HSP Scale are associated with differences in brain morphology and predictable differences in activation during perceptual tasks.

CLINICAL AND APPLIED RESEARCH USING THE HSP SCALE

A number of studies have employed the HSP Scale in clinical research. Meyer and Carver (2000) explored it and other variables that might be associated with college students rating themselves as fitting the *DSM* description of avoidant personality disorder. Pessimism was related to students' ratings if they were high in SPS or recalled adverse childhood experiences. (However, the authors did not test whether the pessimism–SPS correlation would remain after partialing out adverse childhood experiences.)

Neal, Edelmann, and Glachan (2002) used mailed responses from volunteers who belonged to anxiety and depression self-help organizations to study the relationship of various mental health problems to high sensitivity. Sensitivity was related to anxiety (social phobia, agoraphobia, anxiety, panic disorder) in this group, but not related to depression.

Liss et al. (2005) replicated the HSP-by-childhood–experience interaction we found (Aron et al., 2005, Studies 1–3) but measured depression and anxiety separately rather than as a single negative affect (neuroticism) variable. In their study, SPS was related to depression only for those with poor parental care, but was related to anxiety regardless of parental care.

Meyer et al. (2005) used a sample that was 50% college students and 50% from the general London area to look for the antecedents of avoidant and borderline personality disorders and found no main effect relationship between high sensitivity and either these disorders or negative childhood experiences. However, when breaking the HSP Scale down into subscales (an issue discussed later), there were some relationships.

Benham (2006) found that among college students, scoring high on the HSP Scale correlated with self-perceived stress and self-reported physical symptoms of ill health. In the same year, Kemler (2006) separated athletes into those scoring high and low on the HSP Scale and found that after participating in an athletic event, those who were high on the scale reported more anxiety, shame, and more of a discrepancy between how they viewed themselves and their ideal and also between how they viewed themselves and how they ought to be. (A possible alternative interpretation is that their anxiety led to poorer performance and perhaps the other emotional outcomes followed from that.)

Hofmann and Bitran (2007) explored the relationship of scores on the HSP Scale to social anxiety disorder in a sample of persons diagnosed through clinical interviews with the disorder. Although the interviews had generally validated the administered test for social anxiety disorder, being highly sensitive and diagnosed with the disorder did not correlate with scores on the test. Sensitivity did correlate with a generalized subtype of social anxiety and agoraphobia, as well as a measure of harm avoidance, as if those who were highly sensitive had an atypical social anxiety disorder. Another way to think of these results is that the sensitive patients diagnosed with the disorder through clinical interviews did not in fact have it, since the test that normally validated the diagnosis did not do so in their case.

Evers, Rasche, and Schabracq (2008) studied the effect of high sensitivity on work stress: not finding work manageable, meaningful, or comprehensible and work producing alienation, low self-efficacy, and negative affect. Using volunteers recruited through friends who then recruited more in a snowball effect (it is not clear if they knew the purpose of the study), Evers et al. found most of the predicted negative effects of sensitivity were present for the whole HSP Scale and those two subscales measuring negative aspects of the trait. SPS did not correlate with finding work lacked meaning or that work led to low self-efficacy.

Bottom Line: A number of others have used the HSP Scale in various ways, including replicating the interaction of sensitivity and a troubled childhood leading to negative affect, specifically depression but not anxiety. The presence of anxiety in all sensitive persons, whatever their childhood experiences, fits with an image of them as persons preferring to watch before acting rather than taking risks. Sensitive college students reported more stress and physical symptoms than their nonsensitive counterparts, and sensitive college athletes suffered more shame and anxiety following a game. Sensitive persons were not found more likely to have avoidant or borderline personality disorders or to fit the full criteria for social anxiety disorder, and in a study on the effects of the trait on work stress, results were mixed.

IS THE HSP SCALE UNIFACTORIAL?

The HSP Scale was empirically based, using interviews to create a large number of items and then seeking a small number that correlated well with one another (Aron & Aron, 1997). Not knowing exactly what we were studying, this was the appropriate process. When the scale was complete, we were surprised to see the wide range of items that correlated well with one another, from sensitivity to pain and startling easily to a complex inner life and conscientiousness. This result caused us to think further about the concept we were uncovering and to suspect it was about processing at a deep level rather than simply having keen senses and being easily overwhelmed by too much stimulation. Further, this type of deep-processing sensitivity led to both pleasant and unpleasant effects and to strategies to avoid the unpleasant effects of overstimulation.

Further, as Aron et al. (2005) and others later discovered, SPS leads to a vulnerability to stressful life experiences that would affect its measurement. Without partialing out some measure of a troubled childhood or similar stress, the scale we had developed was overly correlated with neuroticism and measures of negative affect because a certain percentage of sensitive people in our samples had had difficult childhoods and had been more strongly affected by that than the nonsensitive persons with difficult childhoods. Nevertheless, the HSP Scale has predicted results well, including the neurophysiological studies reported.

In short, it appears to be an imperfect yet surprisingly useful measure. What remains important about it is that it covers such a wide range of phenomena that all seem to result from some single, underlying individual difference. Cronbach's alpha is an indicator of how much a person saying yes to one item is likely to say yes to another. In the studies reporting in terms of Cronbach's alpha (Aron & Aron, 1997; Benham, 2006; Hofmann & Bitran, 2007; Meyer & Carver, 2000; Meyer et al., 2005; Neal et al., 2002), it was typically .85 or higher, suggesting a coherent, unidimensional scale.

Factor analyses are another way of seeing whether a set of items are unidimensional or can be divided into subscales. There is some disagreement as to when a scale can be said to have subscales. Of those studies using the measure for other purposes but reporting factor analyses, some reported the HSP Scale to be unidimensional (Aron & Aron, 1997; Hofmann & Bitran, 2007; Neal et al., 2002). These were generally based on the widely used standard scree plot method, in which one reviews the pattern of eigenvalues (the variance accounted for) as one proceeds from the first to the last unrotated factor, inspecting the pattern visually for the point at which the eigenvalue for each of the remaining factors stretches out like scree on a hillside. (If there is only one factor, the first eigenvalue might be 7 and the next 2, 1.8, 1.7, 1.5, 1.4, etc.) In the studies that have reported the eigenvalues for the first several factors, results have all been similar, with a very large first eigenvalue (e.g., 26% of variance accounted for), the second substantially lower (e.g., 8% or less), and the rest dropping gradually to 0.

However, in some studies, there was a second drop somewhere after the big initial drop, which was then interpreted as indicating that there is more than one factor. Thus, Myer et al. (2005) reported four factors and Smolewska et al. (2006) reported three. Evans and Rothbart (2008), using a different method of identifying the number of factors, reported two. Below we briefly summarize some of the findings of these studies and what they may suggest about the underlying structure of the HSP Scale. Meyer et al. (2005), as noted, interpreted their results as indicating four factors. After rotation, they labeled these factors general sensitivity/overstimulation (accounting for 28% of the total variance), adverse reactions (8%), psychological fine discrimination (7%), and controlled harm avoidance (4%). In their study of avoidant and borderline personality, these factors (treated as subscales) differentiated the two, in that avoidant personality correlated significantly with controlled harm avoidance and borderline with psychological fine discrimination.

Smolewska et al. (2006) labeled the three factors ease of excitation (26%), aesthetic sensitivity (8%), and low sensory threshold (6%). However, the items in the Meyer et al. and Smolewska et al. factors were not the same.

Evans and Rothbart (2008) compared the HSP Scale to Rothbart's Adult Temperament Questionnaire (Evans & Rothbart, 2007), which was developed differently. They began with definitions of traits and included only items that fit these definitions. Using parallel analysis (a recently developed method for determining number of factors) and cross-checking with confirmatory factor analysis, they found the HSP Scale could be broken down into two factors matching their scales of negative affect (specifically its subscale of distress due to sensory discomfort) and orienting sensitivity (specifically its subscale of sensory sensitivity) with only a moderate correlation between them. (Their factor solution maps fairly well onto the three factors of Smolewska et al. in the sense that one overlaps closely and the second contains the other two. There is much less overlap with the four factors of Meyer et al.)

We would note in all of this back and forth that all of our factor analyses are likely to be biased by the interaction with childhood environment. Thus, for example, the Evans and Rothbart sensory discomfort factor may be largely due to the contribution of those with a poor childhood history. Evans and Rothbart, coming from an exclusively temperament perspective, do not review the several studies that found these interactions and may not have been aware of them.

When the HSP Scale is divided in various ways into subscales, some of the subscales have been found to correlate with various disorders (Liss, Mailloux, & Erchull, 2008; Meyer et al., 2005). This is to be expected, given that the overall HSP Scale correlates fairly highly with neuroticism, and scales using items about sensory discomfort correlate with autism spectrum disorders, in which such discomfort is observed, albeit in an inconsistent way. But we would still argue that although some features of sensitivity can be found in those outside the population of sensitive persons, focusing on that feature misses the source. As an anology, women often wear skirts, but men can also wear skirts, and dogs often have tails, but so do many other animals, from salamanders to ponies. But there is also something specific and unique about women, dogs, and sensitive people. The idea here is that the whole cannot be described by its various parts.

If people need a measure of sensory discomfort, they can find it in a subscale of the HSP Scale, although other measures will no doubt evolve that focus more directly on stimulus threshold and discomfort (e.g., Adult Sensory Profile or Brown and Dunn's Sensory Discomfort Scale [2002], which is based on the concept of sensory processing disorder and has its origin in occupational therapy). Such measures, however, would seem to be assessing only negative effects of the sensory sensitivity aspect of high sensitivity. SPS as conceptualized by ourselves and others who come more from a biological and evolutionary perspective view the trait as involving not only sensing more and perhaps being made uncomfortable by that (those with a troubled childhood even more than others), but also processing and responding to stimuli in a different way than the majority do.

In terms of whether the construct is uniform or complex, the jury seems still out among three major possibilities: (a) there are independent, minimally correlated factors (a possibility supported in some studies, but generally not found), (b) there are partially correlated factors, subscales, or "facets" of an overall coherent construct (a possibility consistent with several studies, although the variations across studies in how the overall scale should be divided raises some doubts), or (c) there is a single factor representing a common underlying trait with diverse expressions depending on circumstances such as parenting (a possibility consistent with quite a bit of the data, and especially with the animal research described below, although clearly not definitively established).

Bottom Line: The HSP Scale items are more highly varied compared to most personality or temperament scales. Thus it is no surprise that these diverse items group into subcategories. Rather, the surprise is that such varied questions do correlate with one another as much as they do, as if one basic trait underlies them all. Further, this set of varied questions does appear to separate persons into groups with and without the trait that are measurably different in important ways, including brain functioning and neuroanatomy.

RESEARCH ON SIMILAR TRAITS

The first modern research on temperament, at least in the United States, began when Alexander Thomas, Stella Chess, and their collaborators (Thomas, Chess, Birch, Hertzig, & Korn, 1963; Thomas, Chess, & Birch, 1968) noticed differences that they did not believe were purely the result of childrearing and began a longitudinal observational study to identify these very early occurring traits. At that time, the causes for personality and behavior differences were entirely explained by psychoanalytic and learning theories. After observing a broader sample, they arrived at nine temperament traits, again based only on what could be observed. SPS most looks like two traits that were not always found together—low sensory threshold and withdrawal (vs. approaching). Even if SPS were the underlying trait, what Thomas and Chess could actually observe about children's behavior would be, for example, that some were sensitive to noise, scratchy clothing, and new foods, and others withdrew from new situations and people. The two sometimes went together (the "slow to warm up" child [Thomas et al., 1968]) but not always, since SPS children high in sensation seeking would not be withdrawing. All in all, it would be difficult to see the underlying strategy of processing stimuli or information more deeply.

Others who looked for innate traits by observing infants noticed that some infants cried more easily, so that no doubt in some cases high SPS was instead called "affective negativity" (Marshall & Fox, 2005). As mentioned before, Kagan (1994) developed the term "behavioral inhibition to the unfamiliar" by observing children from 4 months to adolescence and finding some who paused before entering a laboratory setting full of many novel, complicated toys. Kagan related the trait to fearfulness and the amygdala. However, recent neuroimaging studies (Bar-Haim et al., 2009) have found that reward areas of the brain in "inhibited" adolescents are more easily activated as well as fear areas. That is, they seem to be more responsive to all situations, as if their inhibited behavior is best described as pausing to observe a new situation, and depending on what they find, they are either more excited than others by potential rewards or more threatened than others by danger.

Fewer attempts have been made to understand temperament in adults. Adult personality is generally studied without attempts to decide what is innate, except to note the heritability of, for example, the Five Factor Model (or "Big Five"). But heritability only refers to the degree that a trait is present due to genetics, but not that there are introversion or neuroticism genes. (Wearing skirts is highly heritable because of its close association with gender, but there is no gene for skirt wearing.) Evans and Rothbart (2008) have sought to measure the Chess and Thomas temperament traits with the Adult Temperament Questionnaire, reducing the original nine down to five: orienting sensitivity, effortful control, extroversion, affiliativeness, and negative affect. However, as mentioned above, focusing on the degree of awareness of low intensity stimulation (orienting sensitivity) rather than depth of processing of sensory information captures only one aspect of the larger trait.

Carver and White (1994) developed a theory and measure of two adult temperament traits based on Gray's (1985, 1991) descriptions of a behavioral inhibition system (BIS) and a behavioral activation system (BAS). Having one of these two systems more active would be a basic innate individual difference. However, they based their measure on Gray's earlier version of his theory, which equates having an active

BIS to being more oriented to fear. Although Gray originally equated the BIS with anxiety, he questioned that idea himself in the original article (1981). He said his theory would mean that an individual would be more sensitive to threat only, but such an explanation would "be tortuous, assuming it to be viable at all" (Gray, 1981, p. 270). If the task of the BIS were to compare the present moment to the past (Gray's 1985 formulation of it) in order to detect signs of threat or punishment only, it would still have to examine all stimulation, not just threatening ones. Further, BIS functioning, if it were anxiety producing, ought to be generally disorganizing, interfering with the comparison process, but it is not. Rather, the system slows activity as the high BIS individual "pauses to check." In comparison, those who are reward oriented (high BAS), moving quickly toward their goal rather than pausing to check, are the ones behaving in a more anxious, disorganized way (Patterson & Newman, 1993).

Not surprisingly, Gray's theory of the BIS was revised (McNaughton & Gray, 2000), partly using animal observations to differentiate *three* systems. The BIS involves alert interest and processing of information, a balancing or negotiation between the urge simply to satisfy needs (BAS) and the need to stop and consider how best to make use of the immediate opportunity while also attending to other needs, such as safety. The third system governs true fear—fight or flight reactions. To date, those interested in personality differences have continued to identify the BIS with fear of threat and withdrawal. However, as Gray emphasizes in his revised model, once an individual has paused to check, he or she is as equally prepared to advance as to withdraw, depending on what was observed.

The most interesting discussion of what this trait might be comes from studies of other species. Over 100 different species (Wolf et al., 2008) seem to have a strategy of observing before acting as compared to acting quickly and almost randomly. Both strategies have their advantages according to the time and place. Biologists do not see the strategy difference as being mainly due to keener senses. For example, there are "hawks" and "doves" (Korte et al., 2005) in various species, comparable to sensitive and not. "Doves" do pay greater attention to details in the environment—location of food, aggressiveness of other animals, times when potential mates are unguarded by dominant males—but also use this information to develop a variety of strategies according to what "doves" do in their particular species. This neutral perspective of the trait—useful at times, not at others—leads us to the topics of theories about the trait in humans that emphasize the possibility of either highly positive or negative outcomes according to the environment, especially in childhood, where sensitive individuals find themselves.

Bottom Line: Temperament research began with studies of children and has been extended to adults through Evans and Rothbart's Adult Temperament Questionnaire and Carver and White's measure based on the BIS and BAS. All discuss traits closely related to the SPS construct.

THOSE SEEING THE TRAIT AS POTENTIALLY BOTH POSITIVE AND NEGATIVE

The most recent perspective on the trait emphasizes it as a neutral difference bestowing both benefits and disadvantages, according to the environment. This trend began, perhaps, with Boyce and his colleagues (1995) along with Gannon et al. (1989), who used the term "psychobiological reactivity" to describe children who were found to have more injuries and illnesses than other children if they were under stress at home or at school, but fewer if they were not under stress. After exploring this phenomenon further in animals as well as humans, they developed the term "biological sensitivity to context" (BSC; Boyce & Ellis, 2005) and equate BSC or closely associate it with high sensitivity (p. 286). They suggest that BSC could be governed by a gene that allows the offspring of humans and certain other species (notably rhesus monkeys) to adapt to the environment they find themselves in after birth. This would be in contrast to inheriting a fixed survival strategy, as some species clearly do, that will be successful under certain conditions.

Boyce and Ellis (2005) argued that such a plasticity or malleability is needed in humans and other primates, in which the mother–infant attachment is both prolonged and essential for later social and psychological well-being. This mother–infant relationship can vary from providing strong protection from stress to providing none or even being in itself a source of stress. A BSC gene would provide the capacity to "monitor specific features of childhood environments as a basis for calibrating the development of stress response systems to match those environments" (Boyce & Ellis, 2005, p. 271).

Boyce and Ellis go on to argue that a BSC gene would permit three potential scenarios regarding parenting and early stress. In a highly stressful environment, the BSC is activated so that the individual will be maximally alert to subtle signs of danger. This necessary vigilance, however, has many negative effects on health and later personality development. A second scenario, in an environment highly protective and attentive to the infant's needs, also activates the gene. This allows an individual to derive maximum benefit from excellent parents. A third scenario would be one in which stress in the parent–child relationship is moderate. In that case the gene would not be activated, as there would be fewer benefits to using the energy necessary to be highly tuned to the environment.

Along the same lines Belsky and colleagues (Belsky, 2005; Belsky et al., 2007; Pluess & Belsky, 2009) reviewed evidence that favored their changing the term for the trait from negative emotionality, leading to a "differential vulnerability" to depression and anxiety, to a "differential susceptibility" to both positive and negative environments.

The following is some of the research leading to this reconceptualization of the trait as having benefits as well as drawbacks. In a study looking at the interaction of parenting and fearful temperament in conscience formation, Kochanska and Thompson (1997) found that at 2 and 3 years of age, children who were more inhibited in novel environments and more aware of flaws in a toy (aware of subtleties) were also more upset if the situation was contrived to make it seem to them that they had caused the flaw. At 4 years these same children were less likely to cheat, break rules, or be selfish when they had no fear of being caught, and gave more pro-social responses in moral dilemmas. However, this difference remained at 5 years only if their mothers had used gentle discipline, deemphasizing power. Mother–child mutual cooperation and attachment security had similar interaction effects in combination with temperament in producing unusually positive, conscientious behavior in these children.

Quas, Bauer, and Boyce (2004) found that compared to nonsensitive children, sensitive children had better memories of a stressful event in a supportive environment and worse memories in a nonsupportive one, suggesting that in these children defenses such as suppression and dissociation were necessary when parents were not able to help the child process the stressful event but processed it more thoroughly than others if they were in a supportive environment.

Boyce & Ellis (2005) and Ellis, Jackson, and Boyce (2006) also reviewed a number of animal studies demonstrating the same type of interaction, of worse or better outcomes than controls depending on the environment. An important feature of animal studies is that they allow experimental assignment of "reactive" animals to different forms of mothering. For example, as mentioned in Chapter 1, Suomi (1997) cross-fostered rhesus monkeys selectively bred to be high or low in their reactivity—that is, monkeys from each of the two strains were raised by either average or highly skilled mothers. Reactive monkeys raised by average mothers had the poorest outcomes, and those with low reactivity showed little effect from being raised by either type of mother. But the highly reactive infants raised from birth by highly skilled, nurturing mothers had the best outcomes, in that they showed developmental precocity, behavioral resilience to stress, and ascension within the group's dominance hierarchy, often becoming leaders in this group.

Gunnar and colleagues (Gunnar, 1994; Nachmias et al., 1996) used experiments to demonstrate more explicitly the conditions under which sensitive ("inhibited") children in a novel environment either accommodate quickly after an initial stress reaction or become increasingly threatened. In one experiment (Nachmias et al., 1996), toddlers were brought into a room full of highly stimulating, unusual toys while their adrenaline and cortisol levels were monitored. The inhibited children had an immediate rise in adrenaline levels not seen in the noninhibited children. That is, all inhibited children were initially startled. However, those inhibited children previously ascertained to have a secure attachment to their mothers were soon able to involve themselves in the novel play environment, apparently finding nothing threatening in the situation once they had inspected it, as indicated by their normal cortisol levels. But inhibited children with insecure attachments to their mothers did not relax in this environment and evidenced both increased adrenaline and then increased cortisol, suggesting that their pause to evaluate the situation led to a sense of danger.

Gunnar (1994) did a similar experiment by leaving toddlers for a half hour with caregivers who were instructed to be either responsive or nonresponsive and then introducing these children to the same highly stimulating laboratory playroom. When uninhibited children entered the playroom, their response was unaffected by the type of caregiver with whom they had waited. Inhibited children left with a responsive caregiver behaved, and their adrenaline and cortisol tested, as had those with secure attachments. However, inhibited children left with a nonresponsive caregiver behaved and tested as did those with an insecure attachment style. These studies suggest that how sensitive or inhibited children assess their social support and security greatly affects their ability to adapt to new situations.

Finally, numerous studies (e.g., Canli, 2008; for a review see Belsky & Pluess, 2009) have linked certain genes (e.g., the one encoding the serotonin transporter, 5-HTT) to depression and anxiety. For years this was seen as only a risk factor, but studies have found that these genes bestow certain benefits as well (Canli & Lesch, 2007; Strobel et al., 2007) in social cognition and cognitive control. While it is not yet certain, the 5-HTT transporter may well be associated with sensory-processing sensitivity. Certainly a characteristic that creates a vulnerability to depression and anxiety but also turns out to have positive effects does sound familiar.

Bottom Line: Several lines of research indicate that those with a genetic sensitivity or susceptibility to their early environment can benefit even more than others from growing up in a good family and having a relatively unstressful school experience (be healthier, less depressed and anxious, more socially competent) as well as being especially harmed by bad versions of the same.

SIMILAR TRAITS IN ANIMALS

Although knowing more about the trait in animals is not particularly useful clinically, it does enhance a therapist's confidence in its reality and helps to clarify its function. It was assumed until recently that a species evolved to fit a particular ecological niche, and that there was an ideal type for that species living in that niche such that those approaching the idea would survive and others would die out, at least until the niche changed. Recently it has become apparent that variations or types within species occur in the same environment, each having an advantage over the other at different times or in differing areas of the environment where the species dwells. For example, one behavioral variation within the same species of fish will feed in open water in the center of a pond versus the other type that feeds in reeds at the edge (Wilson et al., 1993).

One of the first to describe stable individual behavioral differences within a species was David Sloan Wilson, in his research on pumpkinseed sunfish (Wilson et al., 1993). When a trap was placed in a pond of them, many came around it in curiosity and were easily trapped. Others did not come near it, so they were captured with a net for comparison in a laboratory setting, where the "bold" fish began to feed five times sooner than the "shy" sunfish. Once both types had acclimatized to the laboratory, they did not differ in the lab in their exploratory behaviors in a novel environment, response to being handled, physical reaction to stress, and likelihood of being dominant or subordinate. (Indeed, in the case of this species, the most likely reason for the development of this individual difference was that the shy sunfish had chosen the safest part of the pond, forcing subordinate bold sunfish to more dangerous areas.) Back in the lake, however, the same shy sunfish returned to their original style. They did not approach divers and preferred to stay near other fish. When paired with a bold fish, the shy fish swam close to it. When the bold fish was captured, the shy one hid under a log and could not be captured.

This research may have led to the attempt to apply the Five Factor Model to animals (Nettle, 2006), but, for example, thinking of sunfish as extroverted or introverted does not make sense in a species in which the shy fish swim in groups while the bold individuals swim alone. Sensitivity to their environment seems a more appropriate assessment. Further, a slight confusion was added when shyness versus boldness in pumpkinseed sunfish was found to vary from situation to situation, such that, for example, the boldest fish were only moderately curious about new objects (Coleman & Wilson, 1998). The authors suggest that personality theorists studying humans might ask whether shyness has evolved for very specific contexts. Another possibility is that the shy fish were actually sensitive and carefully observing new objects that less sensitive fish were less interested in.

Two strategies seem to underlie these differences in "personalities," although the resulting behaviors vary widely from situation to situation and from species to species, so that it is difficult to make a generalization about behavior patterns are being inherited. But whatever the actual behavior, the two strategies seem to represent the two possible "bets" on how to survive, as seen in any other gamble. One is "play the long shot with the big payoff" and the other is "study carefully and play the surest thing."

For example, when a species lives with cycles that vary in density of food resources and predators, the type willing to take risks by acting quickly or entering novel environments will fare better when food is scarce and because this type will benefit from a strategy of being the first to venture into what would usually be dangerous zones and take what is available while the conservative type arrives later and finds less sustenance. When food and predators are plentiful, it works better to be careful about where you dine, as even the safest spots will yield sustenance.

In other species and environments, the conservative types have fed in poorer areas during times of plenty, to avoid conflicts, but in lean years know better where food can be found, having had to search more for it. Hence, the difficulty describing the two strategies as specic behaviors across species.

These two behavioral styles have been found in numerous species (e.g., primates, Higley & Suomi, 1989; Stevenson-Hinde, Stillwell-Barnes, & Zung, 1980; Suomi, 1983, 1987, 1991; canids, Beckoff, 1977; Fox, 1972; Goddard & Beilharz, 1985; MacDonald, 1983; Scott & Fuller, 1965; rats, Blanchard, Flannelly, & Blanchard, 1986; Blizard, 1981; Cooper, Schmidt, & Barrett, 1983; goats, Lyons, Price, & Moberg, 1988; and of course sunfish, Wilson et al., 1993).

These differences could be due either to the evolution of actual variations in genes or to a single gene found in all members of a species that permits a wide range of responses according to the situation. In the case of fruit flies (Renger et al., 1999) a single allele or gene variant seems responsible, having been actually identified. It causes fruit flies to develop into either sitters or rovers, two strategies for foraging. Consistent with the idea that the sitters are in some sense observing and processing more, they have greater neuron excitability, synaptic transmission, and nerve connectivity.

One theory (Wolf et al., 2008) is that there has been an evolutionary emergence of responsive and unresponsive types, an inclusive term that would apply to the over 100 species showing these two strategies. The strategy of the first type is to respond to changes in the environment and adapt one's behavior with each change. The unresponsive meet each situation with a response unrelated to the past—that is, basically randomly. The latter would seem disadvantageous, except that there is an energy cost in being responsive. Responsive and sensitive as used here seem to be overlapping or identical concepts.

Bottom Line: Biologists have found two major personality types in over 100 species. One seems to prefer to observe and respond accordingly and the other to observe less and perhaps even respond randomly. The success of the two depends upon changing or slightly different conditions in the same habitat. As long as each type at times has the advantage, both remain as within species variations.

AN ELABORATION ON THE SUBJECT OF SENSITIVITY AND INTROVERSION

Because introversion is such a familiar concept, it is worthwhile comparing it with sensitivity.

The research literature on introversion from the inside, the physiological difference rather than the difference in social behavior, makes it look much like sensitivity. After numerous studies over a decade or more, Koelega's (1992) meta-analysis and Stelmack and Geen's (1992) review of the literature argued that the hallmark of introversion is sensitivity. For example, introverts have been found to be more sensitive to low auditory frequencies (Stelmack & Campbell, 1974; Stelmack & Michaud-Achorn, 1985) and to have lower pain (Barnes, 1975; Haier, Robinson, Braden, & Williams, 1984; Schalling, 1971), electrocutanous (Edman, Schalling, & Rissler, 1979), olfactory (Herbener, Kagan, & Cohen, 1989), and visual thresholds (Siddle, Morrish, White, & Mangan, 1969). As Stelmack wrote in 1997, "In my view, there is a substantial body of evidence in research on the extraversion trait that converges on one general effect, namely the greater sensitivity (or reactivity) of introverts than extraverts to punctuate, physical stimulation" (p. 1239). He added, "What is striking about the sensory reactivity effect is that it is evident for such a broad range of psychological methods" (p. 1240).

Patterson and Newman's (1993) research suggested the depth of processing that is behind this sensory reactivity. In trying to study the problem of impulsive behavior, they focused on disinhibition as a feature of extroversion and carefulness as a feature of introversion. In their studies using rewards and punishments (winning or losing money) for performance on a task with feedback after each try, introverts consistently used more time to reflect on feedback about the nature of their mistakes before proceeding to the next trial and as a result were more successful. The authors suggested that taking time to reflect "promotes semantic depth and differentiation by means of reflection" (p. 724). That is, they process more carefully, enabling them to process even more carefully next time. These behaviors are obviously the opposite of impulsivity. As a result, the authors reconceptualized introversion as reflectivity (an excellent term, except that it cannot be applied to all species or explain a faster startle response or reaction to caffeine).

It seems that sensitivity and introversion could have been equated if researchers had stayed with Jung's (1921/1961) original definition of the term, which was not based on observable sociability. Introversion to him was a method of knowing based on thorough observation and processing of an object, person, or situation, meaning discovering its relation to past experiences and other subjective factors. In comparison, Jung saw extroverts as preferring to gain such knowledge through direct, immediate contact. The problem, of course, is that this subjective preference of introverts cannot be observed. (Before Jung began emphasizing the concepts of introversion and extroversion, he was interested in sensitiveness as the innate individual difference that interacts with experience to produce neuroticism and may have turned to introversion as a more neutral term [Aron, 2004b].) Because we gain most of our knowledge about others from what we observe, it makes sense that introversion and extroversion have become almost exclusively about being sociable and cheerful, which are observable behaviors. What goes on inside of introverts, and why, has been left unexplored, except for finding it involved a great deal of sensitivity.

Bottom Line: Introversion is associated with greater sensitivity of all sorts. Still, we cannot equate the two as long as introversion and extroversion refer mainly to social behavior because 30% of sensitive persons are extroverts by that definition. If we could use the term as Jung originally defined it, a preference for a subjective experience of the world, we could see introversion and sensitivity as both describing a strategy of processing information more deeply.

THE IMPORTANCE OF THE TERM WE USE

Shy, introverted, aloof, high strung, slow, gifted, stupid, thoughtful, thoughtless, inhibited, withdrawn, fearful, neurotic, pessimistic, or just quiet—many terms can be applied to the person who does not act while others are plunging ahead. Each term represents a theory—implicit or explicit, folk or scientific—about what is going on inside a person who is not acting, or not acting as often as others. Naturally, we base our idea on our subjective experience or what we have learned from our culture about people who are not acting. There is not much else to go on.

For example, in the lexical studies (Goldberg, 1990; Saucier & Goldberg, 2003) that led to the Five Factor Model of personality, there is a behavioral specificity about the almost universal description of extroverts. As summarized by Mullins-Sweatt and Widiger (2006), extroverts are seen as cordial, affectionate, attached, sociable, outgoing, dominant, forceful, vigorous, energetic, active, reckless, daring, and high-spirited. In contrast, introverts, who are of course seen doing less, cannot be described in such behavioral terms, so the descriptors are more variable and even contradict one another as they offer up various theories about what is happening inside them. The long list of Five Factor Model descriptors for introverts begins with cold, aloof, and indifferent—all suggesting the observer's theory that not joining in is due to feeling superior. Second, they are described as withdrawn and isolated, implying a theory that they are simply unable to relate socially for some reason. Unassuming, quiet, resigned—a theory that they are less assertive or have given up and probably feel inferior. Passive, lethargic—maybe they just don't have the energy? Cautious, monotonous, dull—being so inactive, they might be boring to be around. Placid or anhedonic—they do less because they have fewer strong emotions and motivations, or worse, they are unable to gain pleasure from what they do or lack strong positive affect. This is quite a range of descriptors and underlying hypotheses.

These terms and hypotheses become prejudices in daily life that seriously affect both quiet people and those who might benefit from relationships with them. For example, Paulhus and Morgan (1997) gave an intelligence test before placing students in a leaderless group for seven weekly meetings. They had members rate one another after each of these meeting. At the outset the groups rated quiet persons as less intelligent, but by the end the ratings were more accurate—those rated at this point by group members as less intelligent actually were less intelligent, verified by testing, and regardless of how much they talked.

What is more disturbing is that mental health professionals make the same mistake. A study by Gough and Thorne (1986) used leaderless groups as part of a 3-day personality assessment and found the ratings by mental health professionals of quiet persons (especially men) were significantly lower on likability, intelligence, and mental health. Yet these clinicians' assumptions about these men were utterly wrong, given other assessments (SAT, GPA, MMPI, etc.) and the ratings provided by those who actually knew the quiet persons—their spouses, or peers in their sorority or fraternity.

For psychotherapists, it is obviously extremely important to sort out our terminology, which in turn expresses our working hypotheses, attitudes, hopes, and fears about a given patient. This is even more difficult and important if the patients already have negative hypotheses about themselves, expressed in self-attributions such as being shy, having a social phobia, or having an avoidant personality disorder. Such a label could be accurate, but it could also be, at least in part, a sensitive person taking others' observations seriously, as they do, and then these becoming to some degree self-fulfilling.

Is sensitivity a better term? It has both positive and negative connotations, but perhaps that mirrors the more recent research and theory pointing to the trait being essentially neutral, bringing with it benefits in some environments and disadvantages in others, rather than merely the innate precursor to fear, anxiety, shyness, neuroticism, and negative emotions generally.

Bottom Line: It matters very much which term we settle on for this trait, whether it is high sensory-processing sensitivity, biological sensitivity to context, responsiveness, or some other. The term will affect how we structure further research, view our patients, and subtlely teach them how to view themselves. This in turn could have major effects on society, depending on whether we develop the potentially best or most troubled aspects of 20% of the population.

OVERALL SUMMARY AND CONCLUSIONS

This review of the research on SPS and related traits has looked at the subject from a variety of perspectives. First, it appears to be a very real individual variation, not only in humans but also in animals. We have considered one way of measuring it, the HSP Scale, which appears to have some value in predicting individual differences in susceptibility to childhood trauma as well as brain activity during perceptual tasks observed by neuroimaging. Other approaches to measuring it, however, may prove to be even more effective.

We have seen how the HSP Scale has been used in applied and clinical settings and under what circumstances possessing the trait could be an advantage or a disadvantage to the individual and to his or her larger community. In fact, having this trait seems to lead to drastically varied outcomes, from becoming a competent, sensitive leader to being highly impaired by a mood or personality disorder. Therapists can play a role in these outcomes, beginning with what we call the trait and how we understand it and explain it to others. All of this will change as the research on the trait evolves. That unfolding will be both interesting and very important to us as therapists.

REFERENCES

Alloy, L. B., & Abramson, L. Y. (1979). Judgment of contingency in depressed and nondepressed students: Sadder but wiser? *Journal of Experimental Psychology, 108*, 441–448.

American Psychiatric Association (APA). (1994). *Diagnostic and statistical manual of mental disorders*, 4th ed. Washington, DC: Author.

Andrew, M., & Cronin, C. (1997). Two measures of sensation seeking as predictors of alcohol use among high school males. *Personality Individual Differences, 22*(3), 393–401.

Aron, A., Aron, E. N., & Norman, C. (2001). Combating boredom in close relationships by participating together in self-expanding activities. In J. H. Harvey & A. E. Wenzel (Eds.), *Close romantic relationship. Maintenance and enhancement* (pp. 47–66). Mahwah, NJ: Erlbaum.

Aron, A., Ketay, S., Hedden, T., Aron, E. N., Markus, H., & Gabrieli, J. D. E. (2007). *Attentional processing neural independence of culture in highly sensitives individuals*. Presented at APA Symposium, San Francisco.

Aron, A., Ketay, S., Hedden, T., Aron, E. N., Markus, H., & Gabrieli, J. D. E. (in press). Temperament trait of sensory processing sensitivity cultural differences in neural response. *Social Cognitive and Affective Neuroscience.*

Aron, A., Mashek, D., & Aron, E. N. (2004). Closeness as including other in the self. In D. Mashek & A. Aron (Eds.), *Handbook of closeness and intimacy* (pp. 27–41). Mahwah, NJ: Erlbaum.

Aron, A., Norman, C. C., Aron, E. N., McKenna, C., & Heyman, R. (2000). Couples' shared participation in novel and arousing activities and experienced relationship quality. *Journal of Personality and Social Psychology, 78*, 273–283.

Aron, A., Paris, M., & Aron, E. N. (1995). Falling in love: Prospective studies of self-concept change. *Journal of Personality and Social Psychology, 69*, 1102–1112.

Aron, E. (1996). *The highly sensitive person*. New York: Birch Lane Press.

Aron, E. (1999). The highly sensitive person's workbook. New York: Broadway.

Aron, E. (2000). High sensitivity as one source of fearfulness and shyness: Preliminary research and clinical implications. In L. Schmidt & J. Schulkin (Eds.), *Extreme fear, shyness, and social phobia: Origins, biological mechanisms, and clinical outcomes* (pp. 251–272). New York: Oxford University Press.

Aron, E. (2001). *The highly sensitive person in love.* New York: Broadway Books.

Aron, E. (2002). *The highly sensitive child.* New York: Broadway Books.

Aron, E. (2004a). The impact of adult temperament on closeness and intimacy. In D. Mashek & A. Aron (Eds.), *Handbook of closeness and intimacy* (pp. 267–284). Mahwah, NJ: Erlbaum.

Aron, E. (2004b). Revisiting Jung's concept of innate sensitiveness. *Journal of Analytical Psychology, 49*, 337–367.

Aron, E., & Aron, A. (1997). Sensory-processing sensitivity and its relation to introversion and emotionality. *Journal of Personality and Social Psychology, 73*, 345–368.

Aron, E., Aron, A., & Davies, K. M. (2005). Adult shyness: The interaction of temperamental sensitivity and an adverse childhood environment. *Personality and Social Psychology Bulletin, 31*, 181–197.

Badaracco, J. L. (2002). *Leading quietly: An unorthodox guide to doing the right thing.* Boston: Harvard Business School Press.

Bar-Haim, Y., Fox, N. A., Benson, B., Guyer, A. E., Williams, A., Nelson, E. E., et al. (2009). Neural correlates of reward processing in adolescents with a history of inhibited temperament. *Psychological Science, 20*, 1009–1018.

Barnes, G. (1975). Extraversion and pain. *British Journal of Social and Clinical Psychology, 14*, 303–308.

Barrett, L. F. (1997). The relationships among momentary emotion experiences, personality descriptions, and retrospective ratings of emotion. *Personality and Social Psychology Bulletin, 23*(10), 1100–1110.

Bates, J. E., & Wachs, T. D. (1994). *Temperament: individual differences at the interface of biology and behavior.* Washington, DC: American Psychological Association.

Beauchamp-Turner, D. L., & Levinson, D. M. (1992). Effects of meditation on stress, health, and affect. *Medical Psychotherapy, 5*, 123–132.

Beck, A. T. (1978). *Beck depression inventory.* San Antonio, TX: Psychological Corporation.

Beck, A. T., Epstein, N., Brown, G., & Steer, R. A. (1988). An inventory for measuring clinical anxiety: Psychometric properties. *Journal of Consulting and Clinical Psychology, 56*, 893–897.

Beckoff, M. (1977). Mammalian dispersal and the ontogeny of individual behavioral phenotypes. *American Naturalist, 111*, 715–732.

Bell, I. R. (1992). Allergens, physical irritants, depression, and shyness. *Journal of Applied Developmental Psychology, 13*(2), 125–133.

Belsky, J. (2005). Differential susceptibility to rearing influence: An evolutionary hypothesis and some evidence. In B. Ellis & D. Bjorklund (Eds.), *Origins of the social mind: Evolutionary psychology and child development* (pp. 139–163). New York: Guilford.

Belsky, J., Bakermans-Kranenburg, M. J., & Van IJzendoorn, M. H. (2007). For better and for worse: Differential susceptibility to environmental influences. *Current Directions in Psychological Science, 16*(6), 300–304.

Belsky, J., Jonassaint, C., Pluess, M., Stanton, M., Brummett, B., & Williams, R. (2009). Vulnerability genes or plasticity genes? *Molecular Psychiatry, 14*, 746–754.

Benham, G. (2006). The highly sensitive person: Stress and physical symptom reports. *Personality and Individual Differences, 40*, 1433–1440.

Berenbaum, H., & Williams, M. (1994). Extraversion, hemispatial bias, and eyeblink rates. *Personality and Individual Differences, 17*, 849–852.

Birmingham, F. A. (1972). Pearl Buck and the good earth of Vermont. *Saturday Evening Post*, Spring, p. 135.

Blanchard, R. J., Flannelly, K. J., & Blanchard, D. C. (1986). Defensive behaviors of laboratory and wild *Rattus norvegicus*. *Journal of Comparative Psychology, 100*, 101–107.

Blizard, D. A. (1981). The Maudsley reactive and nonreactive strains: A North American perspective. *Behavior Generics, 11*, 469–489.

Boyce, W. T., Chesney, M., Alkon, A., Tschann, J. M., Adams, S., Chesterman, B., et al. (1995). Psychobiologic reactivity to stress and childhood respiratory illnesses: Results of two prospective studies. *Psychosomatic Medicine, 57*, 411–422.

Boyce, W. T., & Ellis, B. J. (2005). Biological sensitivity to context: I. an evolutionary-developmental theory of the origins and functions of stress reactivity. *Development and Psycholpathology, 17*, 271–301.

Brodt, S., & Zimbardo, P. (1981). Modifying shyness-related social behavior through symptom misattribution. *Journal of Personality and Social Psychology, 41*, 437–449.

Brown, C., & Dunn, W. (2002). *The adult sensory profile*. San Antonio, TX: Psychological Corporation.

Buss, A. (1989). Temperaments as personality traits. In G. A. Kohnstamm, J. E. Bates, & M. K. Rothbart (Eds.), *Temperament in childhood* (pp. 49–58). Chichester, England: Wiley.

Canli, T. (2008). Toward a neurogenetic theory of neuroticism. *Annals New York Academy Sciences, 1129*, 153–174.

Canli, T., & Lesch, P. (2007). Long story short: The serotonin transporter in emotion regulation and social cognition. *Nature Neuroscience, 10*, 1103–1109.

Cartwright-Hatton, S., Hodges, L., & Porter, J. (2003). Social anxiety in childhood: The relationship with self and observer rated social skills. *Journal of Child Psychology and Psychiatry, 44*, 737–742.

Carver, C. S., & White, T. L. (1994). Behavioral inhibition, behavioral activation, and affective responses to impending reward and punishment: The BIS/BAS scales. *Journal of Personality and Social Psychology, 67*, 319–333.

Cassidy, J., & Shaver, P. R. (1999). *Handbook of attachment: Theory, research, and clinical applications.* New York: Guilford.

Cheek, J. M. (1983). *The revised Cheek and Buss shyness scale*. Unpublished manuscript, Wellesley College.

Chen, X., He, Y., Cen, G., & Li, D. (2005). Social functioning and adjustment in Chinese children: The imprint of historical time. *Child Development, 76*(1), 182–195.

Chen, X., Rubin, K., & Sun, Y. (1992). Social reputation and peer relationships in Chinese and Canadian children: A cross-cultural study. *Child Development, 63*, 1336–1343.

Chess, S., & Thomas, A. (1987). *Know your child: An authoritative guide for today's parents.* New York: Basic Books.

Coleman, K., & Wilson, D. (1998). Shyness and boldness in pumpkin seed sunfish: Individual differences are context-specific. *Animal Behavior, 56*(4), 927–936.

Cooper, D. O., Schmidt, D. E., & Barrett, R. J. (1983). Strain specific cholinergic changes in response to stress: Analysis of a time-dependent avoidance variation. *Pharmacology, Biochemistry and Behavior, 19*, 457–462.

Cutler, S. E., Larsen, R. J., & Bunce, S. C. (1996). Repressive coping style and the experience and recall of emotion: A naturalistic study of daily affect. *Journal of Personality, 64*, 379–405.

Denning, P. (2000). *Practicing harm reduction psychotherapy: An alternative approach to addictions*. New York: Guilford.

Edman, G., Schalling, D., & Rissler, A. (1979). Interaction effects of extraversion and neuroticism on detection thresholds. *Biological Psychology, 9*, 41–47.

Eikleberry, C. (1999). *The career guide for creative and unconventional people*. Berkeley: Ten Speed Press.

Eisenberger, N., Lieberman, M., & Williams, K. (2003). Does rejection hurt? An fMRI study of social exclusion. *Science*, 302, 290–292.

Ellis, B. J., Essex, M. J., & Boyce, W. T. (2005). Biological sensitivity to context: II. Empirical explorations of an evolutionary–developmental theory. *Development and Psychopathology, 17*, 303–328.

Ellis, B. J., Jackson, J. J., & Boyce, W. T. (2006). The stress response systems: Universality and adaptive individual differences. *Developmental Review, 26*(2), 175–212.

Ersner-Hershfield, H., Ghahremani, D., Aron, A., Aron, E. N., Lichty, W., Mazaika, P. K., et al. (2007, November). *Using voxel-based morphometry to compare brain anatomy of adult humans across levels of the normal temperament trait of sensory-processing sensitivity*. Presented at the Society for Neuroscience, Washington, DC.

Ersner-Hershfield, H., Ghahremani, D., Cooper, J., Aron, E. N., Hedden, T., Ketay, S., et al. (2007). *Do highly sensitive people have different brains? A VBM study*. Presented at the APA Convention, San Francisco.

Evans, D. E., & Rothbart, M. K. (2007). Development of a model for adult temperament. *Journal of Research in Personality, 41*, 868–888.

Evans, D. E., & Rothbart, M. K. (2008). Temperamental sensitivity: Two constructs or one? *Personality and Individual Differences, 44*, 108–118.

Evers, A., Rasche, J., & Schabracq, M. J. (2008). High sensory-processing sensitivity at work. *International Journal of Stress Management, 15*, 189–198.

Eysenck, H. J. (1981). *A model for personality*. New York: Springer-Verlag.

Feldman, L. A. (1995). Valence focus and arousal focus: Individual differences in the structure of affective experience. *Journal of Personality and Social Psychology, 69*, 153–166.

Forster, E. M. (1951). *Two cheers for democracy*. New York: Harcourt, Brace.

Fox, M. W. (1972). Socio-ecological implications of individual differences in wolf litters: A developmental and evolutionary perspective. *Behaviour, 41*, 298–313.

Frable, D. E. S. (1993). Being and feeling unique: Statistical deviance and psychological marginality. *Journal of Personality, 61*(1), 85–110.

Funder, D. C. (1991). Global traits: A neo-Alportian approach to personality. *Psychological Science, 2*, 31–39.

Galen, L. W., Henderson, M. J., & Whitman, R. D. (1997). The utility of novelty seeking, harm avoidance, and expectancy in the prediction of drinking. *Addictive Behaviors, 22*(1), 93–106.

Gannon, L., Banks, J., Shelton, D., & Luchetta, T. (1989). The mediating effects of psychophysiological reactivity and recovery on the relationship between environmental stress and illness. *Journal of Psychosomatic Research, 33*, 165–175.

Goddard, M. E., & Beilharz, R. G. (1985). A multivariate analysis of the genetics of fearfulness in potential guide dogs. *Behavior Genetics, 15*, 69–89.

Goldberg, L. R. (1990). An alternative "description of personality": The big-five factor structure. *Journal of Personality and Social Psychology, 59*, 1216–1229.

Gottman, J. M. (1999). *The seven principles for making marriage work*. New York: Crown Publishers.

Gottman, J. M., & Notarius, C. I. (2000). Decade review: Observing marital interaction. *Journal of Marriage and the Family, 62*, 927–947.

Gough, H. G., & Thorne, A. (1986). Positive, negative, and balanced shyness: Self-definitions and the reactions of others. In W. H. Jones, J. M. Cheek, & S. R. Briggs (Eds.), *Shyness: Perspectives on research and treatment* (pp. 205–225). New York: Plenum.

Gray, J. A. (1981). A critique of Eysenck's theory of personality. In H. J. Eysenck (Ed.), *A model for personality* (pp. 246–276). New York: Springer.

Gray, J. A. (1985). Issues in the neurology of anxiety. In A. H. Ruma & J. D. Maser, Eds., *Anxiety and disorder* (pp. 5–25). Hillsdale, NJ: Earlbaum.

Griffin, J. J. (1990). *Sexual fantasy, extramarital affairs, and marriage commitment*. Doctoral dissertation, California Graduate School of Family Psychology.

Grotstein, J. S. (1995). Orphans of the 'real': I. Some modern and postmodern perspectives on the neurobiological and psychosocial dimensions of psychosis and other primitive mental disorders. In J. G. Allen & D. T. Collins (Eds.), *Contemporary treatment of psychosis: healing relationships in the "decade of the brain"* (pp. 1–26). Northvale, NJ: Jason Aronson.

Haddon, M. (2003). *The curious incident of the dog in the night-time*. New York: Random House.

Hagekill, B. (1996, October). *Influences of temperament and environment in the development of personality*. Paper presented at the Occasional Temperament Conference XI, Eugene, OR.

Haier, R. J., Reynolds, C., Prager, E., Cox, S., & Buchsbaum, M. S. (1991). Flurbiprofen, caffeine and analgesia: Interaction with introversion/extraversion. *Personality and Individual Differences, 12*, 1349–1354.

Hallowell, E. M., & Ratey, J. J. (1995). *Driven to distraction: Recognizing and coping with attention deficit disorder from childhood through adulthood*. New York: Touchstone.

Hazan, C., & Shaver, P. (1987). Romantic love conceptualized as an attachment process. *Journal of Personality and Social Psychology, 52*, 511–524.

Hedden, T., Ketay, S., Aron, A., Markus, H. Gabrieli, J. D. B., (2008). Cultural influences on neural substrates of attentional control. *Psychological Science, 19*, 13–17.

Herbener, E. S., Kagan, J., & Cohen, M. (1989). Shyness and olfactory threshold. *Personality and Individual Differences, 10*, 1159–1163.

Higley, J. D., & Suomi, S. J. (1989). Temperamental reactivity in non-human primates. In G. A. Kohnstamm, J. E. Bates, & M. K. Rothbart (Eds.), *Temperament in childhood* (pp. 153–167). Chichester, England: Wiley.

Hillesum, E. (1981). *An interrupted life: The diaries of Etty Hillesum 1941–43.* New York: Washington Square Press.

Hofmann, S. G., & Bitran, S. (2007). Sensory-processing sensitivity in social anxiety disorder: Relationship to harm avoidance and diagnostic subtypes. *Journal of Anxiety Disorders, 21*, 944–954.

Horton, P. C. (1981). *Solace: The missing dimension in psychiatry.* Chicago: University of Chicago Press.

Jaeger, B. (2004). *Making work work for the highly sensitive person.* New York: McGraw-Hill.

Jagiellowicz, J., Aron, E., & Aron, A. (2007). *Sensory-processing sensitivity moderates health motivations and experiences.* Presented at the Society for Personality and Social Psychology, Memphis.

Jagiellowicz, J., Aron, E., & Aron, A. (in press). The trait of sensory processing sensitivity and neural responses to changes in visual scenes. *Social Cognitive and Affective Neuroscience.*

Jerome, E. M., & Liss, M. (2005). Relationships between sensory processing style, adult attachment, and coping. *Personality and Individual Differences, 38*, 1341–1352.

Jockin, V., McGue, M., & Lykken, D. T. (1996). Personality and divorce: A genetic analysis. *Journal of Personality and Social Psychology, 71*(2), 288–299.

John, O. P., Donahue, E. M., & Kentle, R. L. (1992). *The "big five" inventory.* Versions 4a and 54 (Tech. Rep.). Berkeley, CA: Institute of Personality Assessment and Social Research.

Jung, C. (1913/1961). *Freud and psychoanalysis: The collected works of* C. G. *Jung.* Vol. 4. Princeton, NJ: Princeton University Press.

Jung, C. (1921/1961). *Freud and psychoanalysis: The collected works of* C. G. *Jung.* Vol. 6. Princeton, NJ: Princeton University Press.

Kagan, J. (1994). *Galen's prophecy: Temperament in human nature.* New York: Basic Books.

Kalsched, D. (1996). *The inner world of trauma.* New York: Routledge.

Karney, B. R., & Bradbury, T. N. (1997). Neuroticism, marital interaction, and the trajectory of marital satisfaction. *Journal of Personality and Social Psychology, 72*, 1075–1092.

Kemler, D. S. (2006). Sensitivity to sensoriprocessing, self-discrepancy, and emotional reactivity of collegiate athletes. *Perceptual and Motor Skills, 102*, 747–759.

Klein, M. (1935/1984). A contribution to the psychogenesis of manic depressive states. In R. Money-Kyrle (Ed.), *The writings of Melanie Klein* (Vol. 1, pp. 262–289). New York: Free Press.

Kochanska, G., & Thompson, R. A. (1997). The emergence and development of conscience in toddlerhood and early childhood. In J. E. Grusec & L. Kuczynski (Eds.), *Parenting and Children's Internalization of Values* (pp. 53–77). New York: Wiley.

Koelega, H. S. (1992). Extraversion and vigilance performance: Thirty years of inconsistencies. *Psychological Bulletin, 112*, 239–258.

Korte, S. M., Koolhaas, J. M., Wingfield, J. C., & McEwen, B. S. (2005). The Darwinian concept of stress: Benefits of allostasis and costs of allostatic load and the trade-offs in health and disease. *Neuroscience and Biobehavioral Reviews, 29*, 3–38.

Kowal, K. T. (1998). How HSPs can get the most out of their medical visits. *Comfort Zone, 3,* 13.

Kristal, J. (2005). *The temperament perspective: Working with children's behavioral styles.* Baltimore: Brookes.

Larsen, R. J. (1992). Neuroticism and selective encoding and recall of symptoms: Evidence from a combined concurrent-retrospective study. *Journal of Personality and Social Psychology, 62,* 480–488.

Larsen, R. J., & Prizmic, Z. (2004). Affect regulation. In R. F. Baumeister & K. D. Vohs (Eds.), *Handbook of self-regulation: Research, theory, and applications* (pp. 40–61). New York: Guilford.

Lewis, T., Amini, F., & Lannon, R. (2000). *A general theory of love.* New York: Random House.

Liss, M., Mailloux, J., & Erchull, M. J. (2008). The relationships between sensory processing sensitivity, alexithymia, autism, depression, and anxiety. *Personality and Individual Differences, 45,* 255–259.

Liss, M., Timmel, L., Baxley, K., & Killingsworth, P. (2005). Sensory processing sensitivity and its relation to parental bonding, anxiety, and depression. *Personality and Individual Differences, 39,* 1429–1439.

Lyons, D. M., Price, E. O., & Moberg, G. P. (1988). Individual differences in temperament of domestic dairy goats: Constancy and change. *Animal Behavior, 36,* 1323–1333.

MacDonald, K. (1983). Stability of individual differences in behavior in a litter of wolf cubs (*Canis lupus*). *Journal of Comparative Psychology, 97,* 99–106.

Mangelsdorf, S., Gunnar, M., Kestenbaum, R., Lang, S., & Andreas, D. (1990). Infant proneness-to-distress temperament, maternal personality, and mother-infant attachment: Associations and goodness of fit. *Childhood Development, 61,* 820–831.

Marshall, P. J., & Fox, N. A. (2005). Relations between behavioral reactivity at 4 months and attachment classification at 14 months in a selected sample. *Infant Behavior and Development, 28,* 492–502.

Martineau, F. (1992). *The sensitive vein.* Soquel, CA: Moon Dance.

McCrae, R. R., & Costa, P.T. (2003). *Personality in adulthood. A five-factor theory perspective* (2nd ed.). New York: Guilford.

McGue, M., & Lykken, D. (1996). Personality and divorce: A genetic analysis. *Journal of Personality and Social Psychology, 71,* 288–299.

McNaughton, N., & Gray, J. A. (2000). Anxiolytic action on the behavioural inhibition system implies multiple types of arousal contribute to anxiety. *Journal of Affective Disorders, 61,* 161–176.

Mead, M. (1935). *Sex and temperament in three primitive societies.* New York: Morrow.

Mehrabian, A. (1977). A questionnaire mesaure of individual differences in stimulus screening and associated differences in arousability. *Environmental Psychology and Nonverbal Behavior, 1,* 89–103.

Meyer, B., Ajchenbrenner, M., & Bowles, D. P. (2005). Sensory sensitivity, attachment experiences, and rejection responses among adults with borderline and avoidant features. *Journal of Personality Disorders, 19,* 641–658.

Meyer, B., & Carver, C. S. (2000). Negative childhood accounts, sensitivity, and pessimism: A study of avoidant personality disorder features in college students. *Journal of Personality Disorders, 14*, 233–248.

Mullins-Sweatt, S. N., & Widiger, T. A. (2006). The five-factor model of personality disorder: A translation across science and practice. In R. F. Krueger & J. L. Tackett, *Personality and psychopathology* (pp. 39–70). New York: Guilford.

Muraven, M., Tice, D. M., & Baumeister, R. F. (1998). Self-control as limited resource: Regulatory depletion patterns. *Journal of Personality and Social Psychology, 74*, 774–789.

Myers, I. B. (1962). *Manual for the Myers-Briggs Type Indicator*. Princeton, NJ: Educational Testing Service.

Nachmias, M., Gunnar, M., Mangelsdorf, S., Parritz, R. H., & Buss, K. (1996). Behavioral inhibition and stress reactivity: The moderating role of attachment security. *Child Development, 67*, 508–522.

Neal, J. A., Edelmann, R. J., & Glachan, M. (2002). Behavioral inhibition and symptoms of anxiety and depression: Is there a specific relationship with social phobia? *British Journal of Clinical Psychology, 41*, 361–374.

Nettle, D. (2006). The evolution of personality variation in humans and other animals. *American Psychologist, 6*, 622–631.

Park, L. C., Imboden, J. B., Park, T. J., Hulse, S. H., & Unger, H. T. (1992). Giftedness and psychological abuse in borderline personality disorder: Their relevance to genesis and treatment. *Journal of Personality Disorders*, 6(3), 226–240.

Parker, G., Tupling, H., & Brown, L. (1979). A parental bonding instrument. *British Journal of Medical Psychology, 52*, 1–10.

Patterson, C. M., & Newman, J. P. (1993). Reflectivity and learning from aversive events: Toward a psychological mechanism for the syndromes of disinhibition. *Psychological Review, 100*, 716–736.

Paulhus, D. L., & Morgan, K. L. (1997). Perceptions of intelligence in leaderless groups: the dynamic effects of shyness and acquaintance. *Journal of Personality and Social Psychology, 72*, 581–591.

Pavlov, I. (1927). *Conditioned reflexes*. London: Oxford University Press.

Perera, S. (1986). *The scapegoat complex: Toward a mythology of shadow and guilt*. Toronto: Inner City Books.

Pluess, M., & Belsky, J. (2009). Differential susceptibility to rearing experience: The case of childcare. *Journal of Child Psychology and Psychiatry, 50*(4), 396–404.

Quas, J. A., Bauer, A., & Boyce, W. T. (2004). Physiological reactivity, social support, and memory in early childhood. *Child Development, 75*, 797–814.

*Rammsayer, T., Netter, P., & Vogel, W. H. (1993). A neurochemical model underlying differences in reaction times between introverts and extraverts. *Personality and Individual Differences, 14*, 701–712.

Ratey, J. J., & Johnson, C. (1998). *Shadow syndromes: The mild forms of major mental disorders that sabotage us*. New York: Bantam Books.

*Reif, A., & Lesch, K. -P. (2003). Toward a molecular architecture of personality. *Behavioural Brain Research, 139*, 1–20.

Reissman, C., Aron, A., & Bergen, M. (1993). Shared activities and marital satisfaction: Causal direction and self-expansion versus boredom. *Journal of Social and Personal Relationships, 10*, 243–254.

Renger, J., Yao, W.-D., Sokolowski, M., & Wu, C.-F. (1999). Neuronal polymorphism among natural alleles of a cGMP-dependent kinase gene, foraging, in *Drosophila*. *Journal of Neuroscience, 19*(RC28), 1–8.

Robbins, R. N., & Bryan, A. (2004). Relationships between future orientation, impulsive sensation seeking, and risk behavior among adjudicated adolescents. *Journal of Adolescent Research, 19*(4), 428–445.

Robins, R. W., John, O. P., & Caspi, A. (1998). The typological approach to studying personality. In R. B. Cairns, L. R. Bergman, & J. Kagan (Eds.), *Methods and models for studying the individual* (pp. 135–160). Thousand Oaks, CA: Sage.

Rothbart, M. K. (1989). Temperament and development. In G. A. Kohnstamm, J. E. Bates, & M. K. Rothbart (Eds.), *Temperament in childhood* (pp. 187–248). Chichester, England: Wiley.

Saucier, G., & Goldberg, L. R. (2003). The structure of personality attributes. In M. Barrik & A. M. Ryan (Eds.), *Personality and work* (pp. 1–29). New York: Jossey-Bass/Pfeiffer.

Schalling, D., Tolerance for experimentally induced pain as related to personality. *Scandinavian Journal of Psychology, 12*, 271–281.

Scott, J. P., & Fuller, J. (1965). *Genetics and the social behavior of the dog*. Chicago: University of Chicago Press.

Seto, M. C., Lalumiere, M. L., & Quinsey, V. L. (1995). Sensation seeking and males' sexual strategy. *Personality and Individual Differences, 19*, 669–675.

Siddle, D. A. T., Morrish, R. B., White, K. D., & Mangan, G. L. (1969). Relation of visual sensitivity to extraversion. *Journal of Experimental Research in Personality, 3*, 264–267.

Sih, A., & Bell, A. M. (2008). Insights for behavioral ecology from behavioral syndromes. *Advances in the Study of Behavior, 38*, 227–281.

Silverman, L. (1994). The moral sensitivity of gifted children and the evolution of society. *Roeper Review, 17*, 110–116.

Smolewska, K. A., McCabe, S. B., & Woody, E. Z. (2006). A psychometric evaluation of the highly sensitive person scale: The components of sensory-processing sensitivity and their relation to the BIS/BAS and "big five." *Personality and Individual Differences, 40*, 1269–1279.

Sober, E., & Wilson, D. S. (1998). *Unto others: The evolution and psychology of unselfish behavior.* Cambridge, MA: Harvard University Press.

Stansbury, K. (1999). Attachment, temperament, and adrenocortical function in infancy. In L. A. Schmidt & J. Schulkin (Eds.), *Extreme fear, shyness, and social phobia* (pp. 30–46). New York: Oxford University Press.

Stelmack, R. M. (1997). Toward a paradigm in personality: Comment on Eysenck's (1997) view. *Journal of Personality and Social Psychology, 73*, 1238–1241.

Stelmack, R. M., & Campbell, K. B. (1974). Extraversion and auditory sensitivity to high and low frequency. *Perceptual and Motor Skills, 38*, 875–879.

Stelmack, R. M., & Geen, R. G. (1992). The psychophysiology of extraversion. In A. Gale & M. W. Eysenck (Eds.), *Handbook of individual differences: Biological perspectives* (pp. 227–254). Chichester, England: Wiley.

Stelmack, R. M., & Michaud-Achorn, A. (1985). Extraversion, attention, and habituation of the auditory evoked response. *Journal of Research in Personality, 19*, 416–428.

Stern, D. (1985/2000). *The interpersonal world of the infant.* New York: Basic Books.

Stevenson-Hinde, J., Stillwell-Barnes, R., & Zunz, M. (1980). Individual differences in young rhesus monkeys: Consistency and change. *Primates, 21*, 61–62.

Stone, M. H. (1988). Toward a psychobiological theory on borderline personality disorder: Is irritability the red thread that runs through borderline conditions? *Dissociations, 1*(2), 2–15.

Stone, M. H. (1991). Aggression, rage, and the "destructive instinct," reconsidered from a psychobiological point of view. *Journal of the American Academy of Psychoanalysis, 19*, 507–529.

Strelau, J. (1983). *Temperament, personality*, activity. San Diego, CA: Academic Press.

Strobel, A., Dreisbach, G., Muller, J., Goschke, T., Brocke, B., & Lesch, K. (2007). Genetic variation of serotonin function and cognitive control. *Journal of Cognitive Neuroscience, 19*(12), 1923–1931.

Suomi, S. J. (1983). Social development in rhesus monkeys: Consideration of individual differences. In A. Oliverio & M. Zappella (Eds.), *The behavior of human infants* (pp. 71–92). New York: Plenum.

Suomi, S. J. (1987). Genetic and maternal contributions to individual differences in rhesus monkey biobehavioral development. In N. Krasnoger E. M. Blass, M. A. Hofer, & W. P. Smotherman (Eds.), *Perinatal development: A psycholbiological perspective* (pp. 397–419). New York: Academic Press.

Suomi, S. J. (1991). Uptight and laid-back monkeys: Individual differences in the response to social challenges. In S. E. Brauth, W. S. Hall, & R. J. Dooling (Eds.), *Plasticity of development* (pp. 27–56). Cambridge, MA: MIT Press.

Suomi, S. J. (1997). Early determinants of behaviour: Evidence from primate studies. *British Medical Bulletin, 53*, 170–184.

Thomas, A., Chess, S., Birch, M. G., Hertzig, M. E., & Korn, S. (1963). *Behavioral individuality in early childhood.* New York: University Press.

Thomas, A., Chess, S., & Birch, H. (1968). Temperment and behavior disorders in children. New York: University Press.

van der Kolk, B. A. (1996). The complexity of adaptation to trauma: Self-regulation, stimulus discrimination, and characterological development. In B. A. Van Der Kolk, A. C. McFarlane, & L. Weisaeth (Eds.), *Traumatic stress: The effects of overwhelming experience on mind, body and society* (pp. 182–213). New York: Guilford.

Van Horne, B. A. (2004). Psychology licensing board disciplinary actions: The realities. *Professional Psychology: Research and Practice, 35*, 170–178.

Wilson, D. S., Coleman, K., Clark, A. B., & Biederman, L. (1993). Shy–bold continuum in pumpkinseed sunfish (*Lepomis gibbosus*): An ecological study of a psychological trait. *Journal of Comparative Psychology, 107*, 250–260.

Winnicott, D. (1965). *The maturational process and the facilitating environment.* London. Hogarth.

Wolf, M., van Doorn, S., & Weissing, F. J. (2008). Evolutionary emergence of responsive and unresponsive personalities. *Proceedings of the National Academy of Sciences, 105*(41), 15825–15830.

Woodward, S. A., Lenzenweger, M. F., Kagan, J., Snidman, N., & Arcus, D. (2000). Taxonic structure of infant reactivity: Evidence from a taxometric perspective. *Psychological Science, 11*, 296–301.

Yerkes, R. M., & Dodson, J. D. (1908). The relation of strength of stimulus to rapidity of habit-formation. *Journal of Comparative Neurology and Psychology, 18*, 459–482.

Zajonc, R. B., Adelmann, P. K., Murphy, S. T., & Niedenthal, P. M. (1987). Convergence in the physical appearance of spouses. *Motivation and Emotion, 11*, 335–346.

Zuckerman, M. (1993). P-impulsive sensation seeking and its behavioral, psychophysiological and biochemical correlates. *Neuropsychobiology, 28*, 30–36.

INDEX

A

E

F

G

H

I

O